To Cambodia With Love

A Travel Guide for the Connoisseur

To Cambodia With Love
Edited & with contributions by Andy Brouwer
Photography by Tewfic El-Sawy

To Asia With Love series created by Kim Fay
Cover and book design by Janet McKelpin/Dayspring Technologies, Inc.
Copy-editing by Elizabeth Mathews
Book production by Paul Tomanpos, Jr.

Please be advised that restaurants, shops, businesses, and other establishments in this book have been written about over a period of time. The editor and publisher have made every effort to ensure the accuracy of the information included in this book at the time of publication, but prices and conditions may have changed, and the editor, publisher, and authors cannot assume and hereby disclaim liability for loss, damage, or inconvenience caused by errors, omissions, or changes in regard to information included in this book.

For information regarding permissions, write to:
ThingsAsian Press
3230 Scott Street
San Francisco, California 94123 USA
www.thingsasian.com
Printed in Singapore

ISBN-13: 978-1-934159-08-8
ISBN-10: 1-934159-08-5

Table of Contents

Introduction

Imagine that on the eve of your upcoming trip to Cambodia, you are invited to a party. At this party are dozens of guests, all of whom live in or have traveled extensively through the country. Among this eclectic and well-versed group of connoisseurs are contributors to acclaimed travel guides, popular newspaper writers, veteran gourmets, and pioneering adventurers. As the evening passes, they tell you tales from their lives in these exotic places. They whisper the names of their favorite shops and restaurants; they divulge the secret hideaways where they sneak off to for an afternoon or a weekend to unwind. Some make you laugh out loud, and others seduce you with their poetry. Some are intent on educating, while others just want to entertain. Their recommendations are as unique as their personalities, but they are united in one thing ... their love of Cambodia. If you can envision being welcomed at such a party, then you can envision the experience that *To Cambodia With Love* aspires to give you.

Kim Fay
Series Editor, To Asia With Love

How do I describe my love of Cambodia? I'm not the world's greatest wordsmith, so I'll keep it simple. In 1994 I came to this country for five of the most exhilarating, nerve-jangling, and frightening days of my life—and that was it. I was hooked, completely, by a country and a people who've subsequently enriched my life to a degree I never thought possible. Those five days sparked a passion that grew with each of my annual visits, culminating in my migration here three years ago. I truly feel at home, I belong, I love every day of my life here, and I want to share my passion for this country with everyone. *To Cambodia With Love* is the perfect vehicle to do just that.

Fortunately, you don't have to read my inadequate prose to understand the essence of Cambodia. I've joined forces with more than sixty contributors who know this country as well as I do—better in many instances—and who I'm convinced will inspire you to come and see for yourself why this beautiful land is so alluring. Whether it's acclaimed memoirist Loung Ung eating chive rice cakes in the Russian Market in Phnom Penh, journalist Karen Coates exploring a bird sanctuary in Preah Vihear Province, pioneering guidebook author Ray Zepp riding a traditional *norry* along countryside railway tracks, or scholar and Angkor historian Dawn Rooney explaining her favorite time to visit Cambodia's most celebrated temple, there are essays to feed your obsession if you're already hooked, or spark a love that will continue to grow after your Cambodian baptism.

I urge you to discover and unearth Cambodia's secrets, some of which you will find within these pages, others you must find for yourself—and you will, I assure you. Wander amongst the crowded maze of its markets, absorb the slow pace of village life in a rural landscape where few travelers venture, discover the unique lifestyle along the Mekong River, and above all, appreciate a culture and setting that spawned the incredible temples of Angkor, the jewel in Cambodia's crown. Fifteen years ago, I was blessed to see the Angkor temples without the crowds, to experience sunrise over the pineapple towers of Angkor Wat in glorious solitude, and for that I will be eternally grateful. Though the secret of Angkor is now well and truly out in the open—it is one of the most popular tourist attractions in the world—there are still many opportunities to grasp your own special memories and lock them away forever, as I have ... beginning with a few suggestions in this book.

I know it's a bit of a tired cliché that it's the people of this and that country that make it such a wonderful place, but the truth is, they really do. Cambodia is no different. After weathering decades of bloodshed and civil war, poverty, and instability, the Khmer have proved their incredible resilience, and their smile remains as bewitching as it has throughout time. The friendships I've developed over the years will last forever. No one will leave Cambodia without a large chunk of admiration and fondness for the people they encounter. You have my guarantee.

This is not a definitive guide to Cambodia. Far from it. It is about inspiration, discovery, sharing, and above all else, a love and a respect for a country that has changed my life forever, as I hope it will change yours.

Andy Brouwer
Editor, *To Cambodia With Love*

How This Book Works

A good traveler has no fixed plans, and is not intent on arriving.
~Lao Tzu

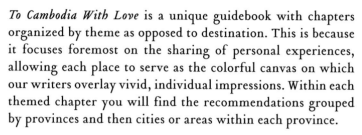

To Cambodia With Love is a unique guidebook with chapters organized by theme as opposed to destination. This is because it focuses foremost on the sharing of personal experiences, allowing each place to serve as the colorful canvas on which our writers overlay vivid, individual impressions. Within each themed chapter you will find the recommendations grouped by provinces and then cities or areas within each province.

Chapters begin in the capital city Phnom Penh, then move on to Siem Reap, home of the Angkor temples. From here the essays travel by province, starting around Phnom Penh (Kandal, Kompong Chhnang, Kompong Thom, and Kompong Cham Provinces) and moving clockwise around the country: Southwest (Kep, Kampot, Kompong Som, Koh Kong, and Pursat Provinces), Northwest (Battambang, Banteay Meancheay, and Oddar Meancheay Provinces), North (Preah Vihear Province), and Northeast (Kratie, Stung Treng, Ratakiniri, and Mondulkiri Provinces). For attractions or experiences by destination, a complete index of cities can be found at the end of this book.

Each recommendation consists of two parts: a personal essay and a fact file. Together, they are intended to inspire and inform. The essay tells a story while the fact file gives addresses and other serviceable information. Because each contribution can stand alone, the book does not need to be read in order. As with an old-fashioned miscellany, you may open to any page and start reading. Thus every encounter with the book is turned into its own distinctive armchair journey.

Additional information and updates can be found online at WWW.TOASIAWITHLOVE.COM/CAMBODIA. Keep in mind that *To Cambodia With Love* is selective and does not include all of the practical information you will need for daily travel. Instead, reading it is like having a conversation with a friend who just returned from a trip. You should supplement that friend's stories with a comprehensive guidebook, such as Lonely Planet or Rough Guide.

Confucius said, "A journey of a thousand miles begins with a single step." We hope that this guide helps you put your best foot forward.

KEY TERMS AND IMPORTANT INFORMATION

ANGKOR: The word *Angkor* is used interchangeably, to refer to the main temple of Angkor Wat and to the Angkor temple complex, which contains Angkor Wat.

BARANG: Foreigner.

KHMER: The Khmer are Cambodia's majority ethnic group, whose empire was responsible for Angkor Wat and many other temple cities. Today, *Khmer* is often used to refer to Cambodians in general, even though Cambodia is still home to many smaller ethnic groups.

METRIC SYSTEM: Although we are an American publisher, we have used the metric system for all measurements. For easy conversion, go to WWW.METRIC-CONVERSIONS.ORG.

MONEY: The few prices noted in this book are in U.S. dollars and Cambodian riel. In general U.S. dollars are accepted—and sometimes preferred—throughout the country, although it is wise to take riel when traveling in more remote areas.

MOTORCYCLE TRANSPORT: There are numerous ways to get around Cambodia, including on the back of a motorcycle. This can be referred to as a moto, motodop, or motorcycle taxi.

SEASONS: Travel in Cambodia can be greatly affected by the rainy season, which runs from June to October. November through May are generally considered the best months to visit certain areas. We have done our best to note the seasonal effects on areas in relevant essays.

SPELLING: The Khmer language is written in script. Because Khmer words are transliterated into English, they often have more than one spelling. We have done our best to use the most common spelling of a word. In cases where an obviously common spelling was not available, we made an executive decision based on our editor's experience.

TELEPHONE NUMBERS: Phone numbers are listed as they would be dialed from within the country, beginning with the area code in parenthesis. For example: (023) 981-888. To dial this number from outside the country, drop the initial zero and add 855. For example: 855-23-981-888.

Praying novice at Wat Damnak in Kompong Phluk village

Moveable Feasts

A tasting menu of exotic flavors

Having traveled to Cambodia annually since 1994 and lived there for three years, I've had the chance to taste my fair share of Khmer flavors. Among my favorites is what is perhaps the country's signature dish, the subtle fish *amok*, a regular order whenever I dine out, which is often. I'm not a big fan of spicy food, so the creamy coconut taste and delicate aroma are simply magical to me.

Then there is my love affair with another Khmer dish, which came about in the aftermath of the passing of one of my closest friends a decade ago. His extended family, all living under the same roof in the Tuol Kork district of Phnom Penh, invited me to join them one evening, and his Aunt Vourch brought out her specialty, Khmer chicken curry (*kari sach moan*), made with her own secret recipe. That was it. I was hooked. I've been back to Tuol Kork many times since. There's just something uniquely special about Vourch's masterpiece, the taste and texture, the bond of true friendship that it represents. I've enjoyed similar dishes throughout Cambodia, but none come close.

It is relationships with local people that give food its special meaning for many of the contributors to this chapter, as well. Caroline Nixon not only eats, but learns to cook, *ban chao* in the kitchen of her "auntie" in Kampot. It is a dish so good that Rachel Wildblood has also written about a takeout version brought to a twilight picnic among Cambodian families outside Angkor Wat. As these essays prove, atmosphere, as much as ingredients, make a meal: you might join Robert Tompkins one night in the regal setting of the Raffles Hotel Le Royal in Phnom Penh, then another night hop across the river with Mark Hotham to drink Beerlao and dine on crispy rice and barbecued crayfish at a waterfront institution.

Given Cambodia's Hindu influences, it's not surprising to find some great Indian food recommendations. Many consider

Indian as local as the most local of fare, from Loung Ung's favorite chive rice cakes to Karen Coates's Kampot crab. Then there are meals for adventurers, including crickets, tarantulas, and yes, *prahok*—fermented fish paste. While the last is one of Cambodian cuisine's most common ingredients, it's pungent, it assaults the taste buds, and it's definitely an acquired taste—one I have yet to come to terms with, unlike Christine Dimmock, who is surprised to find herself enjoying it with grilled beef at a Siem Reap eatery.

As you nibble your way through Cambodia's exotic fruits, brave North Korea's unusual dining traditions, or enjoy a simple airport breakfast, this chapter is a reminder that while Cambodia may be a small country, its food offerings are vast. Better yet, a meal is most always accompanied by warm hospitality, making this country a perfect place to undertake a culinary journey.

PHNOM PENH

*Loung Ung dines
on chive rice cakes in
Phnom Penh*

The motodop stops in front of a row of dusty wooden shops, all selling pirated CDs and DVDs. He announces, "Psar Tuol Tom Pong." Immediately, the smell of fried food beckons me in, making my mouth water and my stomach expand in anticipation. I enter the market, walking quickly past booths selling factory-second Gap T-shirts, blue and white ceramic plates and bowls, bicycle tires, and strange, silver looping wire contraptions that hang from the ceiling like metallic animal innards.

I duck, sidestep, and march my way through the maze of stalls, ignoring the vendors' calls, until in front of me I see my destination, the market's food court—a vision of heaven for those of us who call ourselves foodies. Like vaporous hands, its smell floats toward me and hooks its fingers into my nostrils, pulling me forward. I eye the many stands hungrily. Spread across their tables are rows and rows of pots and plates full of crispy brown egg rolls, red sizzling chicken teriyaki, golden fried dough, hot red curry, cool cucumber salad, and yellow crepes, all making my taste buds stand at attention on my tongue.

Fighting the urge to plant my butt down at every table, I head to the stall where a pleasant looking middle-aged woman stands frying chive rice cakes in a giant skillet. I sit at her booth. We greet each other. I am a regular, and I order for one.

Chive cakes come in two shapes, round and square. For the square cakes, the rice batter and chives are mixed together, while the round one is made with an outer rice cake wrapping and filled with fresh green chives mixed with garlic and salt. Personally, I prefer the round chive cakes for their crispy shell and juicy chives inside, and I watch as the woman silently scoops two brown, crispy cakes with her silver spatula, drops them on a plastic flower plate, and hands it to me. Immediately, another customer calls her attention away.

The temperature at the booth is oppressive, and instantly I go from glowing to sweating like a pig. I watch as Meang hovers over the hot stove, one hand on her hip. The other grips the handle of the heavy spatula. When she adds a ladle of oil to the skillet, it splatters and sizzles, causing bright orange flames to nip at her skin. I am astounded that her face barely glistens as she pushes the round cakes into an upside-down arc, which reminds me of the connected rings of the Olympic symbol.

Most cakes are automatically served with a Khmer sweet-and-sour

PHNOM PENH PROVINCE

sauce. I don't have a sweet tooth, so I like my cakes with soy sauce, hot sauce, and vinegar. I turn away from Meang to add a spoonful of each to my order. I take two plastic chopsticks and split open my cakes, letting the steam burst forth with the fresh aroma of sweet chives and garlic. The first bite turns on the faucet in my nostrils, the second opens the pores in my face and skull, and the third burns the roof of my mouth so that I am hissing and sucking for air as my body empties itself of moisture. But a smile forms on my lips as I chew and swallow, wiping my dripping nose and lips in between each bite.

Once I clean my plate, I give Meang my 50 cents, thank her, and leave, satisfied. Along with immersing myself in authentic flavor, eating at a local stall like Meang's is perhaps the simplest form of paying it forward, and the most appetizing. I love knowing that my money will stay in country and help her provide for herself and her family. To me, it's a win-win situation for everyone.

Chive rice cakes in the Russian Market

While chive rice cakes (*nom kachay*) are sold in most outdoor Khmer markets in the "food court" from eleven-ish in the morning to two-ish in the afternoon, at Psar Tuol Tom Pong, Meang's stall is the only one selling these cakes. To prepare, she and her family wake up

every morning around three to make her cakes. For the day, they will make approximately four hundred each of both the round and square cakes. They use only fresh ingredients. Because they serve many foreign customers, the daughters know a bit of English. Chive cakes are best eaten at the stall when they are still hot and crispy. They generally sell for 800 to 1000 riel. Psar Tuol Tom Pong, also called the Russian Market because of the customers who shopped there in the 1990s, is known by all the tuk-tuk drivers and motodops in Phnom Penh.

Cristiano Calcagno reclaims a restaurant in Phnom Penh

Today a visitor to Phnom Penh has all sorts of restaurants to choose from: French, Mexican, Nepalese, Greek, Korean ... But back in 1991, when I first came here and Cambodia was still subject to an international embargo, none of those places existed.

At that time, the country was desperately poor, and there were very few foreigners around. The eateries in the capital were simple establishments offering local food that I would order from wrinkled menus, with varying chances of getting what I wanted.

As soon as the United Nations came into the country in 1992, these historic places started to disappear. I watched as the first to go was Santepheap (Peace), on the central section of Monivong (then Achar Mean) Boulevard. That little restaurant once sat where the Bayon supermarket is today. Then out went the Bayon café on the other side of the same street, to make way for a modern hotel. Then the Faculté de Médecine, a pleasant outdoor place with excellent food, which occupied part of the grounds of a university.

Progress marched quickly, wiping out the International, which before the Khmer Rouge era had been a meeting place for foreign journalists covering the war. It was replaced by a Lucky Burger outlet. Next came the end for Makara, and finally, in the late 1990s, to my great disappointment, the last survivor of that old dining world and my personal favorite, Chez Lipp, north of the city center in front of Calmette Hospital, closed its doors.

Or so I thought.

It turned out that the restaurant just moved a hundred meters south, reopening with a slightly different name. Chez Lipp was a name the original owner borrowed from a famous brasserie in Paris, back in the colonial days when this part of Phnom Penh was known as the French Quarter. Closed during the time of the Khmer Rouge, the restaurant opened again in 1980, and when it moved to its current location in front of the new Phnom Penh Hotel, the present owner rechristened it Seng Lipp.

At first glance, Seng Lipp does not look particularly appealing: a large dining hall with ordinary furniture and not many customers—which is a shame, as it offers some of the best food in Phnom Penh. It probably suffers from being located away from tourist areas, and perhaps from being neither an upscale place nor at the cheapest end of the spectrum. If there are foreign patrons, they are likely to be French doctors working at the nearby hospital.

The menu offers a wide choice of both Khmer and locally adapted French dishes, but for me the pride of the place is *crabe farci*. Fried stuffed crab. I don't even need to order it. As soon as I step inside, the friendly owner asks, "*Crabe farci, n'est-ce pas?*"

This Khmer delicacy is not common in restaurants. The few that serve it don't make it anywhere close to the taste of Seng Lipp. Not for nothing, this family comes from Kampot, the crab capital of Cambodia.

So, what is this specialty that draws me back again and again? A large red crab is stripped of all ten legs, stuffed full with its juicy meat, and then fried. It comes to the table on a fresh bed of lettuce leaves and tomatoes, and it tastes best with just a sprinkling of pepper. Although it sounds ridiculously simple—and is ridiculously cheap at just a few dollars—I dare you to scoop the meat out of the shell, take a bite, and then tell me you have ever eaten a more delicious crab dish. Impossible, *n'est-ce pas*?

Seng Lipp

Seng Lipp is located in front of the Phnom Penh Hotel (north of the city center), between the Raffles Hotel Le Royal and the Calmette Hospital, both of which are a short walk away. French is spoken here, and English is understood well enough.

46B, Monivong Boulevard
Phnom Penh

Don Gilliland remains loyal to an Indian eatery in Phnom Penh

It's become my Phnom Penh ritual: after arrival at the airport, I check in to my regular hotel, unpack my bags, take a walk one block toward the river, and sit down for a fabulous meal at Chi Cha.

Chi Cha is a small, nondescript restaurant that also houses an upstairs guesthouse. In one corner of the room is a TV that's always playing a Bollywood movie of some sort (decibel level low, thankfully), a few devoted patrons sitting nearby with eyes glued to the screen.

You won't be overwhelmed by the menu, which offers a very basic selection of Indian- and Pakistani-style curries (fish, beef, chicken, or egg) and breads. But what the restaurant lacks in choices, it makes up for with low prices and large servings of very tasty dishes. All of the curry specials, which include several side dishes, will set you back only a couple of dollars, with no hidden taxes or service charges to inflate the bill.

One of my favorite things about Chi Cha is that with each meal I receive side orders of dal, a choice of vegetables, tomato and cucumber slices, chapattis, and as much rice as I can stuff myself with. The polite waitstaff are diligent about offering free extra servings of any of these side dishes that I would like more of. By the time I've finished my meal, I usually have to wave off the nonstop stream of chapattis. If you aren't up for such a gut-busting feeding, you can settle on the small selection of soups and appetizers, including samosas and *parathas*.

As is usually the case when it comes to discovering such little hole-in-the-wall delights, I was introduced to Chi Cha by a Phnom Penh friend. After repeated trips there during my first stay in town, I observed that the restaurant had a loyal following amongst the city's expat community. It's not hard to see why. When you offer consistently good food and good service at affordable prices, you're going to have loyal customers. Count me among them.

Chi Cha Restaurant and Guest House

The restaurant is one block east of the Psar Chas market, going toward the river. It does not serve alcoholic beverages, but allows customers to bring their own.

27, Ang Duong Street (Street 110)
Phnom Penh
(023) 336-065

Mark Hotham feasts on the river in Phnom Penh

It was an office outing to celebrate, well, nothing in particular. The Khmer just love to eat out. We piled into the back of Tri's Toyota Camry and pretended not to be horrified by his driving. He was paying far more attention to us in the back than he was to the road, telling us how Tri was not his real name. When he had briefly joined the military police—because he liked the uniform, he confessed—his name was changed to Tri, as it avoided the paperwork explaining how the last holder of the name had died.

Tri was taking us to the other side of the river, across the Japanese Friendship Bridge, to the outlying town of Prek Leap, where we found restaurant after restaurant vying for the business of the Phnom Penh-ites who flocked each evening to this mecca of fine Khmer cuisine. He drove purposefully past less worthy establishments and turned down a hardly noticeable side road, narrowly avoiding colliding with a family of six on a moped before pulling into the parking area of the Rum Chang Restaurant.

Inside, we found ourselves on a large stone terrace overlooking the Mekong River. A giant tamarind tree sat imposingly in the middle, providing shade in the day and a handy place to string up fairy lights at night. Once seated, we were quickly surrounded by the typical bevy of beer girls, each touting the virtues of the particular beer company that paid her wages. After we selected Beerlao to provide our beverages for the evening, the waitstaff then appeared with an extensive menu complete with pictures for the uninitiated *barang*. Tri chose for us and wasted no time in doing so, as he was eager to indulge in his favorite pastime—eating.

It was not long before plate after plate of exquisite Khmer food began arriving, freshly cooked and smelling divine. Eating is a communal experience in Cambodia, and we all tucked in together, sampling from each dish. The *bai kadang* (crispy rice) was perfectly enhanced by the accompanying prawn sauce. The fresh giant crayfish was barbecued to perfection. And the pork and ginger stir-fry, sour fish soup, beef *lok lak*, and fish *amok* served in a large coconut were all fantastic. My favorite was the *mgiew*, which is a small shellfish cooked in a tamarind-and-basil sauce. Wonderful!

The bill came to just a few dollars a head, including the prodigious quantities of Beerlao that were consumed. Staggering value. Indeed, we staggered out, fit to burst, and collapsed into the back of Tri's Camry.

Rum Chang Restaurant

For traditional Khmer dishes and a peaceful setting, Rum Chang is a top choice. From Phnom Penh, take the road over the Japanese Friendship Bridge and continue straight on for approximately one and a half kilometers to Prek Leap. On the right-hand side you will see a sign for Rum Chang. Turn right down this side road, right again at the bottom, and then left into the car park. When you leave at the end of the night, make sure to pay the car park attendant for "tending" your car. Be advised to allow plenty of time coming and going (thirty minutes), as traffic can be awful in the evenings.

Robert Tompkins dines in le royal style in Phnom Penh

We were met at Restaurant Le Royal with smiles and the folded palms and slight bows of the traditional *sampeah* greeting. Chandeliers hung from the high recessed ceilings, which were creatively painted with a floral motif. The lighting was subdued and enhanced by candles. There were eleven tables, spaced far apart to provide privacy. Only five were occupied by other couples.

While sipping an aperitif, we perused the ten-page menu, which featured international (predominately French) and Khmer cuisine. A separate menu listed the special five-course "Degustation Menu" to which I succumbed, while Doris, whose appetite is far less rapacious than that of her husband, ordered à la carte.

The tasting menu began with an appetizer of cucumber parfait wrapped in a beetroot coat and topped with caviar-laced sour cream—preparing the palate for the following course of goose liver ravioli served with an artichoke essence. Sharing brought further dimension to our meal, as Doris's generously portioned starter of melt-in-the-mouth pan-fried goose liver complemented perfectly the rhubarb compote.

Poised delicately between our starter and entrée, an *amuse-bouche* of duck carpaccio was served to Doris to coincide with my course of salmon confit, which was matched with a slightly tart calamansi-and-lime butter sauce and presented on a bed of lightly spiced eggplant. Then came the high note. Paired with chateau potatoes and sautéed French beans, Doris's entrée of duck *à l'orange* was moist and delicately flavored, while my oven-roasted veal mignons were basted in a tamarind-port wine sauce and accompanied by braised cabbage with glazed sweet potatoes.

Although dessert would indeed be excessive, we surrendered to the temptation. For me, the tasting menu concluded with a wild-berry-and-chocolate charlotte. Doris yielded to the waiter's recommendation of deep-fried port wine ice cream with red pear compote. This final gustatory indulgence left us sated and attempting to aid digestion with cognac.

Throughout our meal the muted background music featured Count Basie, Duke Ellington, and the unmistakable vocals of big-band-era singer Jimmy Rushing. Service was well honed and flawless. Our needs were anticipated and attended to unobtrusively and smoothly, and for just one night, a sense of time and place seemed to slip away. We were no longer in twenty-first-century Cambodia. The real world dissolved into a surrogate of comfortable illusion.

We left to a chorus wishing us a good evening along with a replay of the smiles and *sampeahs* that had greeted us two and a half hours previously. Wrapped in a cozy postdinner lethargy, we sat on our balcony at the hotel. The sultry night was frangipani scented and echoing with cricket calls. Surrendering to the serenity of the moment, we drifted in Le Royal's lost-in-time version of Phnom Penh.

Restaurant Le Royal

Raffles Hotel Le Royal
92, Rukhak Vithei Daun Penh
(off Monivong Boulevard)
Phnom Penh
(023) 981-888

www.raffles.com

SIEM REAP

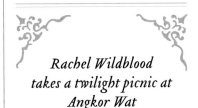

Rachel Wildblood takes a twilight picnic at Angkor Wat

As dusk settles over the temples and the hordes of tourists take their buses back into town, the time has come for me to ride out to a local Khmer restaurant in the Angkor park and buy a *ban chao* picnic. There is nothing more beautiful than Angkor Wat at this time of the evening, when the orange glow of the day fades into nighttime.

Ban chao is a traditional Khmer fast food that you can eat in or take away. A large yellow pancake filled with bean sprouts and chopped pork or prawns, it is served with salad leaves, which you should wrap around pieces of the pancake before dipping the little package in the delicious accompanying peanut sauce. Because I am not accomplished at this kind of dining and tend to make a mess, I need a ready supply of tissues!

The food is tasty, but it needs to be said that it's the setting that makes it. After ordering my vegetarian version of *ban chao*, I head to the edge of the moat outside Angkor Wat.

Gathered here are Khmer families, all with the same things in mind—eating *ban chao* and catching up on the weekly gossip. Each group sits on one of the large rented mats that line the temple walls on both sides of the causeway in the evening. As darkness falls, the picnickers light candles that are sold by industrious children. Sometimes, I might bargain for the rental of mats and candles, but it depends on how bold I'm feeling and how wily the kids are that day.

As the row of mats gets busier, the number of candles flickering in the dark increases. The atmosphere is relaxed and happy, but for me the main pleasure is to sit amongst Khmer families and to escape the foreign restaurants and bars that can dominate Siem Reap. Better yet, all this takes place against the backdrop of Angkor Wat, changing color from purple to red to green as the floodlights illuminate the massive towers against a blackening sky.

After dinner, the only thing left to do is to gather up my plastic boxes and bags and then pay the owner of the mats. By this time, the stream of bright lights from the tourist buses has long since died down, and their thundering engines are replaced with the noise of frogs, insects, and of course much laughter from those who remain, faces glowing by candlelight.

Finding ban chao

Take the tarmac road directly opposite the main steps to the Angkor Wat causeway across the moat. You know you are on the right road because it has an obelisk in the middle. You will pass some toilets and an open templelike building on the right about 50 meters from the obelisk. Walk down the road approximately 150 meters. You will see two restaurants on the right-hand side. Rachel prefers the first restaurant, *Ban Chao*. It has a tattered blue Khmer sign outside it. If you cannot read Khmer, check to make sure that the restaurant next door is called Somnang Kohdot. The pancakes are incredibly cheap, and you can buy soft drinks and beer to take with you too. All the food is packaged for a takeaway, including vegetables and peanut sauce. You can request your pancakes without meat. To read about making *ban chao*, go to page 26.

Keeping it legal

Rachel has not had any problems with going into the outer temple area in the day or night without a ticket, but you may get stopped and even fined if you actually go into the temples themselves. Stay on the public roads around the temples and you should have no problems—this includes the restaurant and picnic areas. Remember that it gets dark quickly here, so try not to leave it too late to sort out a mat and candles for a picnic—tricky in the pitch black.

Soumya James discovers the flavors of home in Siem Reap

"Kama Sutra."

The sign stopped me in my tracks. Was this one of those dubious massage parlors I'd heard about? Or a sex shop, perhaps? Curious, I investigated. Turns out, the Kama Sutra in Siem Reap is an Indian restaurant—tastefully furnished with low lights, simple wooden furniture, and exposed brick walls. No psychedelic pictures of the Taj Mahal or blaring Bollywood music here. And the South Indian co-owner, Karthik, is a soft-spoken and gracious host. To my additional surprise, I soon discovered that the waiter and cook were both from my hometown in Kerala. A small world, indeed.

For the months to come, Kama Sutra became a home away from home for me, where I would sit sipping sweet tea and chatting in Malayalam and Tamil, sampling the eclectic food selection. Unlike most of Siem Reap's other Indian restaurants, which serve mainly North Indian dishes, this one included South Indian fare too. The spicy Kerala crab curry and smoldering fish fry were done to perfection. But the one item for which I would return again and again was the mango juice.

Cambodia's mango season begins in early January, when the little food carts on the roadsides begin selling artistically cut mango sprinkled with spice-and-salt powder. It was mouthwatering just to look at. It was with visions of this succulent fruit floating in my head that I first ordered a mango juice at Kama Sutra.

Chettan, the cook, brought a tall, cool glass of bright green juice. I frowned. There had to be some mistake. I was expecting the usual bright orange color. He smiled apologetically and said, "Well, the mangoes are not ripe yet. But why don't you try this?"

I took my first sip. It did not have the usual thousand-calorie power-packed sweetness of mangoes, but it was a wonderfully uplifting taste, light and mildly sweet with a hint of the raw greenness of the skin. It was, to coin a new word, "ambrosious." It put all the million mango juices I'd had so far to shame. I savored it, taking small sips, trying to make it last for as long as I could.

Chettan stood beside me, smiling. "Good?" he asked.

I smiled back. "Perfect," I said.

Kama Sutra

Kama Sutra is located on Pub Street in Siem Reap. It's impossible to miss, and its delectable food makes it an absolute must on your gastronomic tour. The best time to have the green mango juice is from the end of December until around the first week of January. After that you will get only the regular orange-colored ripe mango juice—the one mere mortals drink.

Christine Dimmock braves a bite of prahok in Siem Reap

I'm dining with Rieng, my favorite motodop driver in Siem Reap. We have come to Somnang Kohdot across from Angkor Wat to eat beef, but while we wait for the food to be served, he asks, "Do you like *prahok*?"

I'm always willing to give anything a go, and my stomach has proved cast-iron so far. "Yes," I lie. When the food comes, the *prahok* is boiling hot, which is something of a relief, because I'd heard that it was raw fermented fish, full of parasites and not to be eaten.

The hot *prahok* is served with slices of melt-in-the-mouth-beef and a bewildering array of accompaniments, including long beans, cabbage, cucumber, mint, basil, slices of green tomato and green banana, chilies, limes, something that translates as river grass, and of course two cold Angkor beers in glasses with ice. Maybe it's the beer, maybe it's the chilies and lime, but I like the beef, which I expected to have the texture of shoe leather, and the *prahok* tastes great—a bit like concentrated fish sauce. The green tomato is fine,

too, but I draw the line at the green banana, which sticks around the gums like some kind of floury, sour paste.

Another night, my driver invites me home to meet his extended family. His mother-in-law makes a special overnight serving of *prahok* for me to take away, and I discover that not all *prahok* is good *prahok*. Served cold, it tastes like yesterday's fish bait with an entire packet of salt added. Take my advice: save your appetite for the beef-and-*prahok* restaurants around the temples. You won't be disappointed.

Somnang Kohdot

This restaurant is located next to Ban Chao (see page 22) near the entrance to Angkor Wat. It sits among many other restaurants also serving similar fare. Another staple from the Khmer kitchen to try here—some even call it the national dish—is *amok*, baked fish wrapped in a banana leaf or served in the shell of a young coconut, with coconut, lemongrass, and chili. This really is one of the most delicious dishes to be tasted whilst dining in Cambodia. To read more about *prahok*, go to page 32.

SKUON

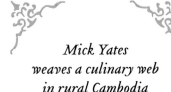

Mick Yates
weaves a culinary web
in rural Cambodia

I had been to the village of O Som once before, to help build a satellite school. It is a poor community, just north of Trapeang Prasat and close to the Thai border in the northern reaches of Cambodia. The district was in Khmer Rouge hands for a long time and only became connected with the rest of the country after Pol Pot's death in 1998.

When I visited, I was both embarrassed and admiring that a group of people so impoverished could be so hospitable, providing a wonderful lunch for our group. We ate well, in the foundations of a new building, with food served by women from the village while the children watched us carefully. It was a happy time, and the odd can of Angkor beer helped move the event along quite nicely.

A year later, we decided to revisit to see the school—but to go at an earlier hour so that there would be no excuse for the villagers to prepare such a feast. Clearly, our itinerary got out somehow. When we arrived at about nine thirty in the morning, lunch was being prepared. Or should I say brunch? Many traditional Khmer dishes were offered, accompanied by lots of rice and vegetables. But one dish in particular caught our attention—tarantulas. Accompanied with garlic, these had been fried, and they looked crispy and seemed a little burned.

I have asked around, and no one is quite sure when this delicacy first hit the Cambodian table. It's possible that it was during Khmer Rouge times, when people survived on anything they could scavenge. Some guidebooks, though, suggest that the spider in question is the Thai zebra tarantula, which apparently has been called the "edible spider" for years. In either case, the crispy creatures were in front of us now.

So, what was it like? I admit to only a little taste. Once I got past the "fear factor," it was pretty bland. Flavorless, really. Dragging the slither of meat from the legs like you would a crab was quite hard to do, but then crunching down on the body was even harder. I could not quite get enough courage to bite through the whole thing ... but my Cambodian friends did, with gusto!

Dining in Spiderville
While deep-fried spiders can be found in many locations across the country, the town of Skuon, known as Spiderville and located on the road between Phnom Penh and Siem Reap near Kompong Cham, is the most

famous place in Cambodia to eat them. Contributor Glyn Vaughan adds: if you find a tablecloth—and atmosphere—necessary when dining on fried spiders, make your way to the Romdeng at 74, Street 174 in Phnom Penh.

www.friends-international.org

KAMPOT

Caroline Nixon cooks ban chao with her Kampot auntie

As we leave Phnom Penh my heart lifts: a trip to beautiful, sleepy Kampot is always a treat. The suburbs give way to rice fields of the deepest green, interspersed with the sugar palm trees that are so typical of Cambodia's coastal plain. We are on our way to see Auntie, who lives in one of the lovely old Chinese-style shop houses near the river. Downstairs is Uncle's carpentry shop, and behind that the heart of the home, the kitchen.

Not only is Cambodian food delicious, its preparation is a great social occasion, a chance to sit and gossip, while chopping, stirring, and tasting. One of my favorite dishes is *ban chao*, a type of pancake with a

savory filling, served with greens and a dipping sauce. My favorite way to cook it is with my friends here in Kampot and my adopted auntie.

After a trip to the market, the preparation begins. The batter, made of rice flour and eggs, is beaten in a big plastic bucket. Pork is minced by hand and fried with onions, spices, garlic, and chilies. Meanwhile, the accompanying salad leaves are washed and prepared. The word *salad* has a whole new meaning in Cambodia. It's not just lettuce leaves, but a range of herbs, some cultivated, some gathered from forest and hedgerow, each with its own intense flavor and aroma.

Soon it's time for the real fun of cooking the pancakes. The wok has been heated to a high temperature on a small charcoal stove. Into it is dropped a cube of pork fat. When the oil is sizzling, batter is poured in. The edges bubble and froth into a lacy golden filigree. The center, where more batter has pooled, forms a thin layer of moist dough. Then the skillful bit: the pancake must be flipped to cook the other side. Once it is flipped, some ground pork is spread inside, and a few fresh prawns laid on top, before it is folded in half to encase the filling. Each freshly cooked pancake is tucked into a banana leaf until enough have been cooked for all.

Everyone has a go, and there is much hilarity at my amateur efforts. But although I am not a professional at preparation, I am one when it comes to eating. *Ban chao* is finger food par excellence. It goes like this—you break a piece of pancake off, roll it in a salad leaf of your choice, and dip it in the piquant sauce. The whole little bundle is then transferred to your mouth, where all the delicious flavors mingle. What more can be desired? Except perhaps a cool glass of Angkor beer!

Eating ban chao around Cambodia

To Caroline's mind, there are only two places to eat real *ban chao*. The first is in a family home. The second at a dedicated *ban chao* restaurant or food stall. For a quick snack in Phnom Penh, excellent *ban chao* can be found in Psar Tuol Tom Pong (Russian Market). For something more leisurely, there's a great open-air *ban chao* restaurant (see page 22) near Angkor Wat. Many of the restaurants in Prek Leap, just outside Phnom Penh, serve it too, but somehow it's never quite as good as in a place that specializes. You can always ask your motodop or hotel to recommend a place.

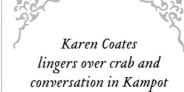

Karen Coates
lingers over crab and
conversation in Kampot

I spot the Phnom Kamchay Thmey restaurant by the Kampot bridge on our first walk through town. A young man invites me in as I walk by. The chairs are plastic; the tables fold; the lights are fluorescent. They'll have good seafood. I know it. I make a mental note to return.

Later that week, my husband and I meet a Swiss man at the Rusty Keyhole bar, where we gather for sunset drinks. He just rode in from Sihanoukville on a dirt bike. He's here on an extended vacation after working for the UN in the former Yugoslavia. Places like this attract people like him. Smart people, worldly people, scientists and diplomats, movie stars and magnates. You'll see them all here. You'll spot Gerard Depardieu traipsing through Preah Khan. Or you'll find a book by Paul Theroux freshly signed by the author himself earlier that morning. You may even get to speak to royalty. It's Cambodia, where the talk of the town is always intriguing.

So we begin a conversation with the Swiss man about postconflict countries and genocides the world has failed to stop. We keep talking, and the sky grows dark. Where to eat? I know just the spot. We take our conversation up the road to

Phnom Kamchay Thmey and order a plate of fried shrimp with citronella and saffron, crab curry, and another crab with Kampot black pepper. Both crabs arrive juicy and sweet, the shrimp infused with aromatic herbs and the subtle suggestion of lemon. We indulge.

The three of us talk on into the night, nibbling our crab, filling our bellies, long after the other customers leave. We are the last lingering patrons. The waitresses have washed tables and stacked plastic chairs for the night. The family owners watch TV in their pajamas in the back corner. When we finish, they are happy to have served us. It's Khmer seafood at its best, with conversation to match.

Kampot dining

Kampot is located along Cambodia's southwest coastline and is reachable by bus or shared taxi in three to four hours from Phnom Penh. You will find Phnom Kamchay Thmey at the corner of Kampot's riverfront street and the bridge. It's open all day for breakfast, lunch, and dinner.

BATTAMBANG

Anne Best takes a balcony seat in Battambang

I visit Battambang in my capacity as an anthropologist to help a local nongovernmental organization, FEDA, which is building a community center in the nearby village of Ksach Poy. My task is to record the oral history of the village, and I am doing this through interviewing four elderly villagers about their lives and traditions spanning the last eighty years. Although it's fascinating, I find the task can be harrowing, too, given what the country has been through over the past decades. At the end of each day, I need to escape. So, as darkness falls, and the question is asked, "What shall we do this evening?" my answer is often, "Let's go to the Balcony Bar."

The Riverside Balcony Bar has rapidly become my haven of choice during my stays in the laid-back former colonial center in northwest Cambodia. To reach it, I head south from the town center along the river road. Past the bridge on my left—and stalls selling fried beetles, spiders, and assorted creepy-crawlies—I find the bar down a short "driveway," located in an old villa. As is the custom, I leave my shoes at the bottom of the stairs.

The place is just as its name describes, a large, airy balcony with a bar and a pool table, wicker tables, and a few comfortable chairs overlooking the Sangker River. It occupies the top floor of a traditional wooden stilt house. It is a bit of a surprise, and a welcome one too, for Battambang, which until recently has not featured significantly on the tourist circuit. Rumor has it that Angelina Jolie spends time here.

The riverside location is special, but what makes it even more so is the owner. John is an Australian who somehow found himself in these parts and ended up as the owner and proprietor of the bar. He runs a simple yet efficient and incredibly laid-back outfit. It is a meeting place for expats, who gather here after supper to enjoy a cool beer or a *krouch-ma* (lemon juice with Khmer simple syrup), or order food and perhaps join friends or friendly strangers for a meal. Another pleasant surprise in this remote Cambodian town: John's chili con carne is to be recommended.

Refreshed, having put my work behind me, I climb back on the moto and head home in the warm, black stillness of the night. Sometimes, en route, I stop at the Chinese grocers near the market, which sells, among other Western delights, Magnum ice cream bars—the perfect indulgence at the end of another long day.

Dining in Battambang

Along with the Riverside Balcony Bar (closed Mondays), Anne recommends the Smokin' Pot, a small pavement café in the center of town, for excellent and fairly priced Khmer food. For Western breakfasts and apple pie, try the Sunrise Café near the market, and for sweet treats, visit the Chinese grocers on the corner between the market and the Sunrise Café.

Making a difference

If you would like to learn more about FEDA or contribute to its work, visit the organization's website. You can also help by purchasing a copy of Anne's book, *The Monk, the Farmer, the Merchant, the Mother*, available through the website and at Monument Books in Phnom Penh.

www.fedacambodia.com
www.monument-books.com

TMATBOEY

*Karen Coates
makes friends in
a kitchen in Tmatboey*

We spent last week in the distant forests of Preah Vihear Province. To get there, go to Angkor and head northeast three hours. Follow the bumpy dirt roads through empty lands, past ancient temples rarely visited, past CMAC camps and fields delineated for land mine clearing. Turn down a sand road to Tmatboey, a village of eighteen hundred people and a couple hundred huts on stilts. There in the nearby Kulen-Promtep Wildlife Sanctuary, you will find two of the world's rarest birds, the giant ibis and the white-shouldered ibis.

That's why we visit, to see the birds, to work on a story about the Tmatboey ecotourism project, established with the help of the Wildlife Conservation Society. Accommodation is rough—a communal room of slat beds and mosquito nets, bath by bucket, car-battery power for one light and a fan at night. But the village is the picture of quintessential Khmer life. And the kitchen: full of good vibes and good food.

A few of the Tmatboey village women have joined the project's cook team, waking each morning by three to feed birders at four before their predawn treks to the field. The women have learned to cook Western dishes such as spaghetti and omelets, but they quickly discover my taste for local food. In the early morning darkness, I forgo bread and jam and ask for rice with fish instead.

"Fish? You like fish?"

They are delighted. The nearest river is many miles away, but the women arrange for a fish to be bought for my benefit. Every meal afterward, I am presented with a personal plate of fish, fried with garlic or mixed in a lemongrass, shallot, and peanut curry. My love of chili intrigues the women further, and along with each fish they serve me a side bowl of hot red peppers.

I make several new friends on this trip, through my interest in their work. We form a bond. And when I leave for Siem Reap, for a return to bright lights and paved roads and telephones, several of the Tmatboey women tell me they will miss me like a loved one; they will love me like a sister.

People ask me why I travel or what makes me go where I go, and it is days like these. Just a few days in a hot wooden house in a faraway forest. Just a few days in a dark kitchen with stoves of fire and women who tend them—and the bond that forms so quickly. They speak no English; I practice my sketchy Khmer. But all we really need to get started is the language of food.

More about Tmatboey
To find out more about getting to Tmatboey and the wildlife sanctuary and bird-watching opportunities there, go to page 119.

GENERAL CAMBODIA

Socheata Poeuv works up an appetite for exotic fruits

What struck me when I visited Psar Thmei (New Market) in the center of Phnom Penh was the bounty of Cambodia's produce. My personal favorite is the amazing range of tropical fruits. The most fantastic looking of them all is the dragon fruit (*sroka neak*). It's a wild-berry-red color with green scales, and you peel back the thick skin to find a juicy-white pulp that's both sweet and tangy, with black seeds flecked all around.

Another favorite is the jackfruit (*khnau*). On the outside, it's large and spiky and intimidating. Inside are pods of sweet and satisfying fleshy orange fruit. The messy part is pulling each pod out, as your fingers get covered with a sticky substance that only a good scrub with some cooking oil can clean.

I also love longan (*mien*), lychee (*kulen*), and rambutan (*sao mao*). Although they are all similar on the inside, each one is progressively more flamboyant—from a boring brown skin, to bright red bumpy skin, to something that looks more like a sea anemone than a fruit. All grow on small trees and are cherry-sized, with a beautiful milky flesh. They are wonderfully mild, with a smooth mahogany pit on the inside. I can easily eat a pound in one sitting.

Of course, I can't forget the delicious mangoes (*svay*), especially during the mango season, which begins in January. I also suggest keeping an eye out for the similarly named but very different mangosteen (*mongkut*). It might escape your eye because it looks like a small plum with a green stem on top. Cracking open the thick skin is like cracking open a jewel box to reveal beautiful, gleaming, gemlike white segments. A tart and delicious surprise.

Everywhere you will go, there are green coconuts (*duong*). If you ever visit a Cambodian family in the countryside, they will automatically send the oldest son to shimmy up the coconut tree and hack off a few. Serving coconut juice is the equivalent of offering guests ice tea. Beware, though, because my mother tells me that too much green coconut can give you a stomach upset. I've never had a problem, but better safe than sorry.

Finally, there is the most mythical fruit in all of Cambodia—the durian (*tourain*). Many claim that it's the most expensive fruit in the world. Perhaps this is because it sometimes takes as long as fifteen years after planting for a tree to bear fruit. I always ask the vendors at the market to pick out the best and crack it open right at their stall. For some reason durian is best within the first five minutes after you open it. If you keep it around your hotel room, that's when it starts emitting that aroma of stinky feet that it is so famous for. Inside are gorgeous, creamy pods with custardlike fruit. Durian is said to be an aphrodisiac, so share it with someone you love. At the very least, it's enough to make you swoon.

Phil Lees follows his nose throughout Cambodia

In Cambodia, something is always rotting.

There is a physical wall of pungency that pummels you as soon as you exit the plane, and it continues to haunt you as you wait in the sterile departure lounge trying to summarize your trip into a pithy précis for when your family inevitably asks, "So, how was your holiday?" The odor is richest in the markets, where the outlandish aromas of tropical fruit battle with fresh fish and other meats in various stages of degradation.

When I first set foot in a Cambodian market, I couldn't help but notice that beneath the trembling crescendo of odor is a consistent olfactory bass line, a distinct earthy undertone that suggests order amongst the pandemonium. That fertile and restrained redolence is *prahok*, Cambodia's national fish condiment.

It is no coincidence that Cambodians named cheese *prahok barang*, literally "foreign *prahok*," as both foods are culinary responses to a rapidly perishable ingredient, and both are artisan produced. To the uninitiated, *prahok* and an aged Stilton may stink. To the connoisseur, both have a distinctive and pleasurable scent.

Unlike the intensified piscine punch of anchovies to which most travelers around Southeast Asia are accustomed, *prahok* is a subtler form of preserved fish and a solution to the seasonality of fish migration along the Mekong and into the Tonle Sap. When the numbers of fish explode with the monsoon season, Cambodia's lake and riverside villages are consumed by *prahok* production. Fish are gutted and filleted by every villager at hand, salted and left in the sunlight for a day to begin the curing process, and then packed with more coarse salt in wooden barrels or ceramic jars to begin the months-long fermentation process. *Prahok* experts can tell the readiness of their paste by the distinctive changes in odor over time;

it begins to reach maturity at around two months.

When sold, *prahok* is graded by the size of the fish used, with the cheapest made from thumb-sized *riel* fish, and the more expensive from both larger snakehead fish and other freshwater varieties. At the top of the *prahok* chain is *maam*, a rich, fermented product made with whole fillets, roasted red rice, and occasionally palm sugar. This is a delicacy that can be added to soups or stocks or—if you are courageous enough—eaten steamed by itself.

Eating prahok

If you eat Khmer cuisine, then it is inevitable that you will eat *prahok*. This condiment adds a depth of flavor and salty clout to typically sour soups such as the herb-rich *samlor machou yuon* or lemongrass-and-galangal-spiced *samlor machou kroueng*. More-adventurous diners will seek out *prahok ktis*—a *prahok*-based dipping sauce served with crudités or alongside barbecued beef. Cambodia's best *prahok* hails from Siem Reap (go to page 24) and the villages surrounding the northern part of the Tonle Sap. The most accessible places to find it are at any of Cambodia's markets, where it will be stored in clear jars or large plastic troughs. Just follow your nose.

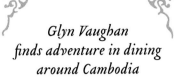

Glyn Vaughan
finds adventure in dining
around Cambodia

When it comes to exotic fare, Glyn Vaughan offers a few recommendations that are sure to challenge your palate. Critters and creatures of all types get their due as he combs the country for adventurous drinking and dining at its finest.

I smell a rat

Some claim that the house rat came to Cambodia quite by accident, slipping in off the old merchant ships that sailed into port from Europe. Upon arrival, this breed joined the several additional varieties of Rattus already inhabiting Cambodia, including the paddy rat. With thickset heads and bodies, coarse shaggy hair, and large front teeth, these rats live in rice fields, burrowing into mounds or termite nests, a habit that frequently damages the farmers' irrigation systems. The Cambodians, however, get their own back. Throughout much of provincial Cambodia, these rustic rats are hounded and chased, cornered and captured, and ultimately digested. The cool season is the best chance to find them on the carte du jour, with the eating houses in the old quarter of Battambang town being as good a place as any to try paddy rat. If you plan to give it a go, let me point out that it is especially tasty if barbecued and seasoned with Worcestershire sauce.

Jiminy cricket!

Crickets are also in season at about this same time. Across the lowlands the traps are laid—one sees them now and then along National Highway 6—and the *jong reut*, as they are known, are caught in the thousands. There are several species, with the *jong reut dike* being the large kind, darkish brown or black as tar. They are mightily aggressive, and Cambodian kids sometimes stage cricket fights with them. The *jong reut doeng* (or coconut cricket) are the edible ones, in case you have a craving. Fried whole, they are bought by the cupful. The egg-carrying females are thought to be the tastiest and are best scoffed with ice-cold beer. *Jong reut* can be bought at the food stalls inside Psar Thmei market in Phnom Penh.

Going batty

Perhaps you are familiar with old stories of the batty rascals of the National Museum, which once emerged at sunset from its rafters, nose to tail, filling the air with the frenzied beat of skinny wings. The spittle of this bat is by Cambodian legend considered something of an alchemist's treasure. In Khmer it is called *teuk moet projeeoo*, and it is a much sought after tonic, taken for strength, wit, and sexual prowess. Word has it, though, that after a bottle or two, the only effect in sight—or not as it turns out—is that it makes you as blind as a bat. Luckily, it is devilishly difficult to find, although it is available at Psar Tuol Tom Pong market, if you're in the mood for taking the risk.

Warts and all

In search of an even more questionable brew? You might consider Kneecaps of the Toad Wine—s*raa angkunh kingkuork*. It alleges simply to cure everything, except sobriety, which it actually counters remarkably well. The label on a bottle I encountered boasts the following: "Kneecaps of the Toad Wine will stop syphilis and gonorrhea, and pain when urinating, and high fever and pain in your kidneys, and chapped lips, rheumatoid arthritis, and testicular inflammation. ... Drink it and your temperature will drop. You will feel cold. It will give you a pot belly and make you look beautiful all over. ... Drink as much as you can take but be careful for syphilis can spread to your wife and children. ... Kneecaps of the Toad Wine is made by the famous herbalist Chhouk Nip Phan, alias Mr. Iron Rod."

While I find this brew interesting to mention, I do not recommend it for evening swilling. It is about as friendly as battery acid. That said, as a keepsake—kept for the sake of one's health, that is, under its original bottle cap—it is a less than ordinary gift to take to a friend back home. Kneecaps of the Toad Wine may be procured from many a *Kru Khmer* (traditional Cambodian healer) and is manufactured down Street 19Z, a little lane running off Street 19, opposite the University of Fine Arts in Phnom Penh, which is itself situated behind the National Museum.

Terrorizing your taste buds

To try a few exotic nibbles in a hygienic setting, take yourself to Romdeng, a nonprofit restaurant run by former street kids, which specializes in food from the provinces. To read about dining on fried tarantulas, go to page 25.

74, Street 174
Phnom Penh

www.friends-international.org

Small Bites around Cambodia

Our writers share more of their favorite restaurants and eating experiences around Cambodia.

Phnom Penh International Airport
Phnom Penh

Before an early morning flight out of Cambodia, I need my coffee fix and some breakfast. Although I could get that in the departure lounge, the coffee alone costs way too much, and it's about the same as airport coffee the world over—not very good. So when I fly out of Phnom Penh, I try to arrive a little early. Check-in desks open two hours before each flight, and once I've checked in, I turn back and walk out of the main exit and cross the road. Directly opposite is another road leading away from the airport, and on the right-hand corner you will find a large table with a glass noodle case on top. Behind that is a little restaurant where I can count on the most amazing bowl of hot noodle soup, brimming with pork, shrimp, herbs, and bean sprouts, not to mention a large cup of *proper* Cambodian coffee—strong enough to stand my spoon up in, all for around $1. If the day is getting hot, the sugarcane juice stall on the opposite corner offers the chance for one last taste of Cambodia before I go. (David Shamash)

Pyongyang Restaurant
Monivong Boulevard
(between Preah Sihanouk and Mao Tse Tung Boulevards)
Phnom Penh

(The restaurant was closed at the time of publication but is expected to reopen soon—when it does, we want to make sure you know about it.)

For a rare culinary experience, head for Pyongyang Restaurant to savor the gastronomic strangeness of the Democratic People's Republic of Korea. The state propaganda machine here may be nothing more than an old TV, but it is sufficient cause for the most gleeful paranoia. There may, after all, be spies in every corner, weighing the sincerity of your awe at those Olympian feats of civil engineering by the tyrannical Kim Jong-il. Cabbage is heaped upon you, as is tripe, knuckle, and tongue. Surprisingly, it is all quite delicious, served up amidst a troupe of dancing waitresses waving their national flags about. Bottle washers, meanwhile, run wildly in from the kitchen with streamers trailing behind, as one of the Dear Leader's virtuosos saws frenziedly on her violin. (Glyn Vaughan)

Psar Tuol Tom Pong
Corner of Streets 155 and 444
Phnom Penh

Of Phnom Penh's many markets, I love Psar Tuol Tom Pong (Russian Market). It has the best range of souvenirs and crafts in the city, and is also a good place to try authentic Khmer snacks. After exhausting my bargaining skills at stalls selling palm leaf manuscripts, lacquerware, musical instruments, and Khmer silk (my favorite), I head for the excellent little coffee stall at the south end of the food section. It serves wonderful iced coffee, made thick and creamy with evaporated milk. Just look for their sign, which reads, "Best coffee in Phnom Penh." It's true. Part of Tuol Tom Pong is roofed with sheet metal, and it can become positively ovenlike by the end of the day, so if I need to escape the heat, I go just outside to an excellent expat-run snack bar called Jars of Clay for a cold drink. And if I'm feeling peckish, I ask my

motodop to stop by Jaik Jien Piseth, a couple of blocks away. The name translates literally as "special fried banana." This is one of my favorite snacks—flavorsome Khmer bananas dipped in batter and deep fried. After that, I might even have the energy to go back and do a bit more shopping. (Caroline Nixon)

Banteay Srei Restaurant
121, National Highway 6
(Right-hand side on the way to Siem Reap airport, a few blocks from Wat Kesaram)
Siem Reap

I am originally from Siem Reap, and although I now live in the United States, I still consider myself a local. When I return, one of the things I look forward to most is seeing the famous Yeay Lok (Grandmother Lok). To the native Siem Reapians' palate, Yeay Lok is the one person who is responsible for making the town famous. She has been in the feasting business for well over half a century, having even been called upon to prepare dishes for the royal family. My own family often ate at her restaurant before I was born. I urge you to try one of her many fish dishes, with the ingredients fresh from the Tonle Sap Lake. My favorite is her signature *plear trey ross*. This heritage dish is a Khmer-style fish slow-cooked in fresh-squeezed lime juice and topped with just the right amount of sliced lemongrass, a variety of mints, and hot pepper. Yeay Lok could very well write a cookbook on the Khmer culinary arts, but she once told me, "My time is better spent cooking in my kitchen!" She shares her vast knowledge and her refined culinary skills with her apprentices, which include her children and adult grandchildren. In this way her legacy is sure to live on. (Ronnie Yimsut)

Sawasdee Food Terrace
Yaklom Hill Lodge
Ban Lung
Ratanakiri Province
www.yaklom.com

In Ban Lung, in the northeast province of Ratanakiri, Yaklom Hill Lodge is an inexpensive and incredibly soul-reviving place to stay. After a long day of exploring—waterfalls, Yeak Laom Lake, hill tribe villages, and Virachey National Park—a great way to enjoy the evening is to take a seat at the lodge's Sawasdee Food Terrace. As I'm a vegetarian, my favorite dishes are the vegetarian green curry and the vegetarian red curry. It takes about half an hour for the dishes to be made, as the ingredients are freshly prepared, with the herbs and spices minced ever so perfectly for the right blend. A bowl of rice is served with the curry, and I like to spoon some of the curry onto the rice and eat it slowly. Whatever you order here, be assured that great care and a little bit of love will be put forth into the dish. (Doug Mendel)

Fresh sugarcane juice
Around Cambodia

On the way to the Takeo countryside from Phnom Penh, my Khmer friend took me to Phnom Chisor. This ancient temple from the eleventh century is on top of a small mountain, and we had to walk up 412 steep steps to get to the top. But first, at the bottom, my friend asked if I'd ever had fresh sugarcane juice before. I hadn't. He ordered two. A vendor took a few stalks of sugarcane, peeled and cut into two-foot lengths, and put them into a juicer, which consisted of two steel cylinders joined by gears and attached to a large wheel that she turned by hand. She ran the stalks through several times until all their juice was squeezed out. Then she poured the juice into little plastic bags, inserted straws, and tied them at the top. Although I had seen locals drinking like this, I never dreamed I would be doing the same. But it was hot, and I was thirsty. I was amazed at how refreshing the juice tasted, sweet and cold. I was hooked. Now, whenever I travel in the countryside, I always stop for sugarcane juice. Stands are everywhere. The juice is generally served with local ice, and while I've been warned against this, I've never been sick. When I seek out sugarcane juice sellers in Phnom Penh, I look for those that keep their carts and glasses clean—they can count on me as a regular customer. (Mariam Arthur)

GENERAL CAMBODIA

SEEING THE SIGHTS

Fresh perspectives on exploring must-see attractions

Cambodia has (arguably) the top tourist attraction in the world: Angkor. And I'm not talking about just one temple. The ancient Khmer civilization encompassed hundreds of temples, centered around the breathtaking Angkor Wat—with the Bayon, Ta Prohm, and Banteay Srei hot on its heels for the honor of favorite among those who have visited. These are the show stoppers, so to speak, the ones that draw the massive crowds. But as the writers in this chapter reveal, it's possible to find a corner among them to call your own, simply by hopping on a bicycle, walking along a less trodden pathway, or even coming during the rainy season.

You can also easily seek out a temple where you can wander, imagine, and have the entire place to yourself. To get started, simply follow me to the satellite temples of Banteay Chhmar, Karen Coates to the tranquil setting of Beng Mealea, Martin Lum to the forest temple of Sambor Prei Kuk, or Dougald O'Reilly to Preah Vihear on the Cambodian-Thai border. The latter is among my personal favorites. Not only does it have the most amazing mountaintop location, perched on a cliff overlooking Cambodia below, but when I visited, there was no pathway for the first hour of the climb, and hanging on to tree stumps, vines, and rocks made it the most physically demanding of my temple adventures. I stayed overnight in a hammock in the shadow of Preah Vihear beneath a full moon and had it all to myself.

Angkor isn't all Cambodia has to offer, though it can sometimes seem that way because, well, it's Angkor. Right outside Siem Reap, you will find Cambodia's quieter charms, from rural villages to amazing sunsets. When not in Siem Reap, travelers usually spend time in Phnom Penh, whose own attractions are a blend of old and new, entertaining and somber. I've tried to offer a bit of each, with essays on topics such as the playful mood at Wat Phnom and the lessons to be learned from the Choeung Ek Killing Fields.

Buddhist monk photographing the Bayon temple

Architecture should play an important role when sightseeing in Phnom Penh, as well as in some of the country's major towns (Battambang, Kampot, Kratie, Kompong Cham). The legacy of the French Colonial era is wonderfully reflected in the buildings that surround the post office square, as well as a few beautifully restored examples around Wat Phnom. Following on, in the 1950s and '60s came a new wave of Khmer architecture, much of it under the leadership of architect Vann Molyvann, whose trademark quirky lines and shapes dominate the Olympic Stadium, university buildings, and the Front du Bassac, now a slum. To my mind, the best way to see these impressive buildings is to take a tour with Khmer Architecture Tours (www.ka-tours.org).

While Phnom Penh and Siem Reap can keep a traveler busy for weeks, I urge you to go farther afield. Whether you join Cristiano Calcagno in a hunt for the Sacred Swords of the Baray, explore an old Pepsi factory with Dickon Verey outside Battambang, brave Khmer Rouge ghosts with Steve McClure in Anlong Veng, or just pedal along the Mekong River outside Kratie with Kim Fay, Cambodia is sure to impress and surprise you with its unconventional character and diversity.

PHNOM PENH

Sheila Scoville finds a playful perch in Phnom Penh

Just before sunset on Christmas Eve, my friend and I finished a daylong tour of trudging the streets at Phnom Penh's namesake pagoda, on the site where the city is said to have been founded. After approaching the hill where Wat Phnom perches above the city, we climbed stairs to the summit and removed our dusty shoes. Crammed inside the pagoda were Buddha images of all sizes, each with its own clutch of precious Cambodian riel weighed down by a lotus bud.

What struck us more than the generosity of Phnom Penh, however, was the pagoda's blend of centuries-old tradition with contemporary kitsch. Behind the main Buddha whirled an electric kaleidoscope. Beside the usual fruit and flowers on the altar, Christmas trees twinkled. To our delight, this anything-and-everything-goes attitude continued outside at a shrine dedicated to the city's guardian, Madame Penh. A sculpture of her smiled sweetly while a large, digital date-and-time keeper flashed above her shoulder.

As we explored the grounds around Wat Phnom, the scene brought to mind a Fellini-esque carnival. Smiling beggars with missing limbs crawled forth, while schoolboys screamingly chased each other, clambering over a large stupa containing the ashes of a long-deceased king. Gaunt slips of men hawked the freedom of caged, twittering birds to pilgrims in need of a few karma points or tourists interested in a new way to part with their money. Even the city's sole remaining elephant, Sambo, played a role, providing rides around the base of the hill for a few dollars.

Running amok at the pagoda's western base were long-tailed macaque monkeys, whose matriarch had to be the most obscenely fat animal we'd ever seen. Thick rolls of silver gray fur encircled her midriff, eliciting from us the snarky nickname Marlon Brando Monkey. Staring with their too wise and world-weary eyes, the macaques sifted the pagoda's refuse. They both impressed and alarmed us with how efficiently they stripped discarded flowers and gulped their tender stamens. Right from our fingers, the monkeys also greedily plucked *cholt*, the inverted-saucer-shaped seed heads of lotuses sold by bonneted women as snacks.

Compared to the many beautiful pagodas and temples in Southeast Asia, Wat Phnom did not take our breath away. But it did provide what a place of worship should—a needed spiritual respite for Phnom Penh's hardworking residents. As for us, the tourists in their midst, it was a sanctuary from moto-clogged streets, and more importantly, a peek at the playful heart of Cambodia, often obscured by the country's rough, scarred exterior.

Wat Phnom

The wat is located at the northern end of the center of Phnom Penh on the only hill in the city. Just follow Norodom Boulevard to the roundabout at the base of the hill. Admission is $1.

CHOEUNG EK

Christine Thuy-Anh Vu learns the lesson of hope at Choeung Ek

When I was fifteen, Dith Pran, a Cambodian photojournalist working for *The New York Times*, came to speak to my high school class. You might recognize his name, because his disquieting eyewitness account of genocide in Cambodia became widely known in the mid-1980s film *The Killing Fields*.

In 1975, Pran was captured. He escaped four years later from being among the 1.7 million Cambodian people slaughtered by the Khmer Rouge. While Pran's story taught us sheltered American high school students about political injustice and the scourge of war, the message he delivered, as well as that of *The Killing Fields*, was about the opportunity for renewal and one's duty to protect humanity.

More than a decade later, I found myself in a place I least thought I would visit: Phnom Penh. But because my parents were war emigrants from Vietnam, and the violence there influenced what Pran faced in Cambodia, I felt I owed it to them and myself to take advantage of my time living in Asia to visit places like Choeung Ek, where twenty thousand victims died, and better connect to my family history and the global history I only understood from a distance.

"The Killing Fields" is a term Pran coined to describe Choeung Ek just as it was: an old orchard converted into a long stretch of pits filled with the remains of murdered victims, who were mostly bludgeoned to death or had their throats slashed. By the time I visited, nearly thirty-five years after the Khmer Rouge took over Phnom Penh, Choeung Ek's ghosts remained half-hidden in the pockmarked terrain of largely excavated pits, covered in layers of plant overgrowth and grass.

I went with my best friend, Jesse, who was visiting a few days before taking off on a bike ride through Cambodia, Laos, and Vietnam. We took a moto, and on our way, the wide, rust-colored dirt road plowed through stretches of empty fields. Large trees with their canopies of glinting leaves protected us from a harsh sun and the lure of winding side paths. Nothing hinted at the past carnage along the way. Not even when we reached the modest gray museum sign or when we walked by the small ticket office.

We arrived rather late, with only forty minutes to roam before the grounds closed. Even with no one around, the gravity of where we were compelled us to tread quietly. An impressive memorial stupa that sits atop a hill displays stacks upon stacks of human skulls, organized by age and gender. While this formal lineup of victims gave us an idea of the numbers murdered, what really affected us were the human bones sticking up from underfoot and a remaining lone tree, which is documented as what babies were smashed against before being thrown into an adjacent pit. Sadly, Choeung Ek is only a modest example of what terror war and oppression can really inflict.

After getting back to town, I was searching for how Pran was able to end his lecture to my class on such a positive note when, to me, visiting Choeung Ek was deeply upsetting. As I stretched my legs with Jesse at a street café and watched a horde of children roaring with laughter in a game of tag, I remembered Pran's parting message—there is always hope for renewal, justice, and change, so long as you believe in it, take part to develop it, and help others to prevent future injustices and atrocities along the way, even if it is just by spreading awareness like he did.

Although many have not had the fortunate experience of meeting Dith Pran, I hope those who visit Choeung Ek are able to come away with something similar—a sense of hope and duty—and that this essay achieves what Pran advocated, playing a small part in passing his message along.

Choeung Ek

Choeung Ek is located fifteen kilometers southwest of Phnom Penh, about a thirty-minute drive from the center of the city. Any motodop or tuk-tuk driver will know the way, and it's up to you to negotiate a fair price for the journey there and back. If you are making your way under your own steam, head for the new Stung Meanchey Bridge and carry on, keeping to the left at the junction with the garage. At fifteen kilometers or thereabouts you will see the signs for the Genocidal Center. The museum is open daily from 8:00 a.m. to 5:00 p.m.

www.cekillingfield.com

Dith Pran

After a devoted career in photojournalism and humanitarian work, Dith Pran passed away in March 2009. You can learn more about his story and the story of other survivors by watching *The Killing Fields* or reading *The Death and Life of Dith Pran*, by his fellow journalist, Sydney Schanberg. Pran is also the author of *Children of Cambodia's Killing Fields*.

SIEM REAP

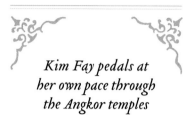

Kim Fay pedals at her own pace through the Angkor temples

"Do you happen to have any with baskets?" I ask the activities desk clerk who is standing in front of two bicycles at the bottom of the front steps of the hotel.

"Baskets are illegal," the young man informs me.

"Illegal?"

"The police don't allow them in the park," he says, earnestly apologetic.

"Really?" I glance at my sister, Julie, whose look says it all: Don't tell me you're actually surprised. After all, I have been traveling in Southeast Asia for nearly fifteen years and lived in Vietnam for four. Vietnam is fraught with weird, illogical rules. Why should neighboring Cambodia be any different?

I use the straps of my knapsack to secure a map on my handlebars, while Julie fastens her camera bag into place. We head out from the hotel that touts itself as being the closest one to Angkor Wat, into steady morning traffic. At the entrance gate, we wait to buy our passes, parked between enormous tour buses sput-tering exhaust into the already hot, heavy air. European and Japanese passengers gaze down on us through high tinted windows, as if we are one of the sights they have come to see.

As we pedal down the side of the wooded road that leads to Angkor Wat, the tour buses pass, and although there are many, they travel at high speeds and are quickly gone, leaving only the oceanic murmur of the forest in their wakes. They may have their air-conditioning, but we have a soft, cool breeze as we cycle leisurely along, listening to the soft humming of cicadas and little gray monkeys in the trees.

The last time I was here, eight years earlier, the main temple of Angkor Wat was well visited but not crowded. Today, it is like Disneyland on a summer day. It is a place where the word *swarm* is not a cliché. We decide to come back later, when it's cooler, just before sunset, and return to the little "parking lot" at the café across the road from the moat.

A few more bikes have accumulated in the lot, and Julie frowns. "Look," she says, pointing to a trio of bikes next to ours. All have baskets. We glance around. There is a bike leaning against a tree. It too has a basket. A spacious wire basket that would be perfect for holding a camera bag or a knapsack. Grumbling with big talk about how we're going to complain to the management when we get back to our luxury hotel that should be above such deceptions, we manipulate our bags back onto our handlebars. But our irritation soon fades.

Cycling away from the madhouse of Angkor Wat toward the Bayon, whose enigmatic sculptured faces provide one of Cambodia's most memorable images, we realize how quiet the park is. Travelers can explore it by motorized tuk-tuk, motorcycles, and private cars, but most come by bus. In a strange way, these buses are a good thing for us. They confine their passengers to two places, the bus or the site, segregating them from the rest of the park, its roadways, forests, small silent yards, and side cafés, which are as enjoyable as the temples, and often more so because they are calm.

We pedal farther into the park, taking turns photographing one another gliding between the elongated stone elephant trunks that flank the South Gate of Angkor Thom. As we approach the Bayon, a pair of smooth, gray sandstone eyes gaze out from the high green leaves. My stomach lurches. I won't go so far as to compare us to Henri Mouhot, the naturalist who stumbled across Angkor Wat in 1860 and brought it to the attention of the Western world, but there is a sense of exhilaration that I am certain does not come to those inside their climate-controlled buses.

This is a feeling of discovering, rather than of being delivered, and it can come only with the pace of a bicycle. Throughout the day, as we follow the Small Circuit road that includes the disheveled ruins of Ta Prohm, we will tread back and forth and back and forth in front of the Terrace of the Elephants, slow down to examine low walls winding through scrub, and stop for nearly half an hour to watch a family of monkeys.

While the monkeys chirrup and squeal and leap on one another in the dusky light, tour buses fly past, most likely to get their passengers back in time for the evening's scheduled Khmer dance performances. I doubt that most of the passengers even notice the monkeys, or us, paused on the side of the road, bags tied sloppily to our bikes, chatting idly as we enjoy the soft early evening air.

Renting bikes

Bikes can be rented from most hotels and guesthouses and should not cost more than $10 a day. Baskets are not illegal. When using a basket, you should tie your bag into it, so you're not a target for thieves.

Parking your bike

Near the entrance of most temples you will find small cafés and parking areas where you can leave your bike. Parking should cost a few thousand riel. Make sure to get a ticket for your bike.

When to go

Get started as early in the day as possible. You can easily do Angkor's Small Circuit in one day, but you will want plenty of time to stop along the way to sip some coconut juice at a street stall and hang out with monkeys. For more about the monkeys of Cambodia, go to page 153.

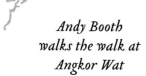

Andy Booth walks the walk at Angkor Wat

Of the hundreds of thousands of people who visit Angkor Wat every year, few take the time to enjoy a leisurely walk along the inner wall of the moat. As this offers a unique perspective on the temple grounds, they miss out on a real treat.

Morning walk

Cross the moat by the east causeway (the less popular one) and turn right before reaching the east *gopura* (entry into the main temple grounds). Give yourself a few good hours to walk all the way around to the western entrance between the moat and the laterite perimeter wall. This side of Angkor Wat is very quiet before noon, and you have a good chance of seeing egrets, wild ducks, frogs, butterflies, and dragonflies. Young boys come here to tether their cattle, buffalo, and horses to graze. Sit awhile and just enjoy the silence. As an added bonus, you will find a few mango trees growing near the perimeter wall. These mangos are small in size but sweet to eat. Bon appétit.

Evening walk

Cross again by the eastern causeway, but this time turn left to follow the wall around the south side of the temple. Cattle and buffalo still abound, but you will also see children playing at the edge of the water whilst moat cleaners wade or use boats to clear weeds. The battle is a constant one between the cleaners and the rampant growth of pondweed that threatens to overtake their efforts. When you reach the *south gopura*, peek inside. There you will find a curious termite mound that has naturally taken on the shape of a Buddha. For the whole of this evening walk, you will encounter wonderfully serene scenes. In June, July, and August the sun (when you can see it through the thunderous rain clouds) will set almost directly over the moat.

Walking Angkor

Even though you are not inside the actual temple, you will be inside the complex and therefore need an Angkor pass. Being inside the complex without a pass may result in a fine.

Soumya James relishes a rainstorm at Angkor Wat

When I saw the storm clouds gathering over the towers of Angkor Wat one November afternoon, my first reaction was *Oh no! There go my chances for some good photographs.* Seeing the darkening sky, most of the other visitors were already beating a hasty retreat to their waiting cars, motos, and tuk-tuks.

I decided to stay.

I climbed to the uppermost tier of the temple and took as many photos as the light would permit. Then the skies opened, and it rained with a vengeance.

Sitting on a window sill at the top, I watched the rain collect in the four courtyards around the central tower. Pattering over the curved *naga* snakes that made up the roof of the galleries, it formed a transparent fluid curtain as it came down to meet the ground below. It flowed over the carved bodies of the *apsaras*, accentuating their sensuous shapes. The verdant trees around the temple glistened with the raindrops and swayed, as though joyously quenching their thirst in the midafternoon heat.

From my perch high above, I watched as the mist rose. It filled the air with that wonderful smell of fresh, wet dirt. There were a few of us up there in the temple that day, but no one spoke. I couldn't. My senses were filled with the sound and scent of this extraordinary display.

Then, abruptly, so typical of the Cambodian monsoon, the rain stopped and the sun emerged. Light glinting off the water collected on the leaves, and the temple set the landscape ablaze. I came down to earth.

Angkor Wat in the rain

Tourists coming to Cambodia are often encouraged to wait until the monsoons are over so that their trips to the temples won't be dampened by heavy rains, but as Soumya points out, monsoon season can bring its own beauty. The season is from May to October, but it is best to plan to visit toward the end of it—this way, most of the day is dry and you can still experience the rains in the afternoon. At this time of year, typically the monsoon rain starts between 1:00 and 5:00 p.m. The good thing about this is that this time is highly predictable. Visit some nearby temples such as Phnom Bakheng or Baksei Chamkrong, and then head for Angkor Wat when you see the clouds approaching.

Dawn Rooney begins the day her way at Angkor Wat

We arrive in the blackness of night, our way lit only by the stars and the descending moon. We walk down the west causeway and through the center entrance, descending the short flight of stairs on the right and continuing southward to the steps, where we settle silently to witness nature's timeless transformation—sunrise.

The morning fog hides the temple, but soon it lifts, slowly at first. The air takes on a mauve hue, and the silhouette of the temple emerges, its vastness filling the sky. The sun rises over the towers. Monks from a nearby monastery file past. A flock of birds flies by. A new day begins once again at Angkor Wat.

Returning to the walkway, we admire the extraordinary bas-relief along the top of the wall on our left. Robust divinities ride fanciful animals within an intricately carved leaflike frame. The female divinities—the *devatas* and *apsaras*—on the inner walls of the porch are some of the most beautiful carvings in the temple.

We leave as we entered and cross the main road for breakfast at one of the open-air eateries. Chez Sophea is my favorite. A baguette warmed on a charcoal grill and a cup of brewed coffee with hot milk. This, for me, is a perfect way to start the day.

As a scholar and art historian specializing in Southeast Asia, I know Angkor well. I have written guides to the temples. I have a favorite path of exploration, and we now follow it, driving to Angkor's east entrance and walking along the earthen path, up the stairs at the southeast corner and through the pavilion where we come face-to-face with a great Hindu epic, "The Churning of the Ocean of Milk." This magnificent wall carving extends forty-nine meters along the Gallery of Bas-Reliefs and is arguably the finest visual depiction of the myth ever created. This story of birth and creation is appropriately placed in the direction of the rising sun, which signifies a new beginning.

At the end of the churning, we seek out the south side of the next level and make our way up the stairs to gaze at the 1,850 *apsaras*, born from the churning. These celestial nymphs have inspired poets and artists throughout history. They are truly, as they have been lovingly described, "visions of perfect grace."

Finally, we climb to the uppermost level (at the south or west if it is open), keeping in mind that we are in the most sacred part of the temple, for a bird's-eye view of the genius of Khmer architecture. Angkor Wat is the largest and most breathtaking of the Angkor monuments, and from this height, at this early hour of the day before the crowds arrive, it feels as if it belongs to us.

Reading about the temples

Kim Fay writes: In my experience, Rooney is the most accessible writer when it comes to learning about the Angkor temples. I consider her *Angkor* to be a classic, as far as guides are concerned. It is divided into two parts. The first is a scholarly (but not overly so) explanation of history, legends, art, and architecture. The second is a guidebook, which takes you through Angkor's temples, citadels, and barays, no matter how small. She lays the foundation for a knowledgeable visit, from types of building materials to the gods encountered on bas-reliefs. Her tour of the Angkor Wat galleries, for example, makes the stories clear without overwhelming with detail. If you have time for only one book, this is it.

Kent Davis is forever changed by the women of Angkor Wat

It's easy to look back and acknowledge pivotal moments in our lives, but beforehand, we never see them coming. So as I walked across the Rainbow Bridge on my first visit to Angkor Wat at 10:35 a.m. on November 2, 2005, I had no idea that my life was about to change.

I was no stranger to Southeast Asia. In the early 1990s I worked in Thailand for five years and traveled the region, passionately studying language, culture, history, and religion. I met my wife, Sophaphan, in 1992, and we've shared our adventures since.

I had waited fifteen years for my Cambodian odyssey. I had no preconceptions or clear expectations of Angkor Wat, but within minutes of entering I was overwhelmed. Not by the magnitude of its soaring structures in the hot jungle setting. I had anticipated "architectural grandeur" from one of the Wonders of the World. I wasn't prepared for the temple's human side as realistic carvings of women began greeting me in my exploration.

The heavenly maidens, called *apsaras* and *devatas*, welcomed me at every entrance, in every sanctuary, and on every level of the massive structure. Their warm stone faces peacefully gazed at me from another century, yet their features were quite familiar. Clearly their daughters are still selling water outside the temple. I had just passed one of their sisters, walking across the rainbow bridge with her wedding party. Even my own wife, born two hundred miles to the north, echoed their beauty.

As the day continued, unanswered questions began gathering deep in my mind. Tourist books dismiss the *apsaras* with a clichéd sentence or two: "The builders decorated the bare limestone walls with lively carvings of heavenly dancers." My guides succinctly commented, "The women were carved to serve the king in the next life. Tonight we see them dancing in a show!"

That night I fell into my bed exhausted but sleepless with my mind ablaze under the *apsaras'* spell. Nearly nine hundred years ago, one of the most powerful Khmer rulers controlled a vast empire. King Suryavarman II built the largest stone religious monument on earth. Yet his will was for women to dominate his temple. He gave them precedence over his own image or that of any male. Even his god Vishnu seems to play a minor role compared to the multitude of 1,850 females, realistically immortalized in stone.

In my heart I knew these women were much more than "decorations." These were portrait carvings, not random faces dreamed up by simple stone carvers. Behind each visage was a woman as real as you and I.

They laughed and loved and dreamed in this world, not in heaven.

Who were they? Where did they come from? How much power did they wield? Why were they glorified at such a fantastic cost to the empire? What happened to them? How could anyone write about Angkor Wat without speaking of them immediately and at length? Does anyone else see what is so clear to me, that this temple is here because of the women?

In my mind's eye, I saw the portraits precisely coded with myriad variations of crowns, jewelry, poses, ethnic features, and attributes. A thorough examination could unlock secrets these women have guarded for so long. I began designing my study. As I drifted off to sleep, I pledged myself to the *apsaras* as they pledged themselves to the Khmer empire so long ago.

The next busy day was filled with temple tours, but I rearranged my schedule to visit Angkor Wat one more time before heading home. I imagined returning to a Western world filled with historical information about these fantastic women. With 140 years of intense study, surely there must be volumes of books written about them.

Instead I found that, perhaps blinded by their beauty, historians and archaeologists have written almost nothing. In 1927, Sappho Marchal, a young French woman, published the only quantitative analysis ever done. Sixty-seven years would pass before K. M. Srivastava wrote the second and only other book about the *apsaras* of Angkor Wat.

My epiphany was more than seeing unrealized significance in the daughters of Angkor Wat. After fifteen years' traveling on the Thai side of the border, I discovered that the Khmer civilization still lived throughout Southeast Asia, even though I hadn't known it when it was right before my eyes.

In 1906, Auguste Rodin wrote, "The Cambodians have shown us all that antiquity can contain. Their classics are as great as ours. It is impossible to see human nature brought to a higher state of perfection. We have only the Cambodians and the Greeks."

Indeed, Cambodia was home to one of the most mysterious high civilizations on earth. Her seed flourished at the fertile crossroads of ancient China and India, giving rise to expressions that sometimes eclipsed those of either parent. To visit a remote Khmer temple is to stand alone with history—your memories, hopes, and dreams becoming one against a verdant backdrop shrill with the sound of cicadas. Here, the powerful currents of past and future flow close to the surface. Cambodia will touch you like no other place. And as it did with me, it just may change your life.

Kent's Khmer studies

Kent Davis is currently working on two books about the celestial female figures of the ancient Khmers. He has set up his own website dedicated to a better understanding and appreciation of the Angkor Wat apsaras and devatas.

www.devata.org

Recommended Reading

Angkor
by Jaroslav Poncar
Edition Panorama

www.poncar.de

Apsaras at Angkor Wat in Indian Context
by K. M. Srivastava
Angkor Publishers

Khmer Costumes and Ornaments of the Devatas of Angkor Wat
by Sappho Marchal
translated by Merrily P. Hansen
Orchid Press

www.orchidbooks.com

Andy Booth travels beyond Angkor Wat for sunrise views

Fumble for the alarm clock in the dark. Light on. Pull on some clothes. Don't forget the tripod—I know, I know—left it in front of the door for just this reason. The elevator is too bright. I pad through the dimly lit hotel lobby, deserted aside from a sleeping security guard and some potted plants, and out into the darkness and unexpected warmth of the Cambodian night.

As an avid photographer I have gone through this routine many times and joined the throngs in front of this greatest of all temples, Angkor Wat. Everyone is waiting for the night to fade and the sun to rise, but for me the real attraction is the journey there. Cambodia is an early morning country. The hotter the season, the more people I see out and about at dawn, trying to steal a march on their labors before the heat of the day sets in.

Despite Angkor Wat's popular photographic potential during the dawn hours, there are other places I prefer to go for the sunrise, mainly due to there being so many people who head to this one temple these days. Chattering crowds and joking backpackers are all very well, but not before six in the morning. So my favorite spots for sunrise are the lesser-known Phnom Krom and—yes, the site famous for its sunsets—Phnom Bakheng.

Phnom Krom, at the north end of the Tonle Sap Lake, is a curious land formation, a hill jutting out of the middle of a perfectly flat plain. Geologists, having found impactites, declared Phnom Krom's setting as evidence that the lake could have been formed by a meteor several kilometers across making a glancing blow on the earth.

The best time to visit is on a rare clear morning in September or October when the lake is close to its high-water level and reaches almost to the foot of

SIEM REAP PROVINCE

the hill. A word of warning: the journey from town in the dark should be taken slowly and carefully, as there is usually a steady stream of people bringing produce from the lake to the markets in Siem Reap, and few have headlights.

An Angkorian temple and a Hindu shrine crown Phnom Krom. While it is not necessary to go to the top of the hill to get a great view of the sunrise, the walk is only thirty minutes or so, and if you are less active, you can usually negotiate for your driver to take you all the way for a few dollars' fuel money. Don't push your luck, though, if it has been raining heavily, as the road can get slippery. Near the top at dawn, you will encounter Buddhist monks, and for a small contribution to their living costs, they are happy to be photographed if shown respect.

The other place to enjoy a marvelous sunrise is at Phnom Bakheng, between Angkor Wat and the Bayon. In the evening hundreds of tourists crowd to the top of this hill, but at sunrise you will share the vantage point with only a dozen or so folks in the know. Afterward, head back toward Siem Reap and take your morning meal opposite Angkor Wat at the Angkor Reach café. Then visit the main temple whilst everyone else is in town eating their breakfast.

Phnom Krom

Phnom Krom is about seven kilometers south of Siem Reap, and the journey from town to the base of the hill takes about twenty minutes. Bring a flashlight (a head torch is best), and make sure to use DEET or some other kind of repellent for mosquitoes. Work backward from the following sunrise times to set your alarm: December 1 (6:04 a.m.), March 1 (6:16 a.m.), June 1 (5:35 a.m.), September 1 (5:50 a.m.).

Phnom Bakheng

To reach Phnom Bakheng, negotiate your way past the crowds assembling in front of the west *gopura* of Angkor Wat and continue toward Angkor Thom. The travel time from Siem Reap is twenty minutes, and the walk to the top takes about fifteen minutes. Again, a flashlight is essential, and mosquito repellent is advisable. For sunrise viewing, use the same times as above.

Angkor Reach

This Angkor Wat-adjacent café provides delicious Western and Khmer breakfasts, including fresh French bread, coffee, fried eggs, fried rice, and pork or chicken. A full meal should cost around $5.

*Mick Yates
gets an education
outside Siem Reap*

Involved in helping Save the Children create an education infrastructure in Cambodia's "reconciliation areas," we had decided to visit one of the project's more difficult spots to access—even though it is only a few kilometers west of Siem Reap. At the village of Puok we turned due north, but we only managed to get about five kilometers before the road disintegrated ... and this was still the end of the dry season. At this point we all needed to "mount up," as we'd managed to get hold of some serious dirt bikes.

The road was long and straight, with small canals on either side, but the houses were spread out, which makes it very difficult to efficiently organize schooling. The farms along the road seemed relatively prosperous, with fields in good condition, although the people themselves looked poor. This entire area was one of the last active battlefields with the Khmer Rouge, even after the fighting stopped around Anlong Veng. Fortunately the mines have mostly gone, and whilst the majority of the people are still ex-Khmer Rouge, there are many migrants, and the area is peaceful and calm.

The trip turned out to be a lot of fun, even though we often had to dismount to get across the hardened, muddy ruts in the road. It only took just over an hour to travel the fifteen kilometers to our first destination of Angkor Chum. As ever, people were amazingly hospitable, and when we visited the new school, we were given a welcome refreshment of coconut milk. After saying our farewells, we headed toward Beng, a small community on the Varin road.

In Beng a tiny grass hut school in bad repair had been replaced with a new, two-classroom "mini-school" that was already being used by almost a hundred children. The children were not in uniform, as the school had only just gotten under way. A lively conversation ensued with the parents and grandparents, all gracefully and patiently sitting on the floor outside the school. We have always been impressed and humbled by the desire of average Cambodians to get a better education for their children than they had. Often it is the well-educated grandparents who survived the Khmer Rouge who quietly help this along.

By now it was midafternoon, and rain clouds were beginning to appear in the sky. However, the people in Beng insisted we visit another village, even though we had no direct involvement. So we steered our bikes across paddy fields to the east. We never did figure out the name of the next village, but it did have a small school recently built, we think by one of the UN agencies. It was a wonderful detour for a few reasons.

The people were warm, friendly, talkative, and happy to have guests. It was nice to see such a crystal clear expression of the family values of the Cambodian people. And we met Myra. She was 101 years old and had obviously survived and seen it all. Yet she had a wicked sense of humor and was more independent than many elderly people we knew. Myra was accompanied by two of her granddaughters, one of her great-granddaughters, and her great-great-granddaughter. In all of our travels in Cambodia, we had never met that many generations of one family in one place—it was truly a memorable event.

All good things must end, and the weather was getting uppity. We said our farewells and headed back to Siem Reap. Even though we got caught in some early rain, the road somehow seemed easier going back. We were very quiet on the bikes, as we each reflected on the day and the significance of the people we had met.

Visiting villages

From Siem Reap you can take guided bike tours of the area Mick visited, and you can find villages like Angkor Chum and Beng all over Cambodia. Veer off the main roads and get into the countryside, where the majority of the population still live. These experiences are priceless, as they give you an authentic look at the lives of the Cambodian people.

KULEN MOUNTAIN

Soumya James searches for ancient sculptures on Kulen Mountain

So vividly portrayed through the words of the early colonial explorers, the monuments of Kulen Mountain, near Siem Reap, beckoned me to partake in a journey of "discovery." After reaching the collection of stalls near the reclining Buddha on top of the mountain, I met a local man who promised to show me some of the sites.

I eyed his decrepit moto with some trepidation but decided to take my chances and struck a deal. We rattled off at full speed on the suspension-free two-wheeler, with me on the back, holding on to anything that would help me remain on the seat. After this experience, I could easily win a rodeo championship.

From the relatively flat and well-marked road, he abruptly turned off on a small path, heading straight into the jungle. For a stretch we rode over rocks and pale white-gray sand, which had a peculiar soothing effect in this otherwise desolate landscape. It was beautiful.

Then we plunged into the jungle, and the motorbike snaked along a narrow path. As the leaves brushed my face and arms, I looked up at the towering trees. They obliterated my sense of direction completely. The sun winked between the leaves as we sped along. As we wound our way around the forested land, with its sinuous roots and branches, I understood why the forces of nature are an integral part of both the Cambodian culture and the landscape. It was not difficult to imagine the power of these forests claiming at one time even the mightiest of monuments within its folds—which surely explains the belief in the potency of forest and mountain spirits that has survived from ancient days into contemporary Cambodia.

After an hour-long drive we came to a stop. There in a small clearing were four stone images: an elephant, two lions, a frog, and a bull. Like giant denizens of the forest, these eroding monoliths stood tall and silent. There was no temple within sight that these jungle statues could be part of, and from the artistic aspect, they were larger and somewhat differently rendered from those that belonged to the temple complexes I'd seen.

Suddenly the quiet of the forest was shattered by a herd of cows that crashed into the clearing, as surprised by my presence as I was by theirs. Civilization was not far off, even at this isolated site. While I didn't get to see grand temples lost in the misty jungle, I took home the exhilarating experience of the journey through the forest and the image of the seemingly immutable stone sculptures as they retraced their steps back to their natural origin.

Phnom Kulen

Phnom Kulen is a sacred mountain for Cambodians, as it was here that the great Khmer Empire began in 802 AD, when Jayavarman II proclaimed himself a god-king. There's a small *wat* at the top of the mountain (Preah Ang Thom), a substantial reclining Buddha carved from a massive sandstone boulder, and a large waterfall with smaller bathing areas above it. There are also riverbed carvings including numerous lingas, and near the top of the waterfall is the ruined ninth-century temple of Prasat Krau Romeas. Elsewhere on the Kulen plateau are as many as twenty other minor temple sites, including Sra Damrei, or elephant pond, where Soumya found her giant stone animals. It's important that you stick to the paths on Kulen as land mines are a real concern in this remote area. A visit to Kulen Mountain is not included in the Angkor temple pass and requires a separate fee of $20.

BENG MEALEA

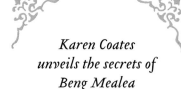

*Karen Coates
unveils the secrets of
Beng Mealea*

I used to take my notebook to a lonely corner of Preah Khan, and I'd sit in a doorway of cobwebs, gazing out on ancient stones. I reveled in my solitude there, thinking and writing and listening to the muffled buzz of bees. I still love Preah Khan in its crumpled state, though that state changes day by day, month by month, as its pieces are restored. But an even bigger change has swept through the Angkor temples in recent years. That solitude, those quiet corners—nearly impossible to find anymore in the ruins along the main tourist paths.

My husband, Jerry, and I would dangle our feet from the stoop of the library facing Angkor Wat. We'd crack open a beer and watch the sun fade, nearly alone. No more. The crowds keep pouring through. We climbed the steps of Phnom Bakheng and watched the sunset with just a dozen others around us. Not today. Today, the mountain jams with hundreds of people, cameras poised, all pointing in the same direction, toward the setting sun in a fireball sky.

Here's what most tourists miss: the untrammeled temples, the places way out there, the destinations not noted in guidebooks. Plenty of those gems remain in Cambodia, all across the country, and I won't tell you where they are. You must explore to find your own. That you can do this is one of Cambodia's greatest attractions.

Still, I will tell you about Beng Mealea, which is listed in guides and does see a relatively small stream of tourists each day. It's two hours by tuk-tuk from Siem Reap, and it requires a drive through fields so remote you can stop for a potty break and hear nothing but the wind. I love this temple for the way nature is an essential facet of its character. Tree roots spread like tentacles through the ancient stones. Shrouded in jungle, Beng Mealea can transport the average tourist to a bygone era of intrepid travelers. So it feels, anyway.

On getting here, we start from the main highway out of Siem Reap heading toward Phnom Penh. We are soon in the painting of Cambodia as I see it in my head: red dirt, blue sky, puffy clouds, luminous paddies with palm trees reaching forth. Toss in an ancient bridge, a few workers in the fields, and there you have it: the classic image of countrified Cambodia. Now sniff the air. It smells of *m'aohm*. Later, you'll eat this pungent herb in a bowl of sour fish soup. Continue on down the highway, eventually turning left on a secondary road. Don a *krama* scarf to combat the dust. When you reach Beng Mealea— its creaky boardwalks and creeping jungle—you're on your own.

Getting to Beng Mealea

In Siem Reap you can hire a tuk-tuk driver to take you to Beng Mealea, just over sixty kilometers east of town. Plan on two hours' driving each way, plus a couple of hours at the temple. You'll take National Highway 6 heading toward Phnom Penh, before turning north just after the market at Damdek village. The road is mostly paved, as of this writing, but conditions vary depending on the season. Expect a lot of dust. You don't need an Angkor pass to visit Beng Mealea, but you'll pay a separate entrance fee. If you're feeling peckish along Highway 6, stop for a bamboo tube of sticky rice with coconut, sold at the roadside in the small village of Khchass. Just peel the bamboo like a banana, and eat.

TONLE SAP LAKE

Gordon Sharpless floats through the villages of the Tonle Sap

When you are based in Siem Reap, it seems that life revolves around the temples, and in a manner of speaking that's true. Siem Reap relies on tourism, and the temples bring in the tourists. But if you're going to talk about what Cambodian life really revolves around here, the answer is not a bunch of old stones, as magnificent as they may be, but the very much alive Tonle Sap Lake.

The Tonle Sap, the largest freshwater lake in Southeast Asia, and its feeder, the Tonle Sap River, are an ecological anomaly. In early June, as the annual rainy season commences, the water level of the Mekong River rises substantially enough to divert part of its flow off its course to the South China Sea and redirect it into the Tonle Sap River. This forces the current of this hundred-kilometer-long river to reverse direction, beginning a process that by the end of October will see the area of the Tonle Sap Lake grow from twenty-five hundred square kilometers to as much as twelve thousand square kilometers. Its boundaries will extend anywhere from twenty kilometers to as much as fifty kilometers inland, and its depths increase from a mere one to two meters to as deep as ten.

The Tonle Sap is one of the most fish-abundant lakes in the world, and the silt deposits left behind by the annual floods have created fertile ground for agriculture. It's no surprise that one of Asia's greatest ancient civilizations developed near this lake, and today much of Cambodia's livelihood still depends on its output.

Due to time constraints, most tourists to Siem Reap that choose to observe life on the Tonle Sap limit their trip to the mostly Vietnamese floating village of Chong Kneas. I'm undecided as to whether this is a good thing (only one village gets destroyed by mass tourism) or a bad thing (tourists miss out on much of what the lake is really about).

Farther away there are flooded forests, hidden fishing villages, bird sanctuaries, and even an island. I've made numerous trips to the other Siem Reap Province villages—Kompong Phluk, Kompong Khleang, and Moat Khla—as well as one trip around the entire perimeter of the lake, stopping at numerous villages in Battambang and Pursat Provinces.

Kompong Phluk, at twenty-five kilometers from Chong Kneas, is the easiest village to visit. It is small, made up of perhaps one hundred houses completely within the confines of the lake. Unlike Chong Kneas, this is a permanent village with houses standing as much as eight meters off the ground. I've seen the village when the surrounding land was completely dry, the houses soaring up above almost like skyscrapers in a city, and at the end of the wet season when the Tonle Sap Lake was literally inches below the floorboards.

Aside from the hundred or so homes, Kompong Phluk has a pagoda, a small school, and a police station. Ethnically, the village is Khmer, and the economics are relatively good, with shrimp harvesting being the main source of income. This fact is readily observable when you visit, as piled on mats adjoining many of the homes are huge mounds of shrimp lying out to dry.

The nearby flooded forest is best seen when the water levels are high. On my first visit, at the tail end of a particularly wet rainy season, I was traveling with a friend, and our heads nearly scraped the canopy of leaves as two young girls expertly weaved through the foliage in small canoes. Just above us monkeys jumped from one treetop to another, and we encountered an elderly man rowing through the forest with two young children. Then, deeper in, balled up in a branch just overhead, was a three-meter python, scaring the two young boys in charge of our boats, who quickly rowed us out of their personal danger.

Back in Kompong Phluk the kids would excitedly tell the village of the great snake and their bravery in confronting this dangerous foe. Conveniently they left out that it was soundly asleep in a tree.

Chong Kneas

There are four main floating villages within Siem Reap Province: Chong Kneas, Kompong Phluk, Kompong Khleang, and Moat Khla. Chong Kneas is the village touted by tour guides and guesthouses everywhere. If you want to visit, any moto driver, taxi driver, or tour guide can sort this out for you.

Kompong Phluk

Kompong Phluk is best visited from June to January. From February onward the flooded forest turns almost to mud flats, and access becomes more problematic. Although you can reach Kompong Phluk from Chong Kneas, it is better to arrange a trip from Siem Reap town that will take you overland by way of the Roluos market. A trip should include a motorized boat to and around the village and a switch to canoes for the flooded forest. The trip takes about six hours and can be arranged by most tour operators as well as quite a few guesthouses.

Kompong Khleang

Kompong Khleang is the largest village on the lake and like Kompong Phluk is built on stilts, although a small floating village exists nearby. While lacking the ecological attraction of Kompong Phluk's flooded forest, this village has a sheer enormity that gives the best insight into the commercial aspects of the Tonle Sap. Kompong Khleang can be visited at any time of year and is, unlike Kompong Phluk, particularly interesting when the water levels are low, as the entire village soars eight or more meters above the ground. A trip there can take about seven hours. Access is by land and can at the right time of year be combined with a trip to Kompong Phluk.

Moat Khla

Moat Khla is a small floating village at the extreme southern tip of Siem Reap Province that sees very few tourists. A trip here would take a full day and can include trips to Kompong Phluk and Kompong Khleang.

UDONG

Steve Goodman encounters a world of religion in Udong

Seeking a glimpse of Cambodia's Buddhist history, I was excited to visit Udong, which had served as the country's capital city at various times between 1618 and 1866 AD. Atop Phnom Udong, a big hill located about an hour and a half north of Phnom Penh, are numerous Buddhist temples in various states of ruin, some from age, but most from deliberate destruction by the Khmer Rouge in the 1970s.

After the hot and crowded bus ride up National Highway 5, we hired motos to drive us to the foot of the hill, where we were greeted by an assortment of elderly beggars, Buddhist pilgrims, local children, and 509 steps leading to the complex of pagodas strewn across the hill's rambling ridge. The view from the new temple built at the top is stunning,

KANDAL PROVINCE

and we enjoyed the cooling breeze as we surveyed the plains below: rice paddy as far as the eye can see, small villages, and the ubiquitous and stoic sugar palms that dot the Cambodian landscape.

We were joined on our jaunt through the hillside region by several small boys who eagerly insisted on being our guides, and we also kept running into groups of pilgrims visiting from nearby provinces. Moving on down the path along the ridges, we came upon older stupas containing the remains of several former monarchs, including King Monivong, the namesake of one of Phnom Penh's main thoroughfares. Some of the destruction of these sacred spaces by the Khmer Rouge, especially at the large temple of Vihear Preah Ath Roes, still seemed fresh and raw despite so many decades having passed since those dark days.

I had thought of Udong as a place of Buddhist worship, and so it was with surprise I found, amidst the shrines, the elegantly simple and charming old Ta San Mosque. Here we met the warm and welcoming elderly imam and his wife. Muslims are a minority in Cambodia and represent a scant 1 to 2 percent of the population. From the imam we learned that the sect of Cham at this particular mosque are known as the Jahed and are unique in that they only pray on Fridays, not five times a day like most of the rest of the world's Muslims. The Ta San Mosque site is also significant in that it is where the

man reputed to have brought Islam to Cambodia is buried.

With our curiosity about the local Muslim community piqued, we traveled a bit farther, about twelve kilometers north of Udong to the large—by Cambodian standards— Chrok Romeat mosque. Here we spent time with Ismael, a well-educated and articulate teacher. Ismael was privileged to have made the Hajj in 2001 and is often referred to as Hajji, the honorary title of respect accorded to those who have made the pilgrimage to Mecca.

Exploring the village behind the mosque, we found friendly faces and the typical slow pace of life in a farming village, including a blacksmith shop where workers were forging knives and the small scythes used to cut rice plants by hand. The highlight of this last stop before we returned to Phnom Penh was the mosque's school and the smiles of about two hundred children in their colorful headscarves and skullcaps—a reminder that the religious persecution of the Khmer Rouge, although still evident in the ravaged temples on Phnom Udong, is finally a thing of the past.

Getting to Udong

To reach Udong, take National Highway 5 north from Phnom Penh about forty kilometers. If you go by bus you must tell the driver that you want to stop at Phnom Udong, and he will drop you off in a spot where you can hire a moto to take you off the main road to the foot of the hill. Here you will find a large picnic area with local vendors offering a tasty variety of food, including chicken, fish, frog, and other local delicacies.

Getting to Chrok Romeak

To reach the Chrok Romeak mosque, just continue north on National Highway 5 past the fifty-two-kilometer marker. The mosque is located on the left-hand side of the road. Although the Cham are accustomed to being greeted in the Khmer manner, it is appreciated if you use the traditional Muslim greeting of "As-Salamu Alaykum," to which the reply is "Wa Alaykum as-Salaam."

BARAY

Cristiano Calcagno quests after the sacred swords of Baray

A French book written in the early 1900s by M. Dufosse, a doctor posted in Kompong Thom by the colonial administration, mentions the sacred swords of Baray as one of the most noteworthy attractions to be found in the province and gives a vivid description of them. Eighty-one centimeters long and decorated with inscriptions in Sanskrit, Pali, and Khmer on their blades, two swords were kept in the house of a *bakou*, an isolated descendant of Indian Brahmanic priests who lived in the village of Chhuk Khsach, a few kilometers east of the district center. Dufosse estimated them to date back to the fifteenth century, that mysterious dark age that followed the collapse of the Angkorian Empire.

Once a year, the swords were sent to Phnom Penh on the occasion of a royal ceremony. They were highly revered by the local population, but there was one person who was not allowed to see them: none other than the local ruler, the governor of Baray, as it had been predicted that if he did, unspeakable misfortune would befall him, his family, and the whole territory he administered.

Having been so lucky to discover that old rare book in the first place, I decided I would try to find out what had become of the swords. I did not have much hope, considering what the country had gone through in the decades that had passed since. I did see, however, that in the main square at Baray there was a small column-like monument topped by three concrete swords, as the emblem of the small town. At least the memory, I thought, had not been totally lost.

I went to meet with the commune chief of Chhuk Khsach, a kind, lean, elderly man. Yes, he knew about the swords, and he told me the rest of the story, as if picking up from where

Dufosse had left it. He said there were in fact four, all similar in shape, although only two carried inscriptions. During the civil war in the early 1970s, the keeper of the swords at that time decided to bury them under a tree in a forest in order to save them from destruction. Later on, when the Khmer Rouge seized power, that man became one of many who did not survive.

Then, after 1979, the horrors ended and life resumed with some degree of normalcy. A villager had a dream and led a group of fellow farmers to the site that his dream had directed him to, in a forest some fifteen kilometers away. They dug under a tree ... and there the swords were, though only three remained. They took them back to Baray, and the column was erected to celebrate their retrieval.

So where are they now? I wanted to know.

They are kept at the office of the district governor, which was considered the safest location. I went there and asked, and—simple as that—the governor showed them to me. A precious treasure indeed, for both their artistic and symbolic value. They are still in their original sheaths of lacquered wood. Their square-section handles are ivory, with an animal engraved on each facet: a lion, a tiger, a bull, and an elephant. The blades are double-edged, with one side of two of the swords carrying the ancient inscriptions.

I cannot say how thrilled I was at the success of what I had assumed was going to be a hopeless quest.

I did not mention the prediction reported by Dufosse about the local governor. Perhaps that referred only to the governor of that time, or perhaps it has already been fulfilled through the tragedies of the Khmer Rouge. In any case, it appears to have been forgotten, while the swords have not, and are still there along with the people of Baray who, like them, have survived the most tragic of times.

Getting to Baray

Baray town is situated 115 kilometers north of Phnom Penh, or 200 kilometers southeast of Siem Reap, along National Highway 6. The central square of the small town opens directly on the main road, and at its center stands the three-sword monument. The office where the sacred swords are kept is on the south side of the square.

KOMPONG THOM

Martin Lum mingles with the spirits of Sambor Prei Kuk

We sat shaded under a thatched shelter in the fork of a sandy road, while villagers scurried from their squatting repose to prepare our meal. The menu was simple. Chicken and rice or nothing. At first we had thought there was no choice at all, until one young man brought a scrawny bird for inspection.

Stretched out, it struggled, its black and gray feathers revealing that it was not ravaged by disease—although they also failed to disguise a lack of any substantial flesh. Suddenly, ritual unfolded. The chicken was taken from view, but its final squawk was audible, and our appetite squeamishly diminished as blood fell to the dusty soil. The horror! There is a brutal honesty here in the simple act of eating. It is confronting, it is life, it is death, it is the endless cycle of karma, *samsara*, suffering.

We were learning this lesson in the precinct of Sambor Prei Kuk. Once a magnificent city, it was now deserted and visited only by the hardy trekker or obsessed temple fanatic searching for more than the glamour of Sambor's younger sibling, Angkor. Next to the rustic shack where we silently ate our bony chicken was a simple stone box. Plain, bunkerlike—a room without the inspired carvings of Khmer tradition.

Pocked with bullet holes, the box had the elegance of a gun turret. It stood in a field, strawlike grass camouflaging the undulating ground where craters overlap. This was neither modern bunker nor symbolic heavenly place of worship. The ashram once housed ascetic hermits who meditated on suffering and enlightenment. Could they have contemplated the destruction and explosive ordnance dropped here by B52 bombers?

And yet, amidst its poverty and war-torn history, there was still great beauty.

We had arrived at Sambor Prei Kuk from Kompong Thom before the sun. The air was chilled, and a small fire glowed with warmth among a stand of trees. Smoke filled the canopy, floating like mist among the silhouettes of the odd-shaped squat structures. These were older, shorter than the Angkorian towers—the elevation of masonry had yet to be mastered when this place was built. But the rudiments of decorative devotion were evident. In one building a cornice figure rested, eyes closed as if in prayer. Its features struck me—without stylized adornment the face resembled an Afghan Buddha of a distant land, and a distant time. They were, of course, neither Buddhist nor Afghan, but the resonance was haunting.

Streams of light began to filter through the edges of the trees, revealing a heavy carpet of fallen leaves. There was an intense quiet and a peaceful serenity. The cries of bygone battles had dissipated. I was reminded of imaginary, magical worlds—a Lothlorien queen wandering among the ruins and shadows of men. Enchanting, ethereal, these spirits at dawn in the forest at Sambor Prei Kuk.

Getting to Sambor Prei Kuk
Sambor Prei Kuk contains Cambodia's most impressive group of pre-Angkorian monuments. It was the capital of the Chenla state of the Funan kingdom during the seventh-century reign of King Isanavarman. It's located approximately thirty kilometers north of Kompong Thom on a good, well-signposted road. Travel takes approximately an hour from Kompong Thom and two from Siem Reap. Entry fee: $3.

BATTAMBANG

*Dickon Verey
catches that Pepsi spirit
in Battambang*

Cambodia is a country of myths and fables, where gossip in the street becomes fast fact in minutes. I would wager that sorting fact from fiction would be a very lucrative business here if anyone found a good way to market it.

I spent almost three years of my life in the town of Battambang, which has a quiet provincial charm and laid-back ease. It also has its fair share of rumors and legends. I used to spend days driving around on my motor-bike, following hearsay, happy in idle discovery. One time, I was in the Balcony Bar describing an adventure to Kompong Puoy Lake. My drinking partner looked at me, smiled, and said, "Bet you've never been to the Pepsi factory. That place gives me the creeps."

"Eh?" I said, cocking my ear. I had always assumed that Western corporations stayed away from Cambodia due to corruption. Furthermore, why would fizzy drinks frighten this character?

"Yeah, it's an old Pepsi factory from Lon Nol times. Now it lies empty. Scary place. Apparently the Thais had an exclusive contract with Coca-Cola, so Pepsi built a factory in Battambang and shipped the stuff across the border. You can find it just outside of town on the road to Ek Phnom."

Fact or fiction?

To find out, the next morning I hit the road. Three kilometers later and there it was; a large 1960s-style complex of warehouses and buildings. On the largest sat the old Pepsi logo. I drove up to the entrance and parked my bike. It appeared that the factory was in use. A group of ladies was cleaning plastic bottles. They looked at me in surprise. In broken Khmer I asked if I might look around.

"*Ot panyahar!*" (No problem!)

I walked into the second room and stepped back in time. All the bottling machines were there, along with what must've been ten thousand old bottles. There were classic Pepsi, green Miranda, Singha Soda Water, and Teem. Could I take a couple?

I was given the go-ahead. I then explored some more. The factory was suffering from age, but other than a few bullet holes and shell damage to one of the warehouses, it seemed largely untouched.

When I got home I noticed that the bottles had "72" etched on the bottom. I assumed that was the year they were made and that consequently they had never left the warehouse, as the surrounding countryside at that time was full of Khmer Rouge. The sense of history was palpable.

I decided to do some more research and talked to a friend of mine who spoke fluent Khmer. A few weeks later we headed back to the factory. As we wandered around outside, a band of giggling kids approached us. My friend asked one of them if he knew anything about the place.

"Speak to my dad," the kid said.

A man of about sixty approached. My friend started chatting to him in Khmer. He seemed delighted that anyone was interested in the factory. He told us he delivered water that was processed by the people who were working there now.

"Where do you live?"

He waved at some shacks a few meters away.

"Have you lived here long?"

He laughed and explained that he had always lived there.

"Do you remember the time when the factory made Pepsi?"

He laughed again and told us that he had delivered the stuff around Battambang. He didn't remember if the product was shipped to Thailand but thought it likely. The factory had closed when Pol Pot's people came, he said. However, every Khmer New Year the Khmer Rouge opened the factory for five days and made ice. In a rare act of generosity, they gave the ice to the villagers, and then they shut the factory again. When the Vietnamese occupied the country, they reopened the ice factory. When they left, the factory lay dormant until the water company came a few years ago.

On my last visit the factory was still there, so go and have a look yourself. Sure, Cambodia may be a country of myth and fable, but this is one story that's definitely true.

Getting to the Pepsi factory

Battambang is located in the northwest of Cambodia about three hundred kilometers from Phnom Penh along National Highway 5. From the center of Battambang, take the road to Ek Phnom. Keep your eyes peeled for the Pepsi bottling factory, which is located about one mile from town.

BATTAMBANG TO SIEM REAP

*Anne Best takes
the slow boat from
Battambang to Siem Reap*

During much of the year, depending upon the water levels of the Tonle Sap Lake, it is possible to journey by boat from Battambang to Siem Reap and vice versa. I have been warned that the boats break down, the riverways are dangerous, that angry fishermen take potshots at the vessels—in general, this is not a good idea. However, loving anything to do with water, I am determined not to be put off.

The day before my departure, I head down to the bustling bus station/ river port in Battambang and, with a certain degree of difficulty, manage to learn that a boat is due to leave around seven the following morning. I buy my ticket in advance, show up on time, and unsurprisingly, the departure is delayed. What should be a four-hour trip ends up taking over six. No matter. In my view, the extended length of the journey is a bonus.

For the first couple of hours we travel on the Sangker River past villages that are a hive of early morning activity. Mist rises from the water as busy

fisherman in small boats set out lines and floats and pull in small silvery fish. Our captain takes great care to weave a course between the fishermen to avoid damaging their nets. Contrary to rumors, no gunshots are fired.

Suddenly, the landscape changes and we find ourselves motoring through a very narrow waterway, scarcely wide enough for two boats to pass. High reeds and willows crowd in. Then this stretch opens out into a vast flooded area dotted with trees and clumps of vegetation and water plants. This is the Tonle Sap. From now on the villages comprise houseboats clustered together. Houses, shops, schools, police stations—all floating. As we pass, children run excitedly onto the verandas waving and shouting with delight.

A brightly painted pagoda occupies dry land with the monks' quarters floating alongside. As far as I can see, long lines of nets are staked out in the shallow water. The lake's landscape is vast, and although white flags mark out the channel, it is not surprising that our captain takes a wrong turn or two as he seeks a route through the flooded vegetation.

We finally dock at Chong Kneas at the edge of the Tonle Sap a few kilometers south of Siem Reap. A clamoring group of hopeful moto drivers meets us upon arrival, many holding up signs for the various hotels in town. I manage to find my hotel's driver and head off. I have a few days of sightseeing at the Angkor Wat temples ahead of me, but already I can't wait to get back on the boat for the return journey to Battambang.

Purchasing a boat ticket

In Battambang, go to the bus station past the iron bridge to find the boat trip ticket sellers. Depending on the time of year and height of the water, boats of various sizes and speeds make the journey. Anne traveled on a smallish boat with rows of seats under cover. The sides were open, which was good for breezes and views. A toilet was available on board, but otherwise services were nonexistent—take food, water, sun cream, and toilet paper. Tickets were $15 one-way, and Anne would advise purchasing a ticket the day before traveling. The boat trip should get you to Siem Reap just in time for a sunset visit to Angkor Wat. You can enter Angkor Wat free after 5:00 p.m. for the sunset as long as you buy a pass that begins the following day.

BANTEAY CHHMAR

Andy Brouwer hunts for hidden temples at Banteay Chhmar

Spoken of in hushed tones when I first went to Cambodia in the early 1990s, the remote temple of Banteay Chhmar was in the midst of the battleground between Khmer Rouge and government forces and off-limits. A decade ago it was in the news for all the wrong reasons, as indiscriminate and large-scale looting robbed it of many of its priceless treasures. Today, it has found new life and has opened its doors to adventurous travelers as archaeologists repair its walls, and it may soon even attain UNESCO World Heritage status.

One of the major temple cities built by King Jayavarman VII during a twelfth-century construction frenzy, Banteay Chhmar is famed for its massive size, giant face towers, and wild location. I was hoping to enjoy the romance of a quintessential lost Khmer city when I paid my first visit in 2001. What greeted me was a giant jigsaw puzzle of fallen masonry, collapsed galleries, towers, and jumbled blocks of sandstone.

In the previous week an army of wood-cutters and leaf-clearers had descended on the site, removed much of the vegetation, and with it, the enchantment of my hoped-for lost city. Some sections of the temple's intricately carved perimeter wall were in good condition, others were covered in lichen and moss, whilst large sections had simply disappeared altogether, removed by looters. Chisel and drill marks were much in evidence, and only two of the original eight multiarmed Lokesvara carvings were still in situ. Graffiti and headless *apsaras* made me angry, reminding me that the temple's remote location, away from prying eyes, made it a perfect target for this type of desecration.

I returned to Banteay Chhmar four years later on a mission to uncover some more of its secrets. I was adopted by half a dozen local teenagers on my arrival. The ringleader was the only girl, India, "like the country," she beamed, eagerly showing me the best bits as we ambled around the temple. We used large sandstone blocks that littered the floor as stepping stones and climbed onto the roof of galleries to get a better view of the three remaining towers with the enigmatic, giant, smiling faces of the Bodhisattva Avalokitesvara (or Jayavarman VII, depending on your point of view)—one of the face towers had fallen and shattered into many pieces a few months before. Despite the occasional bout of laughter from my companions, who couldn't keep quiet for longer than a minute, as we walked through the inner sanctuary the birdcalls and stillness gave the temple an undisturbed and tranquil presence, so unlike the crowds and trappings of the main Angkor site.

India whetted my appetite for further discovery with talk of additional satellite temples nearby. The first was located behind her village, in the center of a moat surrounding a tree-festooned island where a giant Bayon-style face peered over the treetops. Prasat Ta Prohm reminded me of a slimmer version of one of the main gates of Angkor Thom, with four massive faces at the four cardinal points, still in very good condition though lacking any lintel carvings.

One had lost its nose, but apart from that the faces—carrying a serene expression with closed eyelids and thick, slightly curled lips—were identical to those at the main Banteay Chhmar site.

I engaged the services of fifteen-year-old Sita, with his machete, to act as my guide, and we set off on our adventure to find the other temples. The two badly ruined towers of Prasat Toch offered little by way of excitement. Prasat Mebon was on an island in the center of a huge *baray*, but again was in poor condition, though it hosted some interesting wall carvings. Prasat Yeay Pum, a sandstone temple surrounded by a laterite wall, showed obvious evidence of theft, with blocks of sandstone containing the heads of carved *apsaras* missing from the wall.

We continued north for another few minutes and came to a large, water-filled moat and a seemingly impenetrable undergrowth-covered island. It proved impossible to cut a way through the eastern approach, as we came under attack from the spiky thorn bushes, equally vicious red ants, and itchy *kha* pods, so we tried the western entrance, with more success. After ten minutes of inching our way through the tangled, thick bush, we entered the dark interior, under a canopy of tall trees. Adjusting my eyes to the darkness and to the large tower in front of me, I could make out a giant face. The temple, called Prasat Chiemtrei, was similar to Ta Prohm in the form of its main tower, though only two faces remained, with two sides of the structure having fallen down. This was temple exploration at its most exciting and challenging.

After lunch we located Prasat Yeay Chor in a clump of bushes, but with little to see we moved on to Prasat Yeay Chy. Surrounded by a dry moat and dense vegetation, this was another large gate tower with giant faces on two sides, north and east, but missing from the other two compass points. Farther west through a forest of trees and across a series of dry rice fields, we arrived at another moat, this time filled with water. The path into the complex of Prasat Samnang Tasok was easy aside from the ferocious red ants, but the floor of the temple was covered in thick bushes, so it was best to clamber along the walls and roof of the outer *gopura* to make our way to the inner sanctuary, which was topped by four more giant faces and other carvings.

Like the majority of the hidden gems I'd located, not another soul was anywhere to be seen, and the only sounds to be heard were birds and the occasional rustle of a lizard amongst the undergrowth. On the way out, I was perched precariously on the lintel of a gateway when two red ants bit into my stomach after crawling up my trousers, reminding me that temple exploration has an occasional downside.

After years of exploring, Banteay Chhmar is one of my top picks amongst Cambodian temples. It's a genuine ruin where you have to clamber over the fallen remains and shimmy up onto the roofs of galleries. There's something special to see in all of its nooks and crannies, and the thrill of adventure to be found within—and outside—its walls takes me back there time and again.

Banteay Chhmar

Andy adds: On my most recent trip, I saw the Global Heritage Fund conservation work underway. The fund is currently developing a master plan for the temple to preserve and protect the site, which has been receiving international press coverage and will soon apply for World Heritage status. I've a feeling it won't be long until this temple changes forever, with roped-off pathways and more tourists, so try to make a trip as soon as you can.

Banteay Chhmar is sixty kilometers north of Sisophon. Finding the satellite temples will require the services of a local guide. The community offers overnight homestay options and can be contacted through the phone number and email address below. Temple admission: $5.

(017) 782-156
aplc@online.com.kh

ANLONG VENG

Steve McClure documents Khmer Rouge ghosts in Anlong Veng

Most Khmer believe in ghosts, and after a trip to the former Khmer Rouge stronghold of Anlong Veng, I can definitely see why. I wasn't quite sure what to expect as we made the treacherous three-hour drive from Siem Reap—nothing like a potholed dirt road to get the blood flowing. But I was making a documentary about the Cambodian holocaust, and Anlong Veng was an important piece of the country's history.

At first glance, this small border town looks as if it never left the 1970s. It reminded me of something out of the Wild, Wild West, only much, much poorer. Rows of tin shanties lined the dusty, orange dirt roads. Traffic was mostly either on foot or bicycle. This was the epitome of "simple" Cambodian living.

Upon arrival we made our way up the Dangrek Escarpment toward the border with Thailand to see Pol Pot's grave. Along the drive up the steep, rocky road, a truck was making its way down the mountain. "Smuggling gasoline in from Thailand," our guide told us.

Interesting. I hoped the smugglers didn't mind witnesses.

A small walking path led us to the gravesite. "Don't stray off the path," our guide reminded us. The area, of course, was still not cleared of land mines. We braved the narrow path and soon landed upon the grave of the man responsible for the deaths of millions of his own people. How fitting, I thought, that it be marked only by a small tin shed, scattered with a few of his personal items, such as the remains of his porcelain toilet.

I imagined what it might have been like to stand in this very same spot back in 1998, when Pol Pot's body was cremated on top of a pile of burning rubber tires. How many souls, I wondered, did his burning ashes join as they rose into the Cambodian sky? It was definitely an eerie feeling to stand so near to this evil despot's final resting place. He was one of the most villainous men in modern history, and here I was, staring at his broken toilet.

Our excursion wrapped up with visits to the former homes of Pol Pot and then that of the one-legged general Ta Mok, which looks out over a swampy lake dappled with the skeletons of dead trees. We interviewed a few former Khmer Rouge soldiers, who were surprisingly quite nice and even offered us food and drink. I wrestled with whether they were lying about their involvement in the regime or just innocent victims themselves. In the end, they were the only ones who could really know.

After the long day, we retired to our guesthouse. It was around eight and amazingly quiet throughout the entire town. What a contrast from the bustle of Phnom Penh. Too quiet, perhaps. Do ghosts thrive on this eerie stillness? I kept one eye on the door, just in case, as I restlessly dozed through the night.

Getting to Anlong Veng

Anlong Veng is located 118 kilometers north of Siem Reap, along the paved National Highway 67. On the way, you will pass Bantey Srei temple and Kbal Spean, both worth a stop. There are a few choices for guesthouse accommodation, and if you want to explore, you should hire a local guide for the day. Additional points of interest include Ta Mok's gravesite in a pagoda about seven kilometers toward the Thai border.

Dining in Anlong Veng

Contributor Geoff Pyle writes: Anlong Veng is unremarkable except for the remnants of the Khmer Rouge era, including Pol Pot's last resting place, a macabre lake of dead trees surrounding the home of Ta Mok, and one of the top breakfasts in Cambodia. Pkay Preuk, which means Morning Star, is a thatched-roofed affair where you can enjoy the best baguette this side of the French Alps, with orange marmalade and/or a foil-wrapped portion of Laughing Cow cheese-

perfect to set you up for a day of traveling. Also recommended are the Khmer/Chinese breakfast menu and the curried chicken for lunch. To find Pkay Preuk, start at the Anlong Veng roundabout with painted figures in the middle. Go straight over the bridge with the lake on your right and keep following the main road. Set back on the right side, with a sign out front, Pkay Preuk is around 1.8 kilometers from the roundabout.

Rain Falls from Earth

Released in 2009, Steve's documentary about the Cambodian genocide is narrated by Sam Waterston, who was nominated for an Oscar for his lead role in *The Killing Fields*.

www.rainfallsfromearth.com

PREAH VIHEAR

Dougald O'Reilly is rewarded by his arrival at Preah Vihear

Seeing the ancient, lichen-covered stones of the cliff-top temple of Preah Vihear looming out of a thick, swirling mist is a sight I will not soon forget.

To witness this felt like a reward for a punishing journey on motorcycles through the Cambodian jungle from Siem Reap. Pushing on to the Cambodian-Thai border through the overgrown track late into the night, nearly out of petrol and out of water, our small party encountered armed illegal loggers, traversed quagmires, forded neck-deep rivers, and fought off legions of insects.

After climbing a steep, poorly paved incline, we arrived at Preah Vihear in the afternoon. Covered in mud from head to toe, our party drew stares from the well-manicured Thai tourists who had arrived on a double-decker bus from the Thai side of the border. One man in a pressed golfing outfit exclaimed, "What happened to you?!" and nodded knowingly when we explained we had come from the Cambodian side.

That night we were invited to bunk down at one of the demining camps, as a member of our party knew the commander. Perched on the precipice, the camp ran with military precision. At five the tents disgorged scores of men into the chill morning air to wash and prepare for the day's dangers—the odious task of removing land mines from around the temple ruins. We took the opportunity to rise with them and explore in the heavy mist that gave the temple an ethereal quality, reminding me of the seventh-century depictions of temples floating on clouds that decorated some of the brick shrines at Sambor Prei Kuk.

Aside from the temple itself, the most memorable aspect of this adventure was the hospitality of a family we met on the way, who made their living off the land. As we arrived at their humble home in the middle of the night, they welcomed us, slaughtered a chicken, sent their boy to fetch gas, and offered us their well to bathe in—the latter was the cause of much curiosity and laughter among the extended family. While this kind of generosity may seem unusual in the West, it is not in Cambodia. The people may have little, but they will often offer it regardless, making every step of the journey just as valuable as the destination, even if that destination is a place as unforgettable as Preah Vihear.

Getting to Preah Vihear

At the time of writing, the cliff-top temple of Preah Vihear was a war zone between Cambodia and Thailand. Access is only available from the Cambodian side, and overnight stops are no longer possible, under any circumstances. If you do go there, though, the views from the top of the mountain, perched high on the Dangrek escarpment, are breathtaking and worth the journey. The temple itself was built by a succession of Khmer kings, beginning in the ninth century and ending in the twelfth. There are guesthouses at the foot of the mountain, but their continued existence is not guaranteed, as there are plans to build a museum and car park and create an exclusion zone around the temple.

KRATIE

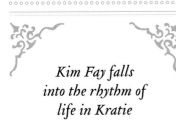

Kim Fay falls into the rhythm of life in Kratie

Kratie at seven in the morning is similar to Kratie at noon and Kratie at sundown. Mellow. Midway up the Mekong River between Phnom Penh and Stung Treng, this is an old colonial town that does not know how to *not* relax. Even progress goes at its own pace here, as a cement mixer passes by on the back of a pony cart. Kratie has a sedative quality, and it was in this state that I set out from my guesthouse on a rented bicycle, with a water bottle, a camera, and a *Mekong Discovery Trail* booklet tucked into my basket.

I headed north on the road that trailed the river, and I made it just a few hundred yards beyond town when I realized that it was already uncomfortably hot. Turning back, I stopped at the first stall at the market, bought a big hat and shawl, and covered myself from head to toe. Wrapped in this cocoon, with only the backs of my hands showing, I cycled for hours while the river ebbed and flowed from view, the shadows of sugar palms skipped over the road, and people went about their daily business in the shade of their modest wooden homes, which were lifted off the ground on stilts.

When I returned to my guesthouse that afternoon, I was addicted and asked if I could rent the bike again the following day. I set out even earlier, my muscles already aching from my first ride. This time I did not go for the countryside surrounding Kratie, but clumsily carried my bicycle down the steep steps to the boat landing. There it was hauled onto a canoelike wooden boat (so small it had only two facing benches) that was the ferry to Koh Trong Island in the middle of the river.

Along with a handful of locals, I was deposited on a vast, flat beach, where a cow that was curled up for a nap could not even be bothered to glance at us. I dragged my bike across the sand to a bumpy, slatwood path, which led to a deeply rutted trail up a hill to the dirt road that circled the island. The morning was so quiet, and as I set off, I was intensely aware of everything around me. The petals of flame trees scattered on the ground. Butterflies drifting as if a breeze had come to life. Chickens pecking at fallen jackfruit. Spirit altars like small bird houses perched in front of homes on stilts. I cut off on a side path through the center of the island, and the landscape opened, its pastoral fields smelling of wood smoke, hay, and the lanky grazing cows. Without the shelter of trees over the road, every passing cloud was a gift, a relief from the sodden heat.

It was possible to pedal for great stretches without seeing a single person. When I did, it would be a grandfather napping in the shade of a roadside food stall or a naked child emerging up a bank with an armload of mangoes. The mango trees were laden at that time of year, and when I passed the one group of children I saw the whole day, they did not go crazy shouting "hello! hello!" but just smiled and gave a nonchalant wave before returning to eating the ripe green fruit.

It was as if, by coming out to the island, a person belonged, no matter her hair or skin color. To be there was just that: to be. The feeling stayed with me throughout the afternoon and back to town, where the day came to a close in perfect Kratie style, with a cold beer at one of the little café tables on the promenade while the sun set over the river.

Getting to Kratie

Buses to Kratie leave Phnom Penh from Psar Thmei market, usually around 8:00 a.m. Numerous companies make this journey. Kim used the Phnom Penh Sorya Transport Company, whose office is at the market. While tickets can be purchased the morning of travel, she suggests buying in advance, to get decent seats at the front of the bus. Buses are basic, and the ride takes six to eight hours, with stops along the way for food and toilet breaks. Food at the roadside restaurants is acceptable, but not terrific. The same goes for the toilets. Bring your own toilet paper.

Biking around Kratie

Although it's not essential, try to pick up a copy of *Mekong Discovery Trail* while you're in Kratie. This booklet has basic bike route information, including the road north out of town and around Koh Trong Island. A bike with good tires and brakes can be rented from the You Hong II guesthouse (see below). Make sure to bring lots of water, a hat, a scarf/shawl, and your own sunscreen, since purchasing sunscreen at the market is nearly impossible. Don't underestimate the sun. The backs of Kim's hands—the only part of her body exposed—were blistered for days after her two rides. Also, keep in mind that there are no public toilets anywhere on these bike rides.

www.mekongdiscoverytrail.com

You Hong II (U Hong II)

Accommodation choices are limited in Kratie, and not all are appealing. The first night, Kim stayed in a guesthouse that was swarming with cockroaches. When she mentioned this as the reason for leaving, the manager shrugged and said, with little concern, "They come in to play with the light." This led her to the You Hong II, which she highly recommends. The rooms are clean, the fans work, and there are en suite bathrooms—all for less than $10 a night. The ground floor restaurant is also quite charming (especially during blackouts), serving good food to travelers as well as those few expatriates working in town. A copy of the *Mekong Discovery Trail* can be borrowed here. The guesthouse is located just off the river, off the road at the south end of the market.

Riverside dining

Of eating and drinking in Kratie, Peter Walter adds: Walking along the river, I stumbled onto a long stretch of drink and snack huts basking in the glow of the late afternoon sun. After picking a spot, I was soon enjoying a bottle of ice-cold beer. The proprietor, a middle-aged mother of two girls, offered me some snacks, including the local favorite of an unhatched chick still inside its egg. Sticking with my drink, I closed my eyes and enjoyed the last rays of the setting sun before it disappeared behind the opposite bank of the river.

Once it was dark, the lady and her teenage daughter caught me by surprise as they started racing around their tables, lunging after fat, buzzing, cicadalike insects that had arrived under the cover of dusk and were flying all around the place. The pair successfully caught about two dozen of the critters, methodically plucking off the wings and legs before skewering the meaty remains and cooking them in a small charcoal oven. The proprietor explained that they planned to bring them home as a snack for her other daughter, who was still a toddler.

RATANAKIRI PROVINCE

Christine Dimmock experiences a grave moment in Ratanakiri

Voices are approaching, and I half expect to be accosted for trespass. I sneak around quietly until the sounds fade into the distance. I am in Ratanakiri, the most northeasterly province of Cambodia on the banks of the Sesan River, north of the town of Ban Lung. More importantly, I am fighting my way through the undergrowth of an overgrown burial ground at Kachon village, home to one of the ethnically distinct groups that makes up the population in Ratanakiri.

Because my mother engendered in me an affinity for old cemeteries, I can't help but be drawn into this one. I soon realize that it is the most unusual

RATANAKIRI PROVINCE

graveyard I am probably going to see in my life. In fact, from the moment my motodop "had relations" with the minority villagers—that is, he sought their permission—I have been falling over myself in a flurry of discovery.

Adventure travel writer Ray Zepp and others reported seeing Polynesian-style funerary statues here, and as I enter I stop at the closest grave, which has a rectangular fence, an elaborately shaped metal roof painted in bright geometrical patterns, and life-size carved wooden figures of a man and a woman at two corners. At the remaining corners are large pairs of carved tusks. Household items have been provided for the dead to use in the afterlife.

I do my best to tread lightly out of respect for this deeply spiritual place. More graves appear as I click away with my camera, and I must struggle through prickly vines and red ants. Photography is challenging due to the combination of bright sunlight and deep dappled shade, and first I concentrate on the newer, colored wooden figures. Some wear metal wristwatches, and a female sports a pair of metal sunglasses. There are clothes in red, green, and yellow paint. Several male figures wear military-style caps, and one has a carved walkie-talkie on his chest. Another carries a bow and arrows. His wife wears round metal earrings and a green painted bra top, which matches the large pipe protruding from her mouth amongst the leaves.

While these modern effigies are intriguing, the older figures are my favorites. They are unpainted, less elaborate, softly weathered, and spotted with lichen. Their only adornments are metal eyes and earrings, and in one case a headband. Occasionally there is a touch of red on female lips or black on male eyebrows. Their heads are large and their bodies lack detail. Items for their use in the afterlife are simple—baskets, china plates, bottles, cooking pots, and brown glazed pottery vessels. Several sets of cow and buffalo horns are lying around, suggesting the ritualistic slaughter of animals.

Reluctantly I tear myself away. On the return journey to Ban Lung, I'm surprised by an unexpected visit to another smaller graveyard. The attraction here is a grave adorned with a naive replica of a helicopter painted in army camouflage. The villager buried here may have helped the Americans in the Vietnam War, as did the ethnic minority groups across the border in the central highlands of Vietnam. Looking at this grave, I realize that these sites are much more than just a tribute to the person buried there. They are a record of Cambodia, both its past and its progress, over the course of the last century.

Graveyards around Ban Lung

In Ban Lung, the capital of Ratanakiri Province, you can hire a motorcycle taxi or ask at your guesthouse about gathering a group together for travel by jeep. Voen Sai is thirty-five kilometers northwest of Ban Lung, and Kachon is one hour by boat east of Voen Sai. Admission to the graveyard is $1. Expect to pay around $15 for the boat ride, which will also include a visit to the Chinese and Lao villages on the way back to Voen Sai. For directions to Ban Lung, go to page 128.

BORDER TOWNS

XXXXXXXXXXXXXXXXXXXXXXXXXXXXXXX
ooooooooooooooooooooooooooooo

Peter Walter travels beyond borders in Cambodia

I like borders. I'm not sure exactly why, nor can I pinpoint the first time I discovered this fascination of mine, but there is something about borders that intrigues me. On maps they appear uncomplicated and static—dormant lines separating two distinct countries, or mere points marking the intersection of multiple nations. Sometimes they are formed around natural features in the landscape, while at other times they meander in less explainable ways to create their national divides. Whatever their shape, borders usually have a history that is much richer than their simplicity might suggest.

For travelers, borders offer the unique opportunity to pass instantly from one country into another, an intersection of places, peoples, and cultures. Along borders one can see the transition between countries from the shift in buildings and roads, the distinctly different clothes of the locals, and the languages that permeate the air. At large crossings, the transformation tends to be more gradual, as crowds from both sides meld into a broad swath of "in-between" that gradually fades as one penetrates deeper into the next country. At small, less traveled points, the change is more immediate, with the traveler immersed in the new environment only a few steps after crossing the line.

Cambodia shares its borders with three countries—Thailand to the west/north, Vietnam to the east/southeast, and Laos to the north. However, today's borders are relatively young in many respects, having been shaped over the past several hundred years by power struggles with neighbors, colonization by France, and the more recent Khmer Rouge tragedy and its aftermath. They are also quite fragile. Disputes between Thailand and Cambodia over the Preah Vihear temple complex (see page 71) have heightened national tensions and trigger the occasional exchange of gunfire across the disputed line. In addition, many parts of Cambodia's borders are still riddled with land mines left over from the Khmer Rouge conflict, making it impossible to explore some of the beautiful forests and mountains in those areas.

BORDER TOWNS

Despite these circumstances, seeing Cambodia through its borders is generally safe and well worth the effort. Traveling overland between Cambodia and its neighbors is easy, with numerous places to enter and exit and Cambodian visas now available on arrival at most crossing points. The points differ widely from location to location, reflecting the traffic loads that they see. Some are sleepy and appear mostly unchanged by time, while the largest crossings teem with people and goods flowing in both directions. My favorites are the quiet outposts where few travelers pass. In these places, crossing the border can become more than just a stamp in your passport.

On a trip to Surin, Thailand, with some friends and our respective kids, we made a detour to the southwestern corner of Si Sa Ket Province, to see the Cambodian border crossing at Chong Sa-Ngam/Anlong Veng. Almost as if standing guard, an ancient Khmer temple looms just inside Thai territory, surrounded by jungle on all sides. A rickety metal fence running along the southern face of the temple marks the border, with a small gate in the middle big enough for only a single person to fit through.

The few immigration guards seated in plastic chairs near the gate didn't appear to get many travelers, and were pleased by the sudden arrival of seven energetic foreign kids and their parents. While we didn't have visas to enter Cambodia formally, the guards on both sides kindly let the kids play, straddling the line with one foot in each country at the same time. At the guards' suggestion, the kids were even allowed to run about twenty yards into Cambodian territory, where they excitedly looked back and yelled, "I'm in Cambodia!"

Toward the end of another trip through Laos, I rode my motorbike as far south as I could, reaching the Laos-Cambodia border at Voeung Kam/Dom Kralor in hopes of getting a visa to enter Cambodia. The Laos immigration office on the north bank of the Mekong River was not much more than a bamboo hut lying in the lazy shade of the river's edge. There were no tourist queues here, and from the looks of it, very few travelers came this way at all. Across the river on the other bank, I could see a small clearing in the thick trees, with a narrow dirt road leading up from the water into Dom Kralor on the Cambodia side. Unfortunately, visas weren't available on arrival at the time, but I vowed to return someday and see things from the other side.

In contrast, the busiest crossing between Thailand and Cambodia is at Aranyaprathet/Poi Pet. This gateway is frequented less by general travelers than it is by casino patrons and others making visa runs from Bangkok, and its rapid growth shows the scars of modern development. It is also the fastest route for the overland trip between Bangkok and Siem Reap and, as such, has its merits. Once you come out of the dust of Poi Pet, the Cambodian countryside opens up, with long stretches of rice paddy and sugarcane fields as far as the eye can see.

On a recent trip, I took the opportunity to cross into Cambodia at the southernmost land border crossing from Thailand at Hat Lek/Cham Yeam, near Koh Kong. This area has a rich although somewhat checkered history, as Koh Kong and the surrounding islands in southwestern Cambodia are renowned for their smuggling past. I had come for more honest reasons—to see what the border was like and explore the surrounding country on my mountain bike. The crossing here is much quieter than at Aranyaprathet/Poi Pet, but well organized and easy to get through, even with a bike in tow.

Over the next few days, I criss-crossed the province on two wheels, doing my best to avoid the frequent rains. After a futile attempt to navigate the muddy roads leading up into the Cardamom Mountains, I had better luck riding through coastal villages and beaches, stopping frequently along the way to rest my legs and chat with locals. As I pedaled along, I saw the country in a way most tourists do not, and I felt immensely fortunate for the opportunity to experience Cambodia through the unique perspective of its borders.

Visas on arrival

The availability of visas on arrival at the smaller land borders of Cambodia has apparently improved considerably in recent years. Many Internet sources report that Cambodian visas are available at most border crossing points in Thailand, Vietnam, and Laos—however, the opposite may not be true if you are departing Cambodia and trying to enter these countries. Travelers are strongly advised to check the latest reports prior to their visit, and as a precaution, it never hurts to have a multiple-entry visa to ensure your passage at any point along the way.

Buyer beware

It's not uncommon for Cambodian immigration officials to charge somewhat inflated, Thai-baht-based prices for visas upon arrival from Thailand. Peter can't attest to whether this is also true along the Vietnam border with Cambodia, but travelers should be aware of this and expect to encounter it. As well, in some cases, there have been reports of immigration police trying to charge a 100-baht fee for the normally free entry and exit stamp. This is a scam, and any traveler who encounters this should not pay.

There is no shortage of touts who offer to assist travelers with the visa process at the border. While getting their help is not required at all, some travelers may find the additional guidance welcome. If you do use such individuals, it's generally appropriate to offer something in return, but there is no obligation, and travelers should not be misled.

Secret Gardens

Where to hide away from the touring masses

At one time, this chapter could have been the toughest one in the book for me. I first arrived in Cambodia in 1994 just as the initial, tentative tourists were coming, following the UN elections and the arrival of peace. I saw the country when no one else was around, and that's how I wanted to keep it. I wanted to maintain it, free from the madding crowds, selfishly, just for me.

Then, when I saw how dramatically the fortunes and lifestyles of my newfound Cambodian friends changed and improved with the advent of more tourists, which now exceed two million per year, I changed my opinion. I even played a small part in this growth by hosting a series of Magic of Cambodia days in middle England, simply to promote Cambodia as a safe and beautiful destination. As well, I posted travelogues on my Internet site, which prompted many emails from interested travelers. I had come full circle.

While I still miss the Cambodia of yesteryear, the truth is that those who come now can still uncover their own private Cambodia if they really want to. Most travelers head for the main areas, Siem Reap and Phnom Penh, but even in these places it's possible to retreat. Follow the suggestions on these pages and you can hide away in Phnom Penh at a rooftop pool, among library bookshelves, on an island in the Tonle Sap River, or in the National Museum when no one else is about. As for Siem Reap, take a break from the temples and spend a day cycling back roads with Rachel Wildblood, or accept Ronnie Yimsut's invitation to slow down at his farm, after which you can visit his cousin in the market in Puok for a bowl of "mean noodle soup."

Off the trodden tourist route, just step into rural Cambodia and you'll find yourself in a village where an outsider is still a novelty—evidenced not only in this chapter, but in

---

Guardian statues at the entrance to the Bayon temple

many of the essays in the Into the Wild section as well. All you have to do is give yourself enough time and you can learn the fine art of *dar' layng*—wandering—with Robert Philpotts in Kompong Chhnang, sway the afternoon away in a hammock with Karen Coates in Kep, day trip to the sedate border town of Kaam Samnor with Caroline Nixon, or discover the real meaning of the apostrophe in Koh S'dach with Roy McClean.

As for my secret gardens in Cambodia these days, I have to go farther afield. The villages, for example, in the northernmost Preah Vihear Province that take hours to get to on the back of a moto and where the children come running out when they hear a *barang* has arrived. People fall over themselves to provide a place to eat and sleep, and I stay up late talking to families by candlelight about my own family, my own life, my own dreams ... in this way, my Cambodia of past days returns.

PHNOM PENH

Georgiana Treasure-Evans starts over on a Phnom Penh rooftop

We first came to the Goldiana Hotel nearly two years ago, the night we arrived in Cambodia. Our daughter was asleep in our room, and my husband and I enjoyed a celebratory beer by the rooftop pool. I still remember how the feelings of fear and uncertainty—at having uprooted our lives and moved to this strange new country—vanished as I stepped out onto the roof terrace, instantly replaced with the thrill that this exotic city was to become our home.

The air was warm and mellow, infused with jasmine and frangipani. Looking down onto the streets below, I could see dogs sniffing about for scraps left over from a noodle stall. Its owner had packed up and was making his way home, wearily pulling his cart behind him. Tuk-tuk drivers played cards on the pavement outside the hotel entrance, waiting for their next fare.

We spotted at least five different birds flying around the neighboring terraces, perching on washing lines, their song sweet and unfamiliar.

As the huge crimson sun slid down behind the low rooftops, the birds metamorphosed into playful bats. We could almost hear them laughing as they swooped fast and low over the floodlit water, just missing our heads as we swam.

A soft, dark light filled the sky. It was quiet enough for the gentle sounds of city life to float upward to where we sat—families sitting down to dinner around outdoor charcoal stoves. Spoons scraping dishes clean. Mothers calling their children in from their play.

"There must be a snooker bar close by," I thought, then realized I said it out loud. I was listening to someone rhythmically potting a ball, amazed by their accuracy as it sounded at equal intervals, over and over again.

James looked at me astonished. "You mean you've never heard a gecko before?"

It was funny to me that our daughter would be saying things like this so nonchalantly to her English friends before long. Our new life, I happily realized, had already begun, on this rooftop terrace at the Goldiana Hotel.

The Goldiana Hotel

Georgiana adds: There are several fantastic swimming pools in Phnom Penh, set in the grounds of majestic hotels. Raffles Hotel Le Royal has the fine beauty of the French colonial era; the Himawari is luxurious, situated right on the riverside; and the

InterContinental has a pool bar. But none can beat the slightly scruffy, unsophisticated rooftop pool at the Goldiana for sitting back and absorbing the scents, sounds, and sights of Phnom Penh at night. Whether you go there simply for a cold beer at sunset, to have a meal, or to take a dip with the bats after dark, I recommend you pay this unlikely hotel a visit.

Having lived there for nearly a month, I feel both affection and loathing for the hotel itself. Its dark and oppressive interior is full of chintz. The plants are adorned with sparkly plastic decorations, and fat little gold-painted Buddhas sit intoxicated by the sickly sweet smell of cheap incense burning at every shrine. The staff are delightful but chaotic. The breakfasts were abysmal when we stayed there, but the curries and stir-fries were and continue to be cheap, delicious, and almost always big enough for two. The fried fish in ginger with soy beans goes down great with kids. As for the pool, it is small and deep—there are few pools in this city where your feet do not touch the bottom—and often unoccupied. It is perfect for plunging in and washing away the stress of the day.

If you like people watching, this hotel is the place to come. It is mainly frequented by NGO workers, volunteers, and the odd tourist, but most interestingly, it also has a deal with an Italian adoption agency. Every week couples come to meet their newly adopted child and then stay there for several days, as the families get used to each other. I have seen many such couples come and go. It is both awful and wonderful to watch the babies and children. They arrive so scared and timid, clinging to their new parents, not speaking a word. By the end of the week they are eating well, splashing about in the pool, and calling their parents Ma and Pa. I often wonder what sort of lives they will go on to lead once they return to Italy, and if they will remember how it all began—much like my new life—by the Goldiana pool in Phnom Penh.

#10+12, Street 282
Sangkat Boeung Keng Kang I
Khan Chamkarmon
Phnom Penh
(023) 219-558

www.goldiana.com

Denise Heywood indulges her inner bibliophile in Phnom Penh

A mangy dog slept on the top step of Phnom Penh's library as I approached. He cocked an eye at me briefly and then carried on snoozing in the languid heat. I stepped gingerly around him to enter my favorite building in the city. La Bibliothèque is a gem of French architecture in the old colonial quarter, and while many similarly gracious edifices are crumbling away, this one has been lovingly renovated.

The word *bibliothèque* is painted in brown Broadway font across the top of the yellow, single-story, neoclassical structure. Around the doorway, the original brown scroll motif and proverb have been repainted by students from the School of Fine Arts: *La force lie un temp, L'idée enchaine pour toujours.* Force binds for a while, ideas chain forever. It seems prophetic, as it was written by Francois Baudoin, the *résident-supérieur* in Phnom Penh, long before the time of the Khmer Rouge.

The building was designed in 1924, and it looks as though it should be in Paris, with its two sets of double ionic columns, pair of outer columns, and architectural details picked out in white stucco. Its elegance is enhanced by the surrounding garden, which creates the kind of peaceful atmosphere associated with reading and intellectual pursuits.

With ceiling fans cooling the spacious interior, newly tiled floors, large tables, and original wooden counter, the library once housed sixty-five thousand volumes and a collection of seventeenth-century palm leaf Buddhist manuscripts. In 1953, after Cambodia became independent, hundreds of volumes disappeared after French readers left hurriedly, "without taking the time to return

their borrowed books," according to a report. While disputes attend the division of the collections after the French departed, nothing matched the destruction by the Khmer Rouge.

Eighty percent of the books were burned. The rest were scattered. The library was used—literally—as a pigsty. Pol Pot's Chinese advisers were garrisoned next door in Le Royal Hotel, and pigs were fattened up in the library's gardens to feed them. The shelves were used to store cooking pots. Thirty-five of the forty-one staff members were killed.

Two survivors, He Hin and Yok Kun, returned in 1979 to find the library in shambles. They told me how they retrieved torn fragments from the undergrowth and helped restock the shelves through donations. As a result, there are lots of technical books in Russian from the former Soviet Union ("No one ever looks at them," admitted He Hin), old leather-bound tomes on French civilization, and atlases of *les colonies* Francaises with disintegrating pages ravaged by humidity and insects, as well as rare books on Khmer culture. Repairs have been made with help from the Australian International Development Assistance Bureau, which also donated equipment such as an air conditioner for a room where three hundred restored palm leaf manuscripts are kept.

Today the library is a haven for the city's bibliophiles, and I left its studious atmosphere reluctantly. Outside, the dog hadn't moved in the heat. As I edged past, he yawned, scratched himself vigorously, and went back to sleep. Clearly, he found the library as calming a retreat from the urban mayhem of Phnom Penh as I did.

La Bibliothèque

The National Library can be found on Street 92, a few hundred meters from the Raffles Hotel Le Royal, another architectural gem from Cambodia's colonial past. The National Archives are housed in a building immediately behind the library and used to store the city's blueprints and architectural documents. Despite their turbulent history, both buildings continue to fulfill their original functions.

Kim Fay finds timeless tranquility in Phnom Penh

The first time I came to Phnom Penh, in 1999, I felt as if I had arrived in a small town. I was living in Ho Chi Minh City, which at that time was quiet itself by regional urban norms. But in comparison, Phnom Penh suited the cliché phrase: sleepy backwater. A coup had taken place just a few months earlier, and its aftermath was a lethargy that crept through the streets. During the day, having a drink down on the river, the most action we saw was an elephant strolling by. After dark, the sound of a motorcycle buzzing past stood out in the night.

Ten years later I came back, and I did not recognize the city. Yes, it was definitely now a city. Not only were its sidewalks cluttered with people and streets crowded with cars, it had a completely new energy. A perpetual rush hour vibration—at times it felt even bellicose—that I must confess, I didn't care for. As I explored, I kept looking around for that old narcoleptic mood that for me had been Phnom Penh's greatest charm. What I saw were too many backpackers, apathetic building projects, and a new aggression that I'm sure many would just brush off as the cost of progress. I couldn't do that. I was too depressed.

My second morning in Phnom Penh, I woke early at my hotel, The Pavilion, a lovely little compound that was once a French colonial manor said to have been built for King Sihanouk's mother. I walked out into the streets, which were already threaded with exhaust-spewing motorbikes, and made my way around the Royal Palace, desperate to find a glimpse of my old city in the National Museum. Inaugurated in 1920 as a shelter for artifacts preserved from the Khmer temples, the museum had played a significant role in my first visit to Cambodia, as I was using it to research a historical novel. I could still remember how serene it had been, and I approached hesitantly, fearing that it too had been co-opted.

The museum was not yet open, but there was a woman at the entrance booth, and she sold me a ticket. No one stood in the doorway to take it, and when I went in, the gift counter was covered in a cloth. The main hall was cool and utterly silent. I walked to the opposite door, overlooking the interior courtyard that was surrounded by the hall and three open-faced arcades—no walls at all inside to protect the ancient collection from the elements. Gazing around, I saw that the old beamed ceilings had been covered, to protect the relics from the bats that once nested up there. A small girl slept beneath a bench.

I took a seat in a wicker chair next to a small drinks cart and had a cup of tea. The heat was already beginning to cling, and I asked the woman in charge if I could turn on the ceiling fan. She just nodded to a switch on the wall and smiled, as if to say, "Do as you like." With the air stirring slowly above me, I sat for an hour, and then another.

Not a single tourist came through as the sunlight entered the courtyard garden over the steep ochre roofs, along with a soft, thin rain. The clouds shifted, and the shadows of the east wing receded. The lotus ponds shimmered. I had forgotten how clear the light in Cambodia can be, as if a film has been lifted from the world. Across the way, Vishnu and Lokesvara and dancing *apsaras* spread through the galleries with a cool indifference to the passage of time. For them—and because of them, for me—Phnom Penh would continue to be a place where the past still mattered, and where quiet corners were only a $3 museum ticket away.

The National Museum

The museum is located just north of the Royal Palace on Street 13 between Streets 178 and 184. www.cambodiamuseum.info

The Pavilion

With a nod to its colonial past in its simple but elegant style, and a small poolside restaurant and bar, this boutique hotel is both a sanctuary and a historic treasure. It is perfectly located a few blocks from the museum.

227, Street 19
Phnom Penh
www.thepavilion.asia

The Great Vishnu

Khmer scholar Helen Ibbitson Jessup adds: Among the hundreds of masterpieces in stone, bronze, and wood in the National Museum, it is hard to choose a favorite, but one candidate for me is the bronze image of Reclining Vishnu, or Vishnu Anantashayin. Although 2.2 meters long, it is only a fragment of the original, which would have stretched more than 6 meters, making it one of the largest bronzes ever cast in Southeast Asia.

This statue was found underground in 1936 in a deep well in the temple precincts of the West

Mebon Island, in the Western Baray, a huge reservoir that was created at Angkor in the mideleventh century. What we now have is the head, torso, and two right arms (this manifestation of Vishnu has four arms), plus several fragments. The rest may still lie buried in the mud—a tantalizing thought.

This may be the same sculpture referred to by the Chinese envoy Zhou Daguan in his account of a 1296 visit to Cambodia. He describes a reclining Buddha with water flowing from his navel, possibly connected with a device to determine the water level of the baray. If it is the same sculpture—and we know of no other on that scale—Zhou was mistaken in its identity, as this clearly represents Vishnu in cosmic sleep.

This beautiful creation myth recounts how Vishnu slept at the end of one of the world's cyclic eras, reclining on the serpent Ananta, who floated on the primordial ocean, until the time for a new cycle of existence arrived. At this moment, a lotus blossom rose from Vishnu's navel. In its unfolding petals sat Brahma, god of creation, who then instigated the next cycle.

Dramatic though the history, massive scale, and technology of this Vishnu may be, they pale before the impact of the sculpture on the viewer. For all its monumental size, the face has a benign expression, its sightless gaze (the eyes were once filled with precious gems or metal) projecting an all-knowing benevolence. The patina of the heavy bronze, now a rich verdigris with rusty depths, has an almost living quality. Standing in front of it for a few quiet moments, I never fail to feel the hairs rising on the back of my neck.

Debbie Watkins goes elsewhere in Phnom Penh

Early Friday evening: time to head elsewhere.

I walk into the Elsewhere bar after a busy day and order a happy hour Cosmopolitan. The bartender smiles. "Where would you like to sit?" I survey the options. Bit difficult to choose really ... the benches with their brightly striped cushions by the pool, surrounded by the delicate blooms of the frangipani? The deckbeds, raised platforms with floor cushions sheltering under the palm trees? It all seems a bit surreal—amongst the chaos, dust, and heat of Phnom Penh, this little bar/restaurant, hidden behind pale green gates, that immediately transports me not just to another place, but to another era.

I settle for the deckbed. Take off my shoes, tuck my feet under me, sigh, relax. Stare up through the swaying palm fronds at the sky, intensely blue. Soft music, contemporary but not too heavy, adds to the birdsong and the muffled sounds of the world outside—a world away, it seems.

A few children laugh and splash in the pool. This was once a grand colonial residence. The white-painted shutters, the bold geometric floor tiles, all speak of some forgotten time. A time of cocktail parties, swing bands, croquet on the lawn. Then it was abandoned during the genocide, its perfectly manicured garden falling prey to creepers, its eaves to termites. Now, with new life breathed into it, it is a haven for people like me, hot, tired, and dusty from dashing around the city.

The bartender asks discreetly, "Happy hour finishes soon, would you like another?"

I need no persuading.

Elsewhere

While Debbie's retreat has recently moved location to 2, Street 278 (Golden Street), the ambience is still the same—pool, drinks, and day beds for whiling away the hours.

www.elsewhere2.asia

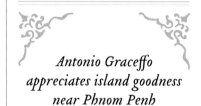

MEKONG ISLAND

Antonio Graceffo appreciates island goodness near Phnom Penh

Sae sat under a shade tree, in the yard of her daughter-in-law's home. Frail and aged, her hands shook as she poured watery rice mix into the stone bowl. With effort, she lifted a heavy crank into place and began to turn it. Slowly, with the patience of ages, a frothy porridge of rice paste began to trickle out of the spout and into the pail.

Sae's rice cakes were a favorite treat for the local children. At 100 riel each (about 2 and a half cents) everyone could afford them. "But some of the children don't pay," she said. She tried to look angry, but it was obvious that the kind-hearted woman was like a grandmother for the entire village. What grandmother could refuse a cake to a child?

I was on Mekong Island, in the Tonle Sap River, only a few kilometers outside of Phnom Penh, but I felt as if I had traveled back to a simpler, more humane time, when people did not work like machines, and when families could live in close community, sharing with their neighbors. Like in

Tevia's village of Anatevka in *Fiddler on the Roof,* everyone knew who he was, and what he was expected to do. Sae made rice cakes. The children helped their mothers spin cloth on traditional looms. All of the family members tended to the vegetable garden, and the fathers were mostly fishermen, who worked the waters of the great river, much as their fathers had for generations.

A fisherman named Noy agreed to take me and my translator, Sawat, on the river. The boats were fashioned from a single palm tree and resembled traditional dugout canoes. A man each perched, precariously, on the absolute bow and aft point, using a long pole to punch the boat along.

We stopped to talk to a family of Cham who lived on their two fishing boats. The Cham are not ethnic Khmers, although they have inhabited the region for centuries, since the Kingdom of Champa. They have their own language and follow a version of Islam that differs dramatically from that practiced in the Middle East. Many Cham are born on boats and spend their entire lives on the water, only coming ashore to attend mosque.

Back on land, Sae's family timidly invited us to lunch. "You are the first foreigner they have seen," Sawat told me. Of course, the food was excellent. The children were cute, keeping their distance at first, but then slowly coming over to stare at the exotic being from another world. I was in the middle of teaching them to box when Sawat said that it was time for us to return to Phnom Penh.

My single day spent on Mekong Island was more of a cultural experience than an entire year in Phnom Penh. Sae and her family didn't understand why I told them I was grateful to them. That may be their most endearing quality. They were good, kind people, who didn't know how rare their goodness and kindness were.

Getting to Mekong Island

Officially called Koh Okhnatey, Mekong Island lies close to Koh Dach. Both can be visited by local ferry from National Highway 6A or by hired boat from the riverside at Phnom Penh.

PHNOM PENH TO SIEM REAP

Cristiano Calcagno pauses between Phnom Penh and Siem Reap

The district of Baray in Kompong Thom Province lies in the exact center of the country. It is rural Cambodia at its most typical: rice plains, sugar palms, small market towns and villages, a couple of Cham settlements, and a number of pre-Angkorian brick towers in various states of ruin.

Visitors usually pass through this area while en route between Phnom Penh and Siem Reap, and very few get a chance of stopping off along the way. But if you can spare the time, follow me and I'll show you a nicely preserved ancient temple that you wouldn't expect to see so far away from Angkor. It is in the countryside some distance away from the main road, quiet and serene, just as you would wish it to be.

With blocks of laterite that have blackened with time, Kuhak Nokor was built in the eleventh century around the era of Angkor Wat. Two ancient ponds lie out front, their stone stairways reaching down to the water. The retaining wall is intact, with a monumental entrance gate to the east and a tower surmounting a chamber in the wall to the west.

Walk through the gate, and you'll be surprised at how the temple grounds have been lovingly tended by the caretaker, who has turned this tranquil space into a small garden of flowers, in the middle of which stands the main sanctuary and a smaller "library" building at its side. The sanctuary, adorned with some fine bas-reliefs, consists of a tower preceded by a gallery, flanked by niches and leading to a narrow central chamber where the altar is located. Behind the altar is the sanctuary tower chamber, teeming with bats.

The old, friendly caretaker keeps a logbook where visitors can write their impressions. He has learned some English and French over the years through contact with visitors and will be glad to show you around. The care he puts in maintaining the site is extraordinary, and the logbook is his personal treasure, with its entries in many languages and from many countries. Be kind and leave a few words for him. He deserves your recognition for maintaining this unsung temple with such grace.

Getting to Kuhak Nokor

Along National Highway 6, 100 kilometers north of Phnom Penh (or 215 southeast of Siem Reap), just north of the provincial boundary between Kompong Cham and Kompong Thom, you will enter the market town of Tangkouk. A few hundred meters south of the very tall, modern, three-story pagoda, a signboard points toward a dirt road branching off to the west through an arched gate. Follow that for 2.5 kilometers until you reach a school compound. Behind that is a pagoda, and within its grounds, just past the main modern sanctuary, is Prasat Kuhak Nokor.

SIEM REAP PROVINCE

SIEM REAP

Elizabeth Briel is seduced into a Siem Reap café

I'd spent the morning running after young photo students at Wat Damnak, showing them different composition techniques. Afterward, I was desperate for a cold drink somewhere in a new patch of shade. My push-bike screeched to a halt next to the Siem Reap River. Behind a colorful gate I was about to discover one of the town's friendliest sanctuaries. "Community space with movies for adults and kids," the sign read. "All welcome. Healthy meals and decadent desserts." Sounds like my kind of place, I thought.

But what really drew me through the Singing Tree's gates was the garden. There are few sights more demoralizing than desiccated urban jungle at the end of the dry season. I had been cycling for weeks past parched plants coated in dust, but this profusion of flowers and waxy palms was five degrees cooler than the scorching, asphalt-coated town outside. Sitting beneath the shade of a traditional wooden Khmer house seemed an ideal way to while away an afternoon in front of an electric fan or three.

I ordered a sandwich—perfectly proportioned for my taste. Then climbed up wooden stairs that had been smoothed by thousands of feet, passing by a sign that said: "Leave shoes and minds behind." I settled into a pile of cushions for an afternoon film.

A man poked his head into the dark, wooden, makeshift cinema and waved. "Hi, I'm Michael," he said. "Thanks for stopping by, and just give a shout if you need anything." After the movie I had a chance to catch up with him. The café's founder, he is an idealist, and unlike many of his kind, is doing something about it. He is a deminer, clearing mines and unexploded ordnance.

As I waved goodbye and hopped on my bike, students began arriving for an early evening yoga class: locals, expats, and tourists, all part of the transient Siem Reap community. The last of the day's sunlight slipped through palm leaves, and I heard someone call out, "Goodbye—see you next time!"

Yes, there would be a next time. And I wouldn't need the excuse of an escape from hot afternoon sun to venture through the gates of this Siem Reap oasis.

Singing Tree Café

The Singing Tree Café, Elizabeth's favorite affordable retreat in Siem Reap, has recently moved to the entrance of Alley

West, just twenty meters from Pub Street. It is not affiliated with the venue now operating at its old location. Opening hours can be "flexible" as it's a family-run business, although usually from 8:00 a.m. until 9:00 p.m. or later, depending on the number of customers. The café is closed on Mondays. It offers free Wi-Fi, and a free computer is available to those who haven't got their own. Various types of workshops, including yoga, meditation, and Khmer arts, can be found on the café website.

www.singingtreecafe.com

Socheata Poeuv stops in her tracks in Siem Reap

I will never forget the day I arrived at the HanumanAlaya Hotel. I had been shooting a documentary film for over two weeks throughout Cambodia. We had visited former Khmer Rouge cadres, Pol Pot's grave, and even the site of the refugee camp where I was born. We had been bumping and rolling for more than five hours over the notoriously broken-down Cambodian back roads from Anlong Veng to Siem Reap. My back and bottom felt like they had been treated with a meat tenderizer.

Parched, sweaty, and cranky, the crew and I crawled out of our cars. We stopped in our tracks. Beyond a lush green patio was the HanumanAlaya. Named after the home of the monkey king, Hanuman, the hotel was inspired by a traditional Cambodian teak house. Before we could walk inside, we all paused simply to admire the place.

Every square inch of the hotel is accented by traditional Cambodian handicrafts, including luxurious silk bedspreads and exquisite bronze figures of dancing *apsaras*. In the open-air dining room, we were greeted with a tray of Cambodian ice tea, a special blend that came straight from the owner's private plantation. It had the natural sweetness of almonds—the best tea I've ever tasted in my life.

Nearby are the sprawling five-star monoliths known as luxury hotels in Siem Reap, but compared to the exquisite intimacy of the Hanuman-Alaya, those other places seemed like a fraud. After two hard weeks on the road, immersed in the tragedies of Cambodia's not-so-distant past, it felt good to find this oasis, which captures the real beauty and the real soul of the country.

HanumanAlaya

This boutique hotel is located in a quiet corner of Siem Reap, near to the Angkor Conservation Depot.

(063) 760-582
www.hanumanalaya.com

Ronnie Yimsut
slows down at his farm
outside Siem Reap

There is an old cliché: "Everything looks about the same here in Cambodia." Not so, I say. Not if you look carefully and experience Cambodia at "local's level."

What do I mean by that? You can start by walking as far as you can from your hotel or place of residence. If you get tired, then get a bike and go a little farther the next day. If you are really tired or want to go even farther, then perhaps you should consider a motorbike as your mode of transport. Certainly you can't see very much detail from a fast-moving car! That's what I mean by going local. Take everything at a slower pace.

For me personally, I often go on average about thirty kilometers a day on my old yet reliable Honda 60, which I keep in Siem Reap. (You can very well rent one for less than $5 a day.) I ride to all the eight directions on the compass, and getting a little lost is considered as part of the challenge. I get to see and do more. I meet new people and experience new places.

At the end of the day, I always end up at a place that I started building from scratch in 1994. It is known as Nak's Farm, a five-acre fenced-and-gated private oasis. When I first found it, it was just a deep hole in the ground. Today, it is a working farm with free-roaming ducks, chickens, big catfish in the pond below a wooden kiosk, a clean outhouse, and plenty of fruit trees. A good hammock under a cool shady tree is a welcome relief to all visitors, after a nice cool bath from the well.

This place is my own heaven, my escape from the hustle and bustle of Siem Reap. And it is open to the public for the price of asking my caretaker, Mr. Sauth, a farmer who lives next door. Someday, I hope, there will be a bed and breakfast here.

To top it off, nearby are two tourist destinations, the Western Baray (two kilometers directly to the north) and the Angkor Silk Farm (five kilometers west along National Highway 6), where you can get lost for hours, if you wish. These spots, which are also local favorites, should not be missed if you wish to get a small taste of the real Cambodia.

If you go a little farther west to a town called Puok, my cousin Yim Sal, who is also Nak's Farm general manager, cooks a mean noodle soup and other feasts in the main market on the highway. Should you happen to arrive a little too late and there is nothing left to munch, he can point you to several great roasted chicken stalls. This tiny town is famous for its fresh roasted chicken, so try not to miss it as you slow down and enjoy life from a local's point of view.

Getting to Nak's Farm

Nak's Farm is approximately twelve kilometers west of Siem Reap on National Highway 6—just past the airport and the Teukvil market. You have to cross a small bridge next to the governor's impossible-to-miss mansion on your left. Go about five hundred meters along a dirt road that runs parallel to the canal until you reach a crossroad. Take a left, and go about fifty meters. The farm will be on your right. The Western Baray, the Angkor Silk Farm (go to page 155), and Puok town are all west of Siem Reap along National Highway 6.

Rachel Wildblood cycles the rural back roads of Siem Reap

In Cambodia, late afternoon is usually warm and sunny, with mellow gold light enveloping people and buildings. This is a fine time of day to leave town behind and cycle out to the countryside to stumble upon the pastoral scenes that are daily life for the majority of this rural country.

Around three o'clock, I start out of Siem Reap. Soon the tarmac road gives way to red dirt tracks that are generally compact enough for a bicycle. After a few minutes, the ostentatious, concrete, town-style houses give way to more-traditional wooden rural dwellings. I pass people eating, sleeping, talking, and working outside their homes. Labor is hard here. Harvesting, plowing, and fishing have to be done even on the hottest of days.

I cycle through a village and out the other side, to the fields that are seasonally flooded by the Tonle Sap Lake. Here, even the houses fade away, leaving only rice fields between me and the distant, hazy Phnom Krom hill. The traffic noises have ceased. I stop my bike to take in my surroundings.

Depending on the season, the view changes dramatically. From verdant rice fields to cows grazing on brown rice straw, these scenes replace each other cyclically during the year. In the distance is the dull clink of cow bells as the beasts are driven home for the evening. The birds are singing, too, high above the fields. This is something I rarely hear. Although I am near buzzing Siem Reap, I would never know it. I could be a million miles away.

The sun starts its descent. It will get dark quickly. A snake slithers in front of me, crossing the road. I jump on my bike and turn back to town. I leave the glowing sun to set, but allow enough time to a drink coconut juice or perhaps a beer on the way back. Yes, a beer. After all, it has been another hot Cambodian day.

Rachel's favorite bike route out of Siem Reap

From Psar Chas/Old Market go over the bridge, straight on past Passaggio Hotel. Three hundred meters after the hotel, take the first right opposite Wat Bo Road. At the T-junction, go left, and take the first road (a compact dirt road) right.

On the dirt road, after five hundred meters, you will pass a bridge. Then the road becomes tree lined. Ignore the turnoffs, including the main turning on the right. You will pass a sign on the left for Adda, which will be on your return route, so make a note of where it is.

After about ten minutes you will reach a crossroad. Go straight on. (You will also come to this crossroad on the way back.) Cycle for about five minutes until you pass Ecole Primaire Chreav. Just past the school you will reach the Chreav village crossroad.

From Chreav village continue straight on and cycle as far as you feel like along the straight road toward the lake, with Phnom Krom in the distance. Gradually, houses will give way to paddy fields.

When you return from the paddy fields, go left at the village crossroads, past the post and police office, and through the market, depending on the time of day. After five minutes, take the first major road right. It is between two small stores with a temple nearby; the temple stupas are on the left as you turn, about forty meters from the road. Go past the temple buildings, including one on the right with new paintings, including a skeleton.

After about ten minutes, go left at the T-junction. You will immediately be at the crossroads that you passed on the way to the village. Go straight on, back toward Siem Reap.

After about five minutes, turn right at the Adda sign, over a bridge onto a loose sandy road (sorry, but it's not for long). Just before the Adda sign is a blue sign with a yellow arrow for El-lohian Mission Centre.

You will pass the Adda office on your left. After six hundred meters the sand stops and tarmac starts. You will pass the World Food Programme warehouse on your right, just before you hit the main road you started on.

Go left, and you will find yourself back at Psar Chas.

Refreshments along the way

You can buy cold drinks during your outing, near the village crossroads, in the market, and at points all along the road. Look out for large orange/red coolers and rummage around until you find just the drink to quench your thirst.

Pedaling in the wet season

The water levels around you will vary depending on the time of year. Take binoculars if you have them, especially in the flooded season. As you go through the village, you may see some of the water birds that migrate to Cambodia seasonally. The road should stay dry in the wet season for a while; just keep pedaling until you reach the water, which eventually, inevitably takes over the roads.

KAAM SAMNOR

Caroline Nixon
day trips to the border
town of Kaam Samnor

I wanted a break from Phnom Penh's noise and traffic. Just an easy day trip, somewhere picturesque, on the river, and not too touristy. Paradoxically I ended up in a place that dozens of people travel through every day. It's just that almost nobody stops in Kaam Samnor.

Kaam Samnor is a border town between Cambodia and Vietnam. Big ferries pass right through, but local boats still stop for visas to be stamped. To get there I caught an early bus from Psar Thmei market to the town of Neak Luong. The food hawkers that greeted me were particularly entertaining, because of their persistent sales patter and the sheer variety of their not altogether appetizing fare. Getting off the bus I was offered tiny grilled birds covered in sticky sauce and flies, deep-fried grasshoppers, and kebabs of "inside cow" (the local term for beef offal). I fancied breakfast, but perhaps something a little more conventional, so made my way down to the waterfront, where I dined in a small café on noodle soup and coffee.

Asking a motodop to take me to the landing for Kaam Samnor, I was delivered to a restaurant with a jetty, where a mixed bunch of locals and backpackers waited. The boat was a simple wooden one, painted blue. An altercation commenced. Some of the tourists wanted to climb up onto the roof against the wishes of the boatman, who was looking increasingly agitated. As the only person with any degree of linguistic overlap, I ended up translating. The boatman told me that recently a tourist had fallen from a boat, nearly drowning. Since then the police had forbidden anyone to sit on the roof. The boatman faced a big fine if he allowed it. My fellow travelers seemed unconcerned by this, their suntans taking priority.

Despite this disagreement, we arrived at Kaam Samnor two hours later after a scenic river journey and climbed the slippery bank to the customs hut. Behind this was a charming one-street town. It appeared prosperous, with neat little houses, shops, and well-kept gardens. Some girls wore the traditional Vietnamese *ao dai*, a long tunic over loose trousers. A motodop took me to the border to watch a stream of heavily laden motorbikes passing the rickety wooden barrier. Wandering back into town I met a friendly male nurse who spoke English. I asked him if he could recommend a good place for lunch, and he replied "my place." So I dined on delicious chicken curry with him and his family, who then offered me a bed for the night. I never cease to be amazed by Cambodian hospitality.

Thanking them profusely, I explained that I was returning to Phnom Penh that day and was soon on the back of another moto, headed back to Neak Luong. The narrow riverside road was a delight, passing small villages, schools, and pagodas. There were many small tributaries, crossed by bamboo or wooden bridges. Each was the scene of much activity, with people bathing, fishing, or washing their clothes, buffalo, or motorbikes. Despite numerous photo stops I arrived back in Neak Luong by late afternoon, with plenty of time to catch a share taxi to Phnom Penh for supper.

Getting to Kaam Samnor

Kaam Samnor is an ideal day trip or overnight destination and would make a great excursion for motorbikers. Catch a bus or share taxi from Phnom Penh's Psar Thmei market to Neak Luong, which takes just over an hour. Rather than follow the crowd to the ferry, instead turn right and walk along the riverbank for about five hundred meters. A number of small motorboats wait to take people along the river to Kaam Samnor. You can charter one for yourself or wait until a boat fills up. The trip to Kaam Samnor takes about two hours and offers great views of river life, although the boat sticks to the central channel, so you are quite far from the shore. Kaam Samnor has several simple restaurants, a bustling market, and a rather seedy-looking guesthouse. There is a strong Vietnamese flavor about the town, and shops take Vietnamese dong as well as Cambodian riel.

KOMPONG CHHNANG

Robert Philpotts goes nowhere specific in Kompong Chhnang

One breezy morning, having left the Samrongsen, my favored hotel in Kompong Chhnang town, I make my way to the port and am passed by a steady stream of modest and cheerful students, each riding a simple, gearless bicycle. Some greet me with "hello." Some ask, "What is your name?" and then giggle when I give it.

Once at the riverside I have to negotiate a market where, amongst the produce dealers, the signature pots of Kompong Chhnang are on display. I rent a boat for a couple of hours. I make it clear to Pim Seat, the boatman, that I want to *dar' layng* rather than visit anywhere in particular. In Khmer *dar' layng* can mean a pleasurable wandering of any kind. If I were on foot, I would be going for a stroll.

We cast off and head toward the distant Phnom Damrei, the highest of the eastern hills, and we begin to travel through the series of small islands, bars, and strips of land—interspersed with sheets of glinting water—that appear in the dry season. The Great Lake (Tonle Sap) is emptying at this time of year, and the current can be powerful, but poles and a mesh barrier have been erected to reduce the flow into a wide, secondary channel. On each pole a white egret waits, intent on snatching any confused fish swimming too near the surface. Passing through a narrow sluice, we travel across the wind-whipped waves beyond.

The falling river reveals trees that have been substantially submerged, but much vegetation snagged on their branches remains and decays, brown tangles through which new leaves must struggle to grow. As the trees also act as a magnet for creepers, and since rafts of water hyacinth congregate around their trunks, it

is hardly surprising some look worn down by the struggle, but most cling on tenaciously, and occasional displays of large pink and white flowers signify their defiance.

As we chug toward the Tonle Sap, I see signs of work and a Khmer village on stilts on the island where we tie up. Most of the recently emerged land, which is really deep, rich mud, has already been cultivated. I also notice new stock plants being prepared in front of the houses where seedlings, wrapped in tiny leaf containers, are handled with the utmost tenderness. The villagers are farmers for half the year, fishermen for the rest, and must make haste to grow, harvest, and sell their crops before the Great Lake starts to fill back up, reclaiming their fields as riverbeds. Then, as the rains come, they will become dependent once again for their living on the fish, which will feed on the leaves of the long-suffering trees.

After a couple enjoyable hours, we meander back to the dock. Surely there is no better place to appreciate the meaning of *dar' layng* than the province of Kompong Chhnang.

Getting to Kompong Chhnang

Kompong Chhnang town can be reached by a daily bus service from Phnom Penh. It is not blessed with great accommodation options. The Samrongsen Hotel is on the road to the port, a couple of hundred meters from the main market. Tour boats, which take several people at a time, can be rented at the port, which is connected to the middle of town by a single tarmac road a few kilometers long. Pim Seat can be reached by telephone at (012) 359-387. He speaks only a little English and rents his boat at $5 per hour for one to three passengers.

KEP

Karen Coates hangs her hammock by the sea in Kep

Well. Where am I? Paradise lost or paradise found? I'm swaying in a hammock on a wooden platform with a grass roof. The sea slurps to my left. A couple of mynahs sing. A flowery breeze ruffles my hair.

The seaside town of Kep sprawls along the coast. Actually, it lazes and snoozes like the dog at this guesthouse, all of its legs outstretched. There are a few accommodations, a few restaurants, and a rocky road with hardly a car. It's Sihanoukville, circa 1998, but even closer to the sea and quieter by far.

I order a pineapple juice. It comes to me, slowly, fresh and sweet, no tang. It's served in a wineglass with a straw and a little wedge of the fruit.

I sip it in the hammock. We're new in town, haven't seen anything yet, but I know few such coastal treasures like this exist in Southeast Asia anymore.

So many years after the fighting stopped, Kep still looks scarred. Like a resort smoldering in the hot ash of recent war. Quiet. Bikes on the road. Roofless skeletons of bombed-out homes. In some, families camp beneath tarps, and they cook over fires in the yard. Cows wander through these ghostly remains of a town that once thrived with society's richest and hippest holiday goers. All that crumbled beneath bombs and guns and misery.

I'm stunned. I expected at least a few more bungalows, a little more traffic, perhaps an Internet shop by now. But nothing. Not even Khmer tourists to lend this place a little more buzz. To call it "awakening," I think, is premature. It will happen, no doubt. Give it time. Already a couple of Belgians have—quietly—turned a few ruined homes into the country's most expensive and exclusive resort. Others have plans for building a new and improved Kep.

But this is still Cambodia, where plans have a way of taking a nap.

Getting to Kep

You can choose one of the air-con bus companies, such as the Phnom Penh Sorya Transport Company, offering daily service between Phnom Penh and Kampot. Get to the Central Market station early, buy your ticket, and wait at the coffee stall, where you can have a wonderful, hot, sweet coffee with condensed milk before you set off. Though the driver may not announce it, Kep is the first stop after the restaurant break. You'll know it when you spot the sea. The trip is about four hours, through some of the most scenic areas of Cambodia, following National Highway 3, turning south on National Highway 31, and making a loop along the coast on National Highway 33a.

Staying in Kep

These days, Kep offers a wide range of accommodation, from high-end resorts to inexpensive rooms on the sea. Karen usually stays at the Kep Seaside Guesthouse, a simple place with good food, friendly staff, and inexpensive rooms overlooking the water.

(012) 858-571, (012) 684-241

Mark Hotham celebrates the seaside silence in Kep

One of the highlights of the festival calendar in Cambodia, Bon Om Tuk takes place every November to celebrate the turning of the waters in the Tonle Sap and the end of the monsoon season. Thousands upon thousands descend on the capital from the provinces and produce an amazing spectacle of color, aroma, music, and food. Boat races provide a focal point to the intensity, and at night barges armed with fireworks are set along the river to float past the enthralled throng of happy faces.

We had witnessed this festival the two previous years and decided that this time we wanted to get out of town and find a refuge somewhere, just for a few days. Friends suggested a place called Veranda in the small and often forgotten coastal town of Kep. So the morning before the masses arrived, we left, taking a local bus for the four-hour journey.

As we made our way out of the capital southward, the faded colonial buildings, concrete tenement blocks, and warehouses gave way to small villages, paddy fields, buffalo, and giggling children on outsized bikes wobbling their way to rural schools. Arriving in Kep around eleven, we stood on the roadside with our bags as the bus continued its journey on to Sihanoukville. Behind us stood a small row of bombed-out old villas from the 1950s, and opposite, between the road and the sea, the local crab market.

Within seconds a couple of moto-dop drivers arrived and transported us to the Veranda Natural Resort, a two-minute ride up the road and onto a dirt track that climbed a jungle-clad hillside. Veranda proved to be everything we were looking for. Nestled into the hill, surrounded by lush vegetation and tropical gardens, were solidly built bungalows on stilts, connected by a network of walkways overgrown with bougainvillea. Simple but elegant, each one featured a shaded veranda area with cushions and a superb view over the coastline below.

Reclining on our private perch and sipping cold Beerlao, watching the sun set over the bay, we were a world away from the festival in Phnom Penh. It didn't take long for us to come to the conclusion that we had found the best way of all to celebrate Bon Om Tuk.

Getting to Kep
See fact file in previous essay.

Hanging out in Kep
There isn't much to do in Kep, and that's the beauty of it. There are few restaurants beyond the local fish stall and marketplaces. You can hire a boat to take you out to the uninhabited Koh Tonsay (Rabbit Island), where you will find a lovely, unspoiled beach in a quiet bay. The beach offers safe swimming and is hosted by a local lady who provides fresh cooked chicken, fruit, rice, and cold drinks for a remarkably reasonable price.

Veranda Natural Resort
This resort sits on the hill above the town, with fifteen bungalows built of bamboo and stone and great views over the bay. The swimming pool should be complete by the time this book is published.

(012) 888-619, (012) 399-035
www.veranda-resort.com

SIHANOUKVILLE

Georgiana Treasure
–Evans is victorious in Sihanoukville

It was a scorching day in April. The creamy white sand was set apart from the road by a stretch of shady grass. Rows of ramshackle shelters offered freshly squeezed juice and whatever today's catch brought in from the sea. Colorful hammocks hung from their beams. The sea was turquoise and calm. At the far end of the beach, away from the bustle, we stumbled across a perfect hideaway for tired parents and tireless children.

The sand gave way to rocks made for scrambling. A wooden swing hung from a huge tree, whose leafy branches shaded the shallow water's edge. And the best bit? Khmer people were allowed on the beach! While my husband snoozed in a hammock, our eighteen-month-old daughter played with the local kids, and I enjoyed the best foot massage I have ever had.

Hawkers passed quietly by with trays of glistening red barbecued prawns and squid, freshly cut mango and pineapple, and warm, sticky fried doughnuts. After sharing this feast with her friends, our daughter curled up into a round, womblike, cushioned bamboo chair provided by the food stall behind us and slept. A long-tail boat slipped past on the water, and I lay back and watched a child playing on the swing. Hypnotized by the rhythmic swinging back and forth, I too fell into a deeply restful sleep, vowing to come back.

We did, at the height of the monsoon season. I still dream of that day, when the heat and the exoticism of Phnom Penh became too much to bear and I longed for the cold gray days of home. We stripped off in the rain; ran down the deserted beach into the dark, inky sea; and were buffeted about in the rough waves awhile. Soon deliciously cool, we struggled to get back into wet clothes, battling with our modesty behind billowing sarongs while fishermen looked on in shameless fascination.

Afterward, we sheltered from the driving rain in the only beach restaurant still open for business. It was owned by an ancient Frenchman who slapped his young Khmer wife mischievously on her bottom and ordered her to make us some passion fruit crushes. She took it well, responding, somewhat uncharacteristically for a Khmer woman, with equal aggression and raucous foul language. We sat back to enjoy their banter, over plates of freshly caught sole and buttery potatoes, and wondered at the tiny baby this man had apparently fathered, despite his improbable age.

Victory Beach

Victory is Sihanoukville's northernmost beach. It lies off Krong Street, at the bottom of Weather Station Hill—popular with backpackers and budget travelers. Our favorite hangout on the hill is Bungalow Village, owned by a Khmer woman and her French husband. Set in tropical rocky gardens, it has several wooden bungalows on stilts and a lovely restaurant serving Western and Khmer food, including great breakfasts. Hammocks, cushions, and books (for adults and children) abound, and parents like us get the rare chance to lie back, drink coffee, and read the newspaper in peace.

KOH S'DACH

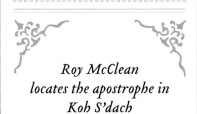

*Roy McClean
locates the apostrophe in
Koh S'dach*

When we arrive late at the pier, we walk purposefully onto the fast ferry, passing aggressive ticket touts and about a hundred Canadian high school students. We have seats, we have cash, I have a slight worry that the seemingly overloaded ferry might sink. We buy tickets on board and speed off.

We know that Koh S'dach is a small fishing island between Koh Kong and Sihanoukville that few people on the ferry ever stop off at. I am glad the high school students don't.

I have a habit of ignoring advice, preferring to make my own mistakes. Koh S'dach takes the opportunity for giving or taking advice out of traveling. There is only one street. It leads to the only guesthouse on the island. I feel a lot more relaxed because of this. I feel I have time to reflect. Time to pause— to stop for breath by the ice factory, then on top of the hill. We choose bungalows by the beach. I stare out of the tiny window for a long time.

I decide we must explore the entire island by moto. We see all of Koh S'dach there is to see in about ten minutes of driving time, but being on the bike breaks up the day: a long rest on the beach looking at the enormous crustaceans that time and fishermen have forgotten, a fun moment to take laughing children up and down some nameless hill, an idle snack on a pier watching sea urchins in the aquarium's clear water, a test of riding skill on a plank over an open sewer.

Almost everything seems made of wood: houses, stores, boats, children's toys. Some of the planks covering potholes in the road are old ships' doors. The quick fix of plastic, concrete, and fiberglass hasn't taken hold here. The times to take a break that really put the pause, the hidden moment, the apostrophe in Koh S'dach continue. We take a seat outside a shop, and five children put on a pantomime and dance for us.

The day happily spent, we avoid the trouser-vibrating guesthouse karaoke and stroll into town. A kind lady stays open late to feed us and entertain us with, yes, karaoke. We turn in for the night and listen to the crash of waves on the shore. I have never really noticed the space between the crashes before. I hope the apostrophe is still in Koh S'dach the next time we visit.

Getting to Koh S'dach

The ferry that plies the route between Koh Kong and Sihanoukville stops off at Koh S'dach. It departs Koh Kong at 8:00 a.m. and Sihanoukville at 9:30 a.m. Cost seems to vary. Hang on to your ticket, as you don't need to pay again if you break up the journey along the way.

Mean Chey Guesthouse

To reach the guesthouse, walk off the ferry and follow the road to the left. You will see some signs marking the way. Turn right just before the ice-making plant (the only building on the island that has an industrial look to it) and walk over the hill to the seaside. There is an open-sided restaurant where you can pick up keys and pay for the bungalows.

The blue concrete bungalows on the hill have cold-water showers and squat toilets. They look serviceable but are charmless. The seaside bungalows are a little of the opposite, each with a window that is just a wooden shutter kept open with a stick. Children like to stand by the window and look in. The same goes for adults, and adolescents pass slowly by on their motos. The toilets (squat) and show-ers (bucket) are just down from the last bungalow and require a key from the guesthouse owner, returned after each use, which is a little inconvenient.

What the guesthouse lacks in luxury it makes up for in setting. Three beaches can be reached by short walk, including the guesthouse beach, a mangrove beach, and a rather primeval-looking rocky beach with great mollusks. Rates run less than $10 per night. (011) 983-806

Dining in Koh S'dach

The guesthouse restaurant is good for dried snacks, coffee, and juice. Meals can be had by pointing at the ingredients and being satisfied with what you get. Roy always was. There are no real late-night food options in town. People here eat early to make more time for karaoke. The guesthouse karaoke is pretty loud and popular, so rent a bungalow as far away from it as possible.

INTO THE WILD

Outdoor experiences for adventurous travelers

Some travelers have to push the envelope. Go where few—or none—have gone before, experience the challenges to be found there, and come up smiling with tales of derring-do and a life enriched by the wonderful discoveries they have made. For these kinds of people, Cambodia is the place. I know because I've experienced it firsthand, and the buzz I get from it is like a drug. That's how I really got hooked on Cambodia, by getting off the beaten path and away from the crowds to discover this beautiful country for myself. I know it's not everyone's ideal holiday, but if you're prepared to put up with some discomfort, you will be rewarded for your adventurous spirit.

When it comes to getting into the wild, personally I'm more of a temple freak than I am a nature buff. But there's enough in Cambodia to satisfy supporters of either persuasion. My own adventures have involved climbing a mountain on my hands and knees, traversing no-man's-land at the border to uncover a forgotten temple, unintentionally walking through a minefield, and overnighting with former Khmer Rouge fighters, to name just a few. I look back now and wince at some of my recklessness, but to be honest, I'd do it all again, in an instant. Cambodia made me feel alive, and that's why I upped sticks and moved here to live—to have that feeling every day of my life.

Clearly the writers in this chapter feel the same way, as they venture into the unknown, quietly view local wildlife, explore an abandoned hill town, or journey to the far reaches to visit remote Mnong tribespeople. Juanita Accardo, Peter Walter, and Peter Leth all relish the joys of travel without a map in Ratanakiri Province—not to mention motorbike breakdowns and meals caught from local streams. Across the country, Gordon Sharpless and Daniela Papi sing the praises of the Cardamom Mountains, where tourism has scarcely scratched the surface. And in an unusual twist, Nick Ray writes about the thrill of *not* visiting a place—it is in his thwarted attempts to return to the temple of Preah Khan that he finds his adventure.

As for those nature lovers among you, Cambodia's parks and preserves beckon. At Ream National Park, Adam Bray finds the perfect antidote to the urban wildlife of nearby Sihanoukville, and on Tonle Sap Lake, Rachel Wildblood learns about the local ecology while taking a much needed temple break. Both Howie Nielsen and Karen Coates are drawn to the bird-watching area of Tmatboey, where rare ibis bring in travelers who discover not only Cambodia's environmental beauty but also ways in which the country is working to incorporate that beauty into the livelihoods of the local people. If for that and nothing else, the majority of the experiences to be had in this chapter are well worth forsaking the small luxuries (toilets, hot water, you get the idea) and going just a little bit wild.

SIEM REAP

Rachel Wildblood supports the environment outside Siem Reap

It is Saturday afternoon, and I decide to reacquaint myself with the Cambodia I originally came here for. I don't mean the temples or lively towns, but rather Tonle Sap Lake. The natural environment in Cambodia is remarkable, and the Tonle Sap is a perfect example of this. I leave Siem Reap behind and head to nearby Chong Kneas to visit the Gecko Environment Center.

The Gecko Center is where I go when I want to get onto the Tonle Sap without any of the typical tourist hassle. It is a relaxing place to wander around, marveling at the lake, which increases its size tenfold every wet season and is fringed by forest that is underwater for several months a year. In this bizarre, watery environment, people live and work, their lives adapting to the ebb and flow of the floods.

Used for teaching local children, the Gecko Center also serves to inform tourists and residents. Environmental awareness is critical to the lake because its natural resources are being exhausted. Since the center is trying to educate the next generation of fishermen and farmers, I am happy to support it. For me, it is a reminder of how delicately and ingeniously people and the land can live together. It is also a quiet place to sit down, bobbing with the waves, reasonably priced drink in hand, and reflect on how much the environment has to offer here.

The Gecko Center drifts in floating Chong Kneas village. I can forget that it is on the water when the lake is still. Then suddenly a boat will go past, booming as a fishermen leaves his house and heads out of the channel that leads to the open lake and rich fishing grounds. I have been told that in the flooded season there is a hierarchy to the location of the floating buildings in Chong Kneas channel. The center seems to lead the way, as it is often nearest the main road, apparently a prime location for floating real estate.

If you make it out to the center, ask for Mr. Vuth, a knowledgeable and ever-present member of the staff. He speaks a little English and is able to help explain the displays, such as tanks of fish, eels, and water snakes, examples of species found in the lake that you would not see if you simply hired a boat. While a trip to the Gecko Center will drag you away from the well-known, and well-trodden, world of the ancient Angkor temples, it more than compensates by showing you how the people of the Siem Reap area live today.

Getting to the Gecko Center

A floating and stilted village, Chong Kneas is approximately ten kilometers from Siem Reap town center. In the rainy season, the Gecko Center is in the Chong Kneas channel usually near to the main road. You can walk onto the center via a gangplank. Around late November, the center is towed into the main area of floating houses, where the channel starts to open up. When the center is here, you will need a boat to access it. Information can be found on the center's website. You can also read more about the floating villages of the Tonle Sap Lake by going to page 57.

http://jinja.apsara.org/gecko

About the Gecko Center

The center contains a wide variety of displays. Information includes how to use traditional medicines from the lake and how the local ecosystem functions. The examples and explanations of fishing gear are useful for observing the countless fishermen all over Cambodia, and the section on reptiles and their uses boggles the mind.

Make sure to take a look at the lovely painting of wildlife on the outside of the building. It was done by a revered monk, and although the pictures need restoration, no one wants to touch them because the monk has passed away.

If you'd like a souvenir, there is a small range of cool fish-related T-shirts on sale—yes, it is possible to be cool and fish related. It's also nice to know that the Gecko Centre is blessed with the only compost toilet for miles, so unlike many village excursions, there is no need for the predeparture dehydration.

Dining on the lake

Soft drinks and beer are available in the Gecko Center, but if you are hungry, excellent food, especially fish and shrimp, is served at the row of restaurants you pass just before you get to the village along the main road. The restaurants are on stilts and extend over the water in the wet season.

BOKOR HILL STATION

Debbie Watkins listens to the whispers of Bokor's past

Bump ... bump ... bump. BUMP! My spine felt as if it had developed a life of its own, jiggling frantically around, trying to escape my body. I cursed myself for my naiveté. Why had I assumed the words "bad road" in Cambodia were in any way similar to the same words back home? This was not a bad road to the top of Bokor Hill Station. It was a virtual assault course, and sitting on the back of a 100cc motorcycle was not the best way to tackle it. My driver, however, seemed totally unfazed. Or maybe the permanent grin was a grimace? But hell, I'd gotten this far. I wasn't going to back down now.

Suddenly, with a turn in the road, everything changed. What had been lush greenery and wild banana trees became scrubby gorse. This was starting to get interesting. Up and up and up we went, and with every twist, turn, and, yes, bump, things were looking less and less like Cambodia and more and more like ... well, Wales!

The road leveled. I heaved a huge sigh of relief. I looked around. All semblance of tropical climes had disappeared once and for all, to be replaced by what could only be described as rolling moors. The air was cool—not just a welcoming breeze in the heat, but genuinely chilly air. I breathed deeply. Over to the left something that looked suspiciously like mist was rolling toward us—not one thick blanket as you'd expect, but waves of it, big clumps that totally obscured the view one moment and left the terrain back in glorious sunshine the next.

"Wow, this is all a bit *Wuthering Heights*," I said to my driver, who looked at me blankly.

"Cold," he said.

Cold it was. The fog was accompanied by a stiff breeze, and I even began to shiver.

Then the fog lifted. I gasped. On my left stood the ruin of what had clearly been a hotel, and to the right of it, what was once, unmistakably, a Catholic church. "What is this place?" I asked.

"Casino, old casino. Rich people come here, before Khmer Rouge, the king too. You want to see?"

Indeed, I did. We bounced through the gorse up to the hulking ruin. As we got close, it took on a surreal, almost spooky feel. The remains were visible of what had been, a sweeping entranceway and intricate patterns on the floor tiles. Shutting out visions of *The Shining*, I tentatively went in.

The formerly sumptuous guest rooms now played host to a thousand shades of mildew. Empty window panes framed the rolling hills. The former banquet hall at the back looked directly over the cliff to the sea in the distance. "This must've really been something," I murmured. Echoes of the past were all around. I closed my eyes, and I could see it, luxurious furnishings, black-suited waiters bearing cocktails, and roulette tables swirling in the mists.

Bokor Hill Station

Bokor Hill Station, a former French colonial retreat, is set in the Bokor National Park forty kilometers from Kampot, along Cambodia's southern coastline. A local company is currently re-

developing Bokor and intends to build a large hotel and golf complex on the plateau at the top. At the time of writing, access to the top has been partially restricted, so visits to the former Bokor Palace Hotel, the old Catholic church, and other bombed-out, desolate buildings—as well as Popokvil waterfall—require a bit of ingenuity. But Cambodia is a country in constant flux, and a place where adventurous types can get great satisfaction from their efforts. It can't hurt to try visiting for a glimpse of the past before it completely disappears.

REAM NATIONAL PARK

*Adam Bray
meditates on a national
park outside Sihanoukville*

I left my beachside room in Sihanoukville early in the morning on a rented motorbike, picking up a rain poncho at a gas station and then a bag of lychees and a baguette sandwich at the local market. I was on my way to explore the lush ecosystem of Ream National Park. Riding first through the hills and past an estuary, I arrived at the ranger's station with its dioramas of local flora, fauna, and cultural relics found in the area.

I learned that Ream encompasses 210 square kilometers of coastal land, including isolated beaches, mangrove forests, the Prek Tuk Sap estuary, two islands, and offshore coral reefs. It is a wildlife enthusiast's dream, since macaques, sun bears, pangolin (spiny anteaters), muntjac (mouse deer), dugongs, freshwater dolphins, and over 155 species of birds can be found there. Although I hadn't come at dawn or dusk—the best time for viewing most of the park's terrestrial mammals—I was still hoping for some sightings as I climbed into a jeep with a ranger and headed for Meditation Mountain.

As we walked up the mountain trail, we passed through pristine tropical forest. Droplets of rain fell from the vines above, pattering on the broad-leafed vegetation below. The ranger pointed out blue-winged leafbirds, iora, and white-rumped shama flittering in the branches. The playful call of the hill mynah (the same birds that are popular as pets) could be heard all around.

Local villagers are said to collect more than two hundred species of medicinal plants in the park, and Meditation Mountain, which they call Phnom Samathik, is the preferred area to gather them. They believe the plants on the mountain are endowed with extraordinary potency by genies that dwell among the boulders. The atmosphere surrounding the trail was eerie as I walked past sticks of incense burning from the rock clefts, left to honor the spirits.

We reached the top of Meditation Mountain with its broad view of the park and surrounding coastline. Cut by a small waterfall, bizarre limestone formations decorated the cliffside. Orchids and delicate pink flowers dotted the edges of the clearing. Standing in that remote landscape, I understood why locals would be drawn there for contemplation. It was one of the most peaceful places I have visited in Cambodia.

Getting to Ream National Park

Officially named Preah Sihanouk National Park, the park is popularly known by the commune where it's located. From Sihanoukville travel eighteen kilometers north on Route 4, then take a right on Airport Road near the *naga* statue. The park office is located five hundred meters farther, opposite the entrance to the airport. The office is open daily from 7:00 a.m. to 5:00 p.m.

Exploring the park

A guide (park ranger) is required for all tours of the park. The Meditation Mountain Walk takes two to three hours, and the O Toul Creek walk three to four hours. Both cost a few dollars per person per hour. Boat trips on the Prek Tuk River take about six hours, and trips to Koh Thmei and Koh Ses can last all day. Boats for one to four persons can cost up to $50. Stops might include beaches, fishing villages, wildlife viewing, and snorkeling (bring your own equipment).

(012) 875-096 (park office)

Supporting the park

Ream National Park is only one of four staffed national parks in the country, and although it is the most established, it officially receives no international support, and development is still in the early stages. Ream is underfunded and the staff paid very little—barely enough to live on, yet they face illegal loggers and poachers with automatic weapons because they believe what they do is important and will lead to a sustainable future for themselves and their families. As Sihanoukville becomes more urban, with all of the problems associated with big cities, the park is even more of a sanctuary for animals and humans. It needs tourist dollars in order to ensure it has any future at all.

CARDAMOM MOUNTAINS

Gordon Sharpless accesses the remote Cardamom Mountains

As tourism reaches most every corner of Cambodia, one area that boasts enormous ecotourism potential still remains largely off-limits—the Cardamom Mountains in the southwest region of the country. Rich in biodiversity, the Cardamoms are accessible only to experienced (and the occasional semiexperienced) motorbike riders and the odd environmental organization given permission to launch a research expedition.

Named after the spice we assume must grow in there somewhere, the Cardamoms top out at 1,771 meters, the tallest in Cambodia. Covering the provinces of Koh Kong, Pursat, Kompong Speu, and a little bit of Battambang, the region comprises the Phnom Samkos Wildlife Sanctuary, the Phnom Aural Wildlife Sanctuary, and a big chunk in between simply known as the Central Cardamoms.

To get an idea of what inhabits the Cardamoms, consider that in early 2000, UK-based Fauna & Flora International conducted an extensive biological survey in partnership with the Cambodian Ministry of Environment and Wildlife Protection Office, identifying at least 30 species of large mammals, over 450 birds, 64 reptiles, 30 amphibians, 30 small mammal species, and scores of plants and insects. Threatened species include the tiger, Asian elephant, Asiatic wild dog, gaur, pileated gibbon, clouded leopard, and perhaps of greatest importance, the Siamese crocodile, as no significant populations of this species exist outside of the Cardamom range. It's also been suggested that Javan and Sumatran rhinoceros may inhabit this area.

What has helped to allow these wildlife populations to flourish is that for several decades hardly anybody has made it into the Cardamoms. Even during the time of the French protectorate, only a handful of explorers and hunters got in. Through the 1980s and into the '90s nobody was there except the Khmer Rouge, who controlled much of this territory, at times skirmishing with the logging companies that began moving in during the mid-1990s.

The major logging companies left a few years ago (though illegal logging continues), and the only way to traverse the range is over the remnants of an old logging road that presently has ruts so deep you could drop an entire motorbike down one. And that's only if you can get past the rivers. Without bridges.

But if you're willing to do the work, the journey is worth it. To this day one of the most spectacular Cambodia images imbedded in my head, right up there with my first sight of Angkor Wat, is standing upon the peak of a high hill in the Cardamoms and looking behind at the trail I just covered. A brown ribbon meandering down and around the mountain, alternately entering and departing from view, surrounded for miles on end by rolling green hills and mountains. Other than that brown stripe, there was not one single sign of human habitation. Oh, we did stumble upon the occasional loggers or old villager making the long supply run from Koh Kong, but we had, or appeared to have, this mountain range almost entirely to ourselves. So far, this hasn't changed.

Official tours of the Cardamoms

Dancing Roads schedule a couple of Cardamom motorbike trips each year, and this is probably the safest and best option. To read about other possible tours, continue on to the next essay.

www.dancingroads.com

Doing the Cardamoms on your own

The basics

If you choose to do a trip without a tour company, do not do it alone, and do not do it without someone who knows the area. Due to the remoteness and lack of facilities of any kind, a bad fall or breakdown can leave you in serious trouble. Use common sense and go in a group of at least three.

If you are leaving from either Battambang or Pailin, plan on three days and two nights to reach Koh Kong or vice versa, though fast riders might get away with two days and one night. You will want to go in the dry season. Forget about the wet season, as you'll never get through the rivers.

Where to stay

For sleeping, bring a hammock and mosquito net. Both are easily purchased in any town market. About halfway to Koh Kong from Battambang or Pailin, the village of Veal Veng is a good place to break the journey. You will have no problem finding someone who will let you pitch a hammock under their house, if not actually invite you inside.

After staying a night in Veal Veng, if you can't make it all the way to Koh Kong the next day, your only hope is the village of O'Saom, seventy-five long, hard kilometers from Veal Veng. Yes, this could take a full day. If heading north you might find yourself sleeping in the jungle. For food and water, bring plenty of your own. You can get fed in Veal Veng, but then it's a long way to O'Saom.

Road conditions

Going south from Veal Veng there are several rivers followed by some very steep mountain climbs with enormous ruts in the road. Once off the mountain, the ride to Koh Kong is pretty much flat and easy,

although going north from Veal Veng to Battambang or Pailin, one word comes to mind: wretched.

Daniela Papi encourages conservation in the Cardamoms

As you fly into Cambodia, the views from a plane show a flat land, sparsely covered with trees. The flooded reflections of the rainy season give way to rich, red earth in the dry months. Although they are not visible when landing in Phnom Penh airport, there are still some lush jungle areas, but the lumber trade is threatening their existence. Protecting this remaining virgin jungle and its endangered wildlife is the priority of many conservation organizations, which are also trying to find a way to make preservation economically attractive.

Many groups concerned with protecting Cambodia's environment have considered opening the southern Cardamom Mountains to travelers through treks and adventure tours, and as a friend began exploratory hikes, I was fortunate to be invited. Looking to escape Phnom Penh for the annual water festival holiday, which doubles the city's population and its chaos, I eagerly accepted the offer. There was no mention of dehydration, leeches, or harrowing vertical inclines in the invitation, but maybe it was better that way. I might have turned down a truly unique adventure.

The week's outing took us through varied terrain: streams, wide rivers, waist-high grass plains stretching for miles, and lush forests whose high shrubs grabbed at my pack as I pushed through the trails that had not been cleared. The leeches preoccupied me at first, and being cold for the first time in months as I shivered in my hammock, I questioned if I would have been better off battling the water festival crowds of Phnom Penh rather than the wilds of the Cardamoms.

Then, on day three, when I looked up at the massive hornbills flying in pairs over me, I finally appreciated what it meant to leave the cement city and go back to a time when Cambodia had once been covered by jungle and the roar of tigers could still be heard. Another highlight was being able to look into one of the famous burial jars, left by an ancient civilization from which the Cambodian royal family claims to have descended. These jars sit hidden in the jungle, having been protected by the local communities as ancient treasures.

I left the Cardamom Mountains having spent my first week in a jungle hammock, learned to ignore leeches, and gained a new appreciation for the wilds of Cambodia. I also came away with the hope that tourism can bring the incentive to preserve the jungle, so future generations can experience the beauty of Cambodia's past through its wilderness areas.

Cardamom Mountains

If you are interested in hiking and biking in the Cardamom Mountains, check out this recent tourism project based out of the town of Chi Phat.

www.mountainbikingcardamoms.com

KOMPONG SVAY

Nick Ray is haunted by the curse of Preah Khan

Not to be confused with *that* Preah Khan on Angkor's Grand Circuit—lest you want to spend several days lost in the jungle—this is the sleeping giant that is Preah Khan in Kompong Svay. A satellite city during the golden age of Angkor, it quite literally fell off the map in recent decades. It was lost in the impenetrable forests of northern Cambodia, but we were resolved to discover its secrets by following an ancient Angkorian highway.

The paths split and reformed like the mouths of the Mekong. Sometimes the trail ran cold—into a confused farmer and his buffalo surprised to see *barangs* in his rural retreat. But east is east, and the ancient Khmers were like the Romans of Europe, distilling culture throughout mainland Southeast Asia via a network of straight highways. Noble sandstone bridges provided historic waymarkers along the route.

Following the devout and destructive before us, we eventually stumbled upon Spean Ta Ong, a seventy-seven-meter bridge guarded by fearsome *nagas*. Camping out under the stars at Preah Khan, I realized how privileged we were to have chanced upon our very own Angkor without the tourists.

But did we inadvertently offend the gods by sleeping in their sanctuary? They certainly did their damnedest to make a return to this marvelous place all but impossible.

On my next try in 2002, I traveled the old Angkor road, scouting for Jean-Jacques Annaud's film *Two Brothers*, a story of tigers in colonial-era Cambodia. The heavens opened, and the trails turned to streams. Before we knew it, we were knee-deep in mud. Annaud took it in his stride, snapping away on his Leica, as we tried to pull the bikes out of the treaclelike mud. "I need to understand the difficulties involved in the locations I am working with," was JJ's philosophy.

But failure wasn't an option on my part, and a dry November convinced me to try again. The gods deigned otherwise. The heavens opened again, and we were soon sliding around like Ski-Doos.

Unrepentant and still oblivious to the curse, I ventured forth once more to conduct a community tourism assessment. This time it was going swimmingly up until the point my colleague, John, took this literally and went up to his neck in a river. I pushed ahead for help.

As dusk was closing in, I came upon a second river, wide and dry. Squirming through the sand, I reached a narrow channel of water. The bank was steep and sandy; the wheels of my bike just churned and spun. Pushing, pulling, raging, cursing, I tried everything, but I couldn't get the bike to budge. I abandoned it and stumbled on to Ta Seng to raise the rescue committee. We found John dazed and delirious on the outskirts of town, carrying a dirty bowl he'd been using to drink from puddles.

The next morning we set off with ox carts in search of our steeds. As we came upon the first river, it had swollen overnight and was now a raging torrent. All I could see was a handlebar sticking sorrowfully out of the water. Stripping off, we hauled my bike out. John swam the river and trekked in search of his bike. Remarkably, it started, and he came roaring out the forest. Mine, on the other hand, was paraded around Ta Seng in search of a mechanic or magician. After taking it apart with the precision of a surgeon, the local mechanic reassembled it and beeped the horn triumphantly. It wouldn't start, but face was saved.

We eventually made it out on a combination of ox carts and motorbikes. It was time to return to civilization. Third time unlucky, and I realized the curse of Preah Khan was upon me.

PREAH VIHEAR PROVINCE

Getting to Preah Khan

There is no public transport to Preah Khan itself, but there are very infrequent trucks to the nearby village Ta Seng. Realistically most visitors are going to get to the temple under their own steam, either by moto, rented motorbike, or chartered 4WD. Getting to Preah Khan is quickest by motorbike from Kompong Thom. Follow National Highway 64 north toward Tbeng Meanchey. After about 80 kilometers, a small track leads west from the village of Phnom Dek through the forest to Ta Seng and Preah Khan. The total distance is about 120 kilometers from Kompong Thom, and it takes about five hours in the dry season.

Coming from Siem Reap, it's multiple choice. By 4WD, take National Highway 6 to Stoeng, before heading north on a long, long dirt road to Ta Seng and Preah Khan. By motorbike there are two options. Easiest is to follow National Highway 6 southeast to Kompong Kdei before heading north on a good dirt road to the village of Khvau. From Khvau, it is forty kilometers east to Preah Khan on a miserable ox-cart track. Or get your kicks on Route 66 …

More adventurous and romantic is to follow the old Angkor road from Beng Mealea east to Preah Khan, which includes about ten Angkorian bridges dating from the twelfth century. Forget about trying this in the wet season, unless you can handle an ox cart. The best time to visit is from January to April, as the trails are reasonably dry.

Where to stay

There is no guesthouse in Preah Khan or the nearby village of Ta Seng, but with a hammock and mosquito net, it is possible to sleep within the walls of the temple or in a private house in the village. While sleeping at the temple sounds romantic, the kamikaze mosquitoes always seem to find a way through the net. If staying in the village, expect to pay villagers a few dollars for the privilege of sleeping on their floor. Basic meals and drinks are available in Ta Seng.

A rose by any other name

There is some confusion over the name of this temple. Most locals refer to it as Prasat Bakan. Scholars officially refer to is as Bakan Svay Rolay, combining the local name for the temple and the district name. Khmers in Siem Reap often refer to it as Preah Khan, Kompong Svay.

On the safe side

Locals say there are no land mines in the vicinity of Preah Khan, but stick to marked paths just in case. Also, isolated incidents of banditry have been known on the remote roads in this area, although so far it only seems to affect locals and not foreign visitors.

TMATBOEY

XXXXXXXXXXXXXXXXXXXXXXXXXXXXXXX
ooooooooooooooooooooooooooooooooo

*Howie Nielsen
watches rare birds in
Tmatboey*

My first real taste of the Cambodian bush was Tmatboey. Just getting there is an adventure that will have you spinning through sand traps in the dry season and slipping and sliding through mud puddles in the wet season. The village and its guesthouse are situated on the country's vast northern plains, with grasslands supporting a beautiful, deciduous forest, and open canopy with little undergrowth, similar in structure to the savannah forests in Africa.

I've had the pleasure of visiting during the different seasons, and it varies from a lush, green, high-grassed forest to a place yellowed and opened up by the dry weather. It's always easy to walk around, following the ox-cart tracks, occasionally encountering families riding along en route to their rice paddy. The slow, methodical strides of the oxen pulling their load and the soft, rhythmical clang of their bells give insight to the pace of life here—one that can hardly be imagined in more-developed parts of the world.

The day's activities start well before dawn as the kitchen crew at the guesthouse prepares packed lunches for its guests, primarily bird-watchers who are interested in getting into the forest by first light. Village cockerels soon join the owls calling in the early dawn. This is the time when bugling giant ibis are heard. Under the house, ducks, pigs, and dogs begin their daily foraging. The shouts and cries of children announce Tmatboey is awake.

The dawn forest is alive with birdlife. The squawks and cries of parakeets, the clear ringing chimes of orioles and mynahs, the mechanical racket of Chinese francolins, and a variety of hooting chants of banded bay and Indian cuckoos and greater coucals fill the air. Spotting and following birds is straightforward with the open nature of this habitat.

I love this area for its ease of birding, just as I love returning to the village, simple and traditional, with more people using ox-carts than motorcycles. Wood is cut by hand, water is hauled to homes, and people live with the animals they will consume. This is about as organic a relationship to nature as I have seen. With a simple "hello" I elicit warm smiles, unless it is a small child, who just as likely will flee in panic at the encounter.

Village life takes place out of doors, and as a tourist I watch the daily rituals of communal bathing at the pump, naked kids wrestling in the dirt, and the local card shark trying to fleece boys of their earnings.

With a bit of trepidation I sample the local cane juice topped off with a little sweetened milk and fruit bits. It is so refreshing I have another and am happy to suffer no ill effects.

Meals are spartan Khmer fare, with rice or noodles, fish or meat, and fresh produce. The green mango salad is a welcome treat, and the fish *larb* we have for dinner one evening is the best I've had in Cambodia. Like everything else about Tmatboey, its meals have me slowing right down, appreciating—and yet not missing—the privileges of my modern world.

Birding in Cambodia

Wildlife Conservation Society (WCS), an international environmental NGO, has a number of sites it is developing with support of the Cambodian government, which are being designed for the protection of several highly endangered bird species and their habitats. WCS is encouraging controlled tourist access to some of these sites as a way of bringing an alternative revenue stream into the poor villages in these areas. The hope is that by creating value, the local people will protect these special creatures.

21, Street 21
Phnom Penh
(023) 217-205

www.wcs.org

About Tmatboey

A village of about 150 families, Tmatboey is located in Preah Vihear Province in northern Cambodia. This area used to support a complex guild of grazing mammals that tragically is close to being wiped out due to thirty years of armed conflict. WCS is trying to create an opportunity for these herds of wild oxen, buffalo, and deer to rebuild. This area is also the home to two of the rarest birds in Asia: giant and white-shouldered ibis.

A visit to Tmatboey takes four hours from Siem Reap and is best done during the dry season. Accommodation is a basic wooden house. It is rustic, with dormitory-style sleeping, bucket shower, and squat toilet. A cook team wakes early to prepare hot packed lunches of fresh, hygienic Khmer food. The women's group even sets up an outdoor lounge serving cold beer, soda, and no doubt a provincial first, gin and tonics.

All visitors to Tmatboey are required to make a donation of $30 to a development fund that is controlled by an elected committee of villagers that decide its use. The project is designed to have the village profit from foreign visitors, in the hope that as more birders and nature lovers come to see the ibis, the ecotourism enterprise will become sustainable.

Arranging your trip

WCS has partnered with Sam Veasna Center for Wildlife Conservation (SVC), a small Cambodian NGO, to manage access to their sites, and requires all visitors to be accompanied by an SVC bird guide. To arrange a village stay, contact SVC via its website or visit the center in Siem Reap, which is located one hundred meters past Angkor Village Hotel.

#0552, Group 12, Wat Bo
Siem Reap
(063) 761-597

www.samveasna.org

Birds of Tmatboey

To read more about the birds living in the Tmatboey preserve, continue on to the next essay.

Side trips

Attractions on the way to Tmatboey from Siem Reap include a remote Angkorian temple (Koh Ker) and other birding rarities (Bengal Florican, Manchurian Reed Warbler). Beyond Tmatboey, a visit to the vulture restaurant in Chhep entails another two days, and the tour price includes the purchase of a cow. SVC will arrange stops at these locations as add-ons to the usual four-day trip to see the ibis.

Karen Coates conserves energy for the birds of Tmatboey

At noonday, I sway in a hammock, sighing and sweating in the languid air. Cambodia serenades me—cicadas and chickens, rambunctious kids and a neighbor banging on an ox-cart. Across the way, a woman bathes at a well, hair coiled atop her head, her body swaddled in a sopping orange sarong. I want to join her, but that would require movement. At dawn, I hiked a few miles, tracing the edges of ancient watering holes. Come two o'clock, I will walk again through forests and paddies looking for birds. But for now, I rest.

The birds are why I'm here. The birds are why, every day or two or three, an air-conditioned vehicle plies the pitted roads and sand paths through Cambodia's northern plains to unload a few visitors on the isolated village of Tmatboey, a farming community of eighteen hundred or so inhabitants within the Kulen-Promtep Wildlife Sanctuary. Here, two of the world's rarest birds, the giant ibis and the white-shouldered ibis, make their home.

Both of these long-legged water birds nest and forage in the deciduous forest, grasslands, and seasonal wetlands surrounding Tmatboey. At the height of the dry season, the birds congregate at man-made ponds

PREAH VIHEAR PROVINCE

called *trapeangs* that date to Angkorean times. For centuries, *trapeangs* have provided water for people, livestock, and wildlife. They nourished the inhabitants of what science has recently revealed to be the world's largest known preindustrial complex: the Angkor empire.

Giant and white-shouldered ibis were once widespread throughout Southeast Asia, but hunting and habitat loss have taken their toll. Perhaps as few as 250 of each species remain. Tmatboey is the only protected nesting site in mainland Asia for the white-shouldered ibis. It is also one of the few places in the world to spot its cousin, the giant ibis, Cambodia's national bird.

For these reasons, the ibis are an economic boon, with avid birders from all over the world descending upon the Northern Plains. In addition to the ibis, there are sarus cranes, various storks, adjutants and eagles, falcons and weavers, Alexandrine parakeets, rufous-winged bush larks, sixteen types of woodpeckers, and many other species. In 2005, the Wildlife Conservation Society (WCS) established the Tmatboey ibis ecotourism project, with hopes of simultaneously saving the birds *and* helping the villagers.

Since the project began, the villagers have enforced a code of conduct prohibiting the hunting of these birds and protecting their feeding and nesting areas. They take pride in the wildlife they are helping to flourish and the tourists who visit their village. And it's working-birds are soaring, and so are the villagers' incomes.

"Before this conservation program, the people didn't know about the birds," fifty-year-old Toem Rung, a member of the cook team, tells me. She and others were hired to prepare meals for the tourists. Rung has not seen an ibis. "I never go for a walk in the forest," she says. But she thanks the birds for her job. "I can make money from the tourists"—up to 6,000 riel ($1.50) per visitor each day. She doesn't even mind rising at two in the morning. "It's normal," she assures me. The wee hours are shared alike by Cambodian farmers and birders.

This morning, I marveled at the sight of a giant ibis in the treetops, peering over a field of hopping frogs as the red sun rose in the distance. A veritable feast for an ibis. This afternoon, I follow the heels of my guide, Dep Kimourn, as we plod in the hot sunlight across the parched, russet earth. It's quiet, but there are birds zipping about—hoopoes and parakeets, drongos and bee-eaters.

I would never be able to find the ibis on my own. "We local guides know the forest and the *trapeangs*," Kimourn tells me proudly. In turn, Kimourn is getting an education on the job. "I want to know about a lot of bird species," he says, "and I enjoy taking knowledge from tourists." Kimourn prefers being a guide to his previous post as a soldier, fighting the Khmer Rouge during Cambodia's civil war. "I faced danger every day as a soldier. As a guide, I learn every day and make money." He also is witnessing the resurgence of his country's national icon.

When we reach the *trapeang*, Kimourn crouches cautiously. A cow grazes at the pond's edge. Perched in a tree beyond is a white-shouldered ibis, its plumage catching the sunlight. It leisurely preens the feathers beneath its wings as we sit like stones for ten minutes, admiring its beauty. Then the ibis flaps away into the distant forest.

A few hundred yards farther on is another *trapeang*. As dusk approaches, we watch dozens of little birds swoop down to the mucky ground to glean insects from this perennial water source. High in the trees behind us, three white-shouldered ibis shatter the air with their startling calls, like the *Jurassic Park* raptors of the big screen.

The venerable sound befits this ancient forest with its age-old *trapeangs*, which nourish not only birds—but descendants of an empire that changed Asian history.

Getting to Tmatboey

Information about conservation projects and arranging your trip can be found in the fact file of the previous essay.

VIRACHEY NATIONAL PARK

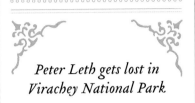

Peter Leth gets lost in Virachey National Park

One day in late 2004, I picked up a copy of *The Cambodia Daily* and read a truly astonishing story. A group of thirty-five Cambodians had been detained by the authorities in the jungles of the southern Lao province of Attapu, ostensibly for "illegal entry" into that country. The governor of Attapu called the governor of Ratanakiri Province, in the most northeastern corner of Cambodia, and transport arrangements were made for their speedy return, after it was determined that the group had innocently stumbled across the border.

What made this story amazing, however, was the fact that the Cambodians claimed to be running from occupying Vietnamese forces in Cambodia. Knowing that the Vietnamese had left Cambodia in the late 1980s, I read on with curiosity. The thirty-five, it turned out, had originated as a group of eight former Khmer Rouge sympathizers (four men and four women) who fled to the mountains along the Lao border in late 1978, as Vietnamese troops were overrunning the country and driving the Khmer Rouge from power. These people naturally feared for their lives. Days turned to months, which turned to years, which then turned to decades, and it wasn't until this moment nearly twenty-six years later that the eight emerged as an extended family of thirty-five.

With no knowledge of the outside world, and fearing that the Vietnamese were always on their trail, this group had stuck to the thickest and most remote parts of the jungle, always one step ahead of the invisible "enemy." They lived a truly primitive and nomadic lifestyle, hunting and gathering from the forest, shifting camp now and then to ensure that they couldn't be tracked. When picked up by the Lao authorities, they were wearing clothing that had been fashioned from leaves and tree bark.

Taking this all in, I realized that the area these people had been in, which today is known as Virachey National Park, must surely be one of the most remote places on the planet. Where else can you go these days to "get lost" for more than two decades? I had to check it out, so a buddy and I took an eight-day trek up some remote canyons in Virachey. It was easy to see how the Cambodian group had remained isolated. Aside from a village or two on the first day, there was no sign of civilization for an entire week.

At night, our guide, who was from one of the local minority highland ethnic groups, set up our camp by hacking some sturdy bamboo shafts from the jungle with a machete and fastening them together with vine string in order to create a boxlike structure around a central campfire where we could attach our hammocks in order to keep off the bug-ridden forest floor. Then he stripped to his underwear, jumped in the stream with a fishing net, and came back five minutes later with dinner in hand! While the untouched jungle landscape continually amazed me, this is my favorite memory of the true remoteness that much of the Cambodian backcountry still has to offer to the intrepid and adventurous traveler.

Virachey National Park

The park headquarters are located in Ban Lung (for directions, go to page 128), the capital of Ratanakiri Province, in the northeast corner of Cambodia known as the "Dragon's Tail." You can book tours of the park here, as all visitors require an entry permit and must be accompanied by a guide. Park headquarters: (075) 974-176.

The two most common access points into the park are the villages of Voen Sai and Ta Veng, both on the Sesan River, roughly two hours by car or motorbike taxi from Ban Lung. Each of these small hamlets has a ranger station at which it is also possible to find out about places of interest, map your approach routes, and negotiate the services of a guide.

Guides are officially park rangers and are generally happy to take you out on one of their patrols in exchange for a modest fee. These men are knowledgeable about life in the jungle, and they will arrange transport, lead you through the network of unmarked footpaths, help set up camp and prepare meals, and even educate you on the flora, fauna, and history of the region, depending on their English or your Khmer language skills.

Be advised that hiking in Virachey is no "walk in the park." No matter how many hours or days you wish to spend out, you are advised to treat all water, take all necessary precautions against mosquitoes (this is real malaria country, a fact to which Peter can personally attest), and prepare to rough it, in every sense of the word. You will need to carry all supplies on your back. Given the heat and uneven terrain, it is easiest to follow the dietary practices of your guides—boil all water, and carry your own rice, noodles, sardines, cooking oil, salt, pepper, and garlic. The guides will supplement with fish and vegetables from the jungle whenever they can be found.

Juanita Accardo is lured into Virachey National Park

Until I visited the Virachey National Park headquarters, my trip to Ratanakiri Province was to involve nothing more than lazy swimming in Yeak Laom Lake near Ban Lung town. But lured by visions of tigers behind every tree, I signed up for a trek into the remote northeast section of Cambodia near the Laos-Vietnam border.

Early in the morning our small party left by motorbike for the Sesan River, armed with mosquito repellent, sunblock, water purification gear, a change of clothing, and some basic food supplies. A wooden longboat with a small outboard engine bore us upriver to Yorn, a Brau tribal village where I spent the first of several uncomfortable nights getting used to sleeping in my hammock.

By the light of the dying fire on one particularly memorable evening, the last thing I saw was a huge spider scuttling into the hollow bamboo pole above my bed. I zipped my mosquito netting closed and stayed put until dawn, despite urgent whisperings and the hasty lighting of a fire during the night. Since I wasn't about to get out of my hammock and investigate, the nonchalant reply to my inquiry—"Don't worry, go back to sleep"—

RATANAKIRI PROVINCE

meant I did just that. During breakfast the next morning, the tale of the "big cat" that had entered our camp was told, and although I'd like to believe it was a tiger, such a creature hasn't been seen in a long while, despite the photo of the last sighting that adorns every trekking poster in the region.

My days were spent wading streams, removing leeches, listening for the calls from invisible wildlife, and hacking through paths of dense bamboo, tenacious rattan vines, and tall trees strung with amazing arachnids. At one point we followed a five-kilometer section of the Ho Chi Minh Trail as it moved southerly, back toward Vietnam after a detour through Laos and Cambodia.

Used for the covert transport of equipment, troops, and civilians during the Vietnam War, the trail was strewn with rusting remnants of vehicles, bicycles, and airplanes. Handguns, mounted machine guns, and small stacks of M16 rifles nestled amongst foliage once destroyed by lethal pesticide. The occasional Viet Cong bunkers could be seen from the trail. Bomb craters littered with shell casings and mines, which may still have been live, transformed the trail into a dangerous shrine to the many who passed through or died during the fighting. Time stood still, and the sounds of muffled shouts, gunshots, and explosions haunted my imagination.

Captured by the past, I traveled back downstream to Ban Lung, a quiet town that now seemed hectic after the peace of the forest. But there would be plenty of time for reflection during the motorbike journey to Sen Monorom in two days' time. Meanwhile, I was ready to enjoy a comfortable bed, several cold beers, and a wash in hot water before taking back off into the unknown.

Virachey National Park

For information on the park, go to the fact file in the previous essay.

RATANAKIRI PROVINCE

Peter Walter gets a lift in Ratanakiri Province

It was my first chance to explore the more remote parts of Cambodia—far from the busy tourist stops of Siem Reap and Phnom Penh. I was headed to Ratanakiri, tucked away in the northeastern corner of the country between Laos and Vietnam. Ratanakiri is one of the least visited and wildest provinces in the country, with abundant mountains, forests, and waterfalls. I couldn't wait to get there to see it for myself.

A day after my arrival into Phnom Penh, I was on my way up-country in a "share taxi," which in Cambodia means an old Toyota Camry stuffed with a driver and six other passengers. I had managed to secure a window seat in the back, but with my six-foot, four-inch frame squeezed in with three other people, there was not much unused space. I felt sorry for the smaller passengers next to me, who had to deal with my shoulders pressing into their ears.

Fortunately, the kilometers passed quickly as we sped through the changing landscapes of the open countryside. While car traffic was sparse, people, animals, and bicycles/motorbikes entered the road constantly, causing the driver to sound the horn in warning. At each stop, I pried myself out of the backseat and walked around to re-start the circulation in my legs. Eight hours later, we had reached Kratie, nestled along the eastern banks of the Mekong River.

The next morning, my share taxi crew and I set out early for Ban Lung, the provincial capital of Ratanakiri. By late afternoon we had arrived, and I settled on the small, pleasant Lodge des Terres Rouges on the outskirts of town, away from the noise and traffic. Over each of the next four days, I headed in different directions from Ban Lung on my rented Chinese motorbike, following the dusty main roads at first, and then branching off down smaller dirt paths and trails, past villages, through forests, and across small streams.

Riding through the cool mountain air was exhilarating, and with each twist and turn of the trail, I was propelled onward by my curiosity to see what lay around the next turn. Fortunately this was the dry season, as the tracks would have been impassable were they wet and muddy. Even now the narrow dirt trails bore the uneven scars of erosion suffered during the previous rainy season, leaving me to contend with deep trenches, highly uneven surfaces, and no shortage of holes, roots, and other obstacles.

While Ban Lung town was already developing rapidly for its small size, with many new shop houses dotting the main roads, the small villages outside of town quickly became more traditional, without much in the way of infrastructure or commerce. Many were largely agricultural and had only basic schools for the village children whose parents could afford to pay for the required supplies. I had brought along quite a few pens and pencils to hand out to local children and soon found these to be so popular that I was in danger of running out too quickly.

Stopping frequently at villages and roadside snack stalls provided a great way to interact with the locals. While my Thai language skills didn't help much here, I was able to get on with some basic Khmer I had learned, along with large doses of sign language and smiles. The people were extremely warm and appeared both amused and confused by my presence, and it was pretty clear that they didn't see too many foreigners. Children called out from their huts as I passed, perhaps hoping that I had bonbons to share.

One afternoon I rode through a large rubber tree plantation whose

RATANAKIRI PROVINCE

RATANAKIRI PROVINCE

canopy of gracefully swaying trees created a surreal atmosphere of premature dusk. The trees showed the exposed, winding cuts in their bark that channel the raw rubber "milk" into the collecting strings and buckets below. I hadn't passed another human being in nearly an hour and was relishing the remoteness of the place. Suddenly my motorbike sputtered and stalled, refusing to respond to my attempts to restart it. I had no choice but to press on, pushing my bike and hoping to find someone who knew more about repairs than I did.

After walking more than a kilometer, I was heartened by the sight of two young men approaching in the distance on a motorbike. They stopped and took a look, quickly identifying the culprit—a worn-out spark plug. Without my needing to ask for help, they devised a rescue plan. Tying my limp bike to theirs with a rope, they signaled for me to ride on the back of their bike, while one of them would steer my bike as it was towed behind.

Given the treacherous conditions of the dirt trails we traversed, it was an incredible feat of control and balance for both of them while I just held on for the ride. We finally reached a small repair shack, and within minutes, my bike was purring again with a brand-new spark plug inside. I asked for the bill and almost fell over upon hearing that the total charge for the tow and repair was a mere 19,000 riel—not even $5.

Before getting back on the road, I thanked my rescuers profusely and reflected on my good fortune. However, as I continued riding, it struck me that I hadn't actually been lucky at all, for it was typical—this Cambodian spirit of hospitality—in this remote and fascinating corner of the world.

Getting to Ratanakiri

The only way to get to the Ratanakiri Province capital of Ban Lung is by road, as all flights to the province were stopped a couple of years ago. It is not possible to cross into Ratanakiri from Vietnam or Laos, although there are rumors of a future Vietnam border crossing. Most likely you will travel there from Phnom Penh or towns along the way. The main highway, National Highway 7, is in good condition these days all the way from Kompong Cham to the northernmost city of Stung Treng. Highway 19, which links Stung Treng to Ban Lung, is also in good shape and should be paved sometime soon. Buses and private minibuses now ply the route all the way from Phnom Penh's Central Market (typically leaving early, around 7:00 a.m.) to Cambodia's most northerly province, though travel times can be as much as eight to nine hours in the dry season. Add a couple more hours when it rains.

In and around Ratanakiri

For information on renting motorbikes and lodging, go to the fact file in the next essay.

Background reading

Peter first became interested in this part of the country after reading about it in the *Ultimate Cambodia Travel Guide*, by Matt Jacobson. This book provided inspiration, as well as many of the practical tips needed to help navigate the way. He strongly recommends it for anyone interested in travel to the more remote parts of the country, and as an excellent source of information on interesting attractions in Ratanakiri Province and throughout the country.

www.ultimatecambodia.com

BAN LUNG TO SEN MONOROM

Juanita Accardo roughs it from Ban Lung to Sen Monoram

I'm never more comfortable than when I'm exploring Cambodia on the back of a motorbike. The event that gave rise to this addiction—followed by the purchase of a secondhand dirt bike—was my recent survival of the infamous back road journey from Ratanakiri Province into Mondulkiri Province via Koh Nhek.

Leaving Ban Lung's incomparable Lodge des Terres Rouges by the rough road west toward Stung Treng, my driver Sophat and I took a southern fork to Ratanakiri Province's former principal town of Lumphat. An hour later, we rolled the bike down a steep bank onto a platform fixed to wooden canoes for the brief ferry crossing on the Srepok River. On the other side, Cambodia's atrocious roads deteriorated further. At times no more than a light footpath could be discerned.

Slash-and-burn agriculture predominates amongst the Phnong people living in this area, so that forest gives way to grassland, groves of bamboo, and poorly defined, exposed agricultural plots of land. It's hot, flat, sandy, deeply rutted, and dusty, but it gave me a pioneering spirit of adventure to pass through such a little-disturbed part of this country, knowing that inevitable change will come with the advent of the "new road" that is in the works.

Various ethnic peoples reside in these eastern provinces, including Kreung, Tampuong, Jerai, and Brau, as well as Phnong, Lao, and Khmer, but this route passes by few settlements, and it's rare to meet more than an occasional pedestrian or ox-pulled cart. We passed a group of around 150 Phnong villagers gathered in the forest to perform a sacrificial funeral ritual to appease spirits, with the blood and organs of various animals arranged around a prepared bower. Invited to share rice wine from large ceramic jars, we made a donation to the celebration, thanked them for their hospitality, and moved on.

Traveling this route requires a lot from the driver—a good sense of direction (Sophat's command of local languages helped clarify obscured trails), accomplished off-road bike skills, and the ability to make repairs en route. As the passenger, my task was to attend to the way ahead, anticipate jolts, hang on to the driver tightly, and shut up. Being agile enough to jump off a sliding bike and walk through sand was useful, too, enabling Sophat to move forward, find a spot in the shade, and lounge with a smug smile on his face, waiting for his sweaty client to finally catch up.

It takes about six hours to reach Koh Nhek village, situated in Mondulkiri Province, then three hours more to Sen Monorom along a wide, prepared-and-pressed red dirt road. Entering this chilly, peaceful town as the sun set, we belatedly bought secondhand jackets, ate ravenously, and fell asleep early.

I was hooked. No more bus tickets for me. Instead of the expected exhaustion, I felt exhilarated, and I soon left for Phnom Penh to shop for a proper motorbike before heading out to explore the rough roads of Cambodia again.

Getting to Ban Lung
Go to the fact file in the previous essay.

In and around Ratanakiri
Motorbikes with drivers and/ or guides can be arranged through a variety of hotels and guesthouses in Ban Lung, including the Lodge des Terres Rouges. Typically both dirt bikes and old scooters are available, and a passport or credit card is required for deposit. You can also contact Juanita's driver/ guide, Thak Sophat. Sophat has ten years' experience as a ranger in Virachey National Park and speaks English, several tribal languages, Lao, and some Vietnamese. His vehicle is a Suzuki 250 dirt bike.

www.ratanakiri-lodge.com

sophat06@hotmail.com
(Thak Sophat)

(092) 61-92-86, (011) 62-38-63
(Thak Sophat)

Ban Lung to Sen Monoram
If you plan to make this ride, note that the turnoff for Lumphat (about twenty-two kilometers from Ban Lung) is poorly signed, and the road is in fair condition. It takes about forty minutes to reach the town from there. The two Phnong villages Juanita passed through on the way to Koh Nhek were Sray Chrey and

Sray Vong (phonetic spellings). Sen Monorom is a worthy destination in itself, with unspoilt tribal villages such as Phulung, many elephants belonging to the Putang villagers, and a beautiful waterfall thirty-five kilometers along the road to Bou Sraa. This is an open, windy area of gentle hills and lovely vistas. Make sure to take lots of water and basic spare bike parts.

SEN MONOROM

Ray Waddington seeks the Mnong of Mondulkiri Province

I wanted to fly from Phnom Penh to Sen Monorom, the capital of Mondulkiri Province, to visit Mnong tribal villages. But no travel agent in Phnom Penh had even heard of the place. Once I pointed to the province on the map, they only acknowledged the existence of Mondulkiri, as if it and Sen Monorom were one and the same. Then they told me it wasn't possible to fly there. So, at seven the next morning, I got on a boat to begin the four-hundred-kilometer river and overland journey.

The boat was so small that I doubted I'd ever reach my destination since we'd be sailing north—against the current of the mighty Mekong River. The only comfortable "seat" was atop the enclosed engine deck. At least it was a warm, dry November day. The Mekong was alive with activity, and time was unimportant as we cruised by village after village. Six hours later we pulled ashore at the small town of Chhlong. My journey was half-complete, and I exchanged river for road.

"Mondulkiri!" I shouted instead of Sen Monorom, remembering my earlier lesson with the travel agents.

The looks I got should have told me what I was letting myself in for. A few men led me to a truck that was departing soon ... for Snuol. At most two hours away, at least it represented progress. Snuol was a different story though. A small pickup truck was waiting to leave for Sen Monorom, but it had only fifteen passengers.

When it was finally packed with about twenty sardines, it set off around five o'clock. From my map I predicted I'd be showering off the dust and sweat by eight. We passed through two tiny villages and ate in one of them. Then as it started to get dark we journeyed on into wilderness. Soon we saw a distant, flashing light ahead of us. As we slowed to a halt, the silhouettes of three men became discernable. Bandits! I thought my life was over. It turned out

MONDULKIRI PROVINCE

their truck had veered off the road and was now four hundred meters down a ravine. That any of them had survived the accident was a miracle.

After somehow finding room for the one man who was injured, we drove even slower than before and got to Sen Monorom hospital about nine thirty. Half an hour later, I was dropped outside a guesthouse. The owner greeted me with a smile and said, "Welcome to Sen Monorom. You're our seventeenth tourist this year. How was your journey?"

While the trip had hardly been rewarding, it prepared me for even-more-challenging travel into surrounding Mnong villages. My experiences in these villages were worth that rough boat-and-truck ride ten times over. I was welcomed everywhere I went and was allowed to spend the night anywhere I asked. I learned about traditional Mnong culture as well as some fascinating, recent Mnong history: the original introduction of literacy (an accidental consequence of the American war in Vietnam and the Khmer Rouge uprising); the current, government-sanctioned development of literacy; and the impact of 9-11. My most enduring memory, though, is of the night I took about forty Mnong village children to "the movies" for a total cost of 2 American dollars!

Getting to Sen Monorom

Sen Monorom is the provincial capital of Mondulkiri Province. It is a very small town set between rolling hills. There is daily bus service from Phnom Penh, but the length of the journey depends on the road conditions, which during the rainy season can be disastrous. It can take up to ten hours even if the conditions are good. At the time of writing, a new road is in the middle of being completed that will reduce travel times considerably.

Cottage on the way to Tonle Sap Lake

WHEN IN ROME

Lessons on living local and making yourself at home

To know a country, a person must live there. Become immersed in the lifestyle. Make friends—the kind of friendships that last a lifetime. But few travelers have that kind of time. So if you're here for only a week or so, what can you do to scratch more than just the surface of Cambodia's character?

I cannot emphasize enough the importance of spending time with local people. As I write this I think about how different my life might have been had I not met Sok Thea. His spirit of adventure and boundless energy to uncover his country's secrets and to promote them to others was a revelation to me. I'd never met anyone like him. Our best bonding session came over a decade ago as we clambered around an overgrown Beng Mealea temple along with five gun-toting soldiers when the area was still heavily mined. Thea died a year later, aged just twenty-nine, and I still miss him. No one has ever understood my love for Cambodia more than he did. His loss was Cambodia's loss. He was the one who prompted me to begin a voyage of discovery that continues to this day.

From the temple keeper of Ta Phrom to an impoverished cyclo driver who shares his life's dreams, Cambodians have touched the hearts of all the writers here. As they describe, opportunities to spend time with such people abound. Cambodia has countless public holidays, festivals that will bring you into contact with Khmer customs and beliefs, as well as the understanding of the importance of family. They are also a rollicking chance to drop your guard, as Debra Groves discovers during the "talcum powder wars" of New Year, and a time to pay your respects, as Anne Best does by honoring the past at the Pchum Ben Festival.

Perhaps the most entertaining way to dip your toe into Cambodian life is to go where the locals go and do what they do: bump and jolt alongside Elizabeth Briel on a train to Battambang, join Mark Hotham in losing a bet to a local at a

Learning traditional dance at Banteay Kdei temple

kickboxing match in Phnom Penh, brave the healing tradition of coining despite Lundi Seng's warnings, or hop a *norry* with Ray Zepp through the countryside.

While every essay in this chapter is valuable, taking you to silk production workshops, traditional dance classes, and karaoke bars, none expresses the spirit of When in Rome like Socheata Poeuv's musings on what it means to be Cambodian. Having left the country at the age of two, she returns as an adult with her parents and brother to visit Angkor Wat. Donning local clothes and speaking the few meager words of Khmer that she knows in order to fit in, she discovers her heritage not in the way she looks or the way she sounds, but in the majesty of the monuments her ancestors created centuries ago.

PHNOM PENH

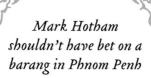

Mark Hotham shouldn't have bet on a barang in Phnom Penh

The toothless old man pressed his palms together, inclined his head, and touched his fingers to his forehead, unable to conceal the grin that was spreading across his face. *"Aw kun charan,"* he said— thank you very much—tucking my money into his shirt pocket. Ten thousand riel. Not so much for me, but for this elderly gentleman, a significant victory.

I had just learnt an important lesson: never bet on the *barang*.

The man and I were sitting high up in the stands on concrete benches in a hot and noisy warehouse-cum-boxing arena, watching an international Khmer kickboxing contest. Hapless *barangs* from Poland, Australia, Russia, England, and France regularly take it in turns here to try their luck against the local champions and inevitably receive a good kicking for their pains. It is always a raucous, entertaining, and—for the Cambodians—proud event.

Contestants climb into the ring amid much fanfare and shouting. Ringside musicians fill the warehouse with what, to the unaccustomed ear, sounds like a kind of discordant snake charmer's tune, accompanied by a rhythmic drum-and-cymbal beat. In time to this beat, the fighters *sompeah* and genuflect to the four cardinal points in an elaborate display of homage to the spirits and the crowd. You can almost hear the cash being slammed down on the concrete benches around the arena.

That night featured a headline fight between the Cambodian heavyweight champion and a young Sudanese contender. It was as they got into the ring, and the contender stood to his full height, that I had been lulled into a false confidence. Well over six and a half feet tall, with legs like flagpoles, he towered over the champion. In a martial art where kicking is everything, how could this guy possibly lose? I slapped down my money.

It was honors for the first few rounds, each fighter gauging his opponent. Then, in round three, the contender unleashed the full length of one of his legs, reaching so high and with such speed that the crowd screamed in delight. Never before had they seen such a fighter, so ridiculously tall, with such dangerous limbs! A worthy man to beat. And that's exactly what happened.

Despite having such weapons in his armory, the contender couldn't break down the defenses of the supremely fit and very stocky champ, who bided his time and administered a few killing combinations. The judges were unanimous, and the crowd went even wilder, as though there was ever any doubt about the outcome. Handshakes and money went round the arena like wildfire, and the toothless old man gave me a knowing wink as he got up to leave, taking my cash with him.

Kickboxing competitions

These kickboxing events are filmed on the weekends at the Channel 5 studios in Phnom Penh, in a large warehouse on the road out to the airport. Any motodop driver will know the way and the time of the next match. Entry is usually a few dollars for *barangs*. Chances are you will be seen on TV, as the matches are broadcast live, most of the male population watches them, and *barangs* in the audience are always picked out for extra coverage. For that reason you may find yourself being ushered to sit at the front near the VIPs, but Mark notes that it is always cooler at the top at the back, which is open to the breeze. Small children ply the bleachers, selling cold drinks, fruit, nuts, etc.

Debra Groves takes a powder in Phnom Penh

Cambodian New Year is a three-day celebration that occurs in the middle of April. It is perhaps the most festive of all the country's holidays. It's a time to start anew, and Cambodians clean out their homes, give each other gifts,

PHNOM PENH PROVINCE

and visit pagodas. It's also a time to pay respect to deceased relatives to keep them happy in the afterlife and ensure good fortune for the coming year. Even the poorest Cambodian families will buy or make New Year decorations and put up shrines and offerings for their ancestors.

There are many traditions associated with the holiday, and the two most obvious ones to foreigners involve water and talcum powder. Traditionally, elders are blessed with a small amount of pure and clean water, and over the years this has evolved into full-scale water fights. The talcum powder is rubbed on faces as a blessing for good luck, and it is with this custom that my story begins.

Having decided to investigate the authentic Cambodian New Year experience, my friends and I prepared ourselves by stocking up on bottles of talcum powder and heading off to Wat Phnom. When we arrived we were amazed to see thousands of people, mostly young Cambodians, getting fully into the festive spirit. Every single person was splashed with talcum powder—some with just a little on their faces, while others were completely covered, brilliantly white from head to toe. Timidly at first, people approached us to dab powder on our cheeks. Soon, though, their gentle approach gave way, when they realized we had come armed not only with talcum powder, but more importantly with a sense of humor.

Before long all four of us were completely covered in powder, and we gave as good as we got.

However, it's important to point out that this New Year ritual is not for the cowardly. At one point, a member of our group found herself in the middle of a full-scale powder pounding, arms and hands coming in all directions to slap fists full of talcum powder onto her face and upper body. This moment had the potential of turning unpleasant, but as mentioned, a sense of humor truly is the most important thing to take with you on a day like this one.

We managed to spend a couple of hours immersed in the crowds, where we wandered and laughed ourselves silly. Finally, we meandered toward home, walking the back streets to a restaurant along the riverside tourist strip. Our walk wasn't without calls from locals wishing us a Happy New Year. With our powdery arms and hands, we waved our well wishes back to them.

Talcum powder tradition

If you want to participate in this New Year custom, be prepared to be engulfed by the swarming crowd and totally covered in powder. Take your camera, mobile phone, etc. at your own risk.

Georgiana Treasure -Evans rides slowly around Phnom Penh

There are times when life in Phnom Penh just gets to be too much. Being six months pregnant in April, preparing dinner in a 40-degree-Celsius kitchen with a toddler tugging at my mosquito-ravaged leg, is one of them. There is only one thing to do. Leave the cooking, get out of the house, and hail a cyclo.

There is something about a cyclo ride that instantly calms me. The shaded seat at the front is just big enough for me to sit back comfortably and wrap my arms around my daughter as she relaxes on my lap. The breeze, as we move silently through the streets, makes this much needed physical closeness bearable for the first time all day.

Our irritation and petty squabbles are soothed away by the gentle, healing rhythm of the cyclo as it winds its way through the back streets of Phnom Penh. Our favorite sunset trip is close to home, in Boeung Keng Kang 1. The streets are quiet, and the evening air is fragrant with jasmine and frangipani.

"Svay! Svay!" cries the old woman heading home from market, pushing a cart piled high with mangoes. The roasted-egg man sees us and presses the button on his trolley to release a loud and strange recorded message, used universally by egg sellers across the city. For months we thought it was election propaganda until we finally saw where the noise came from. Street boys, collecting rubbish, peer curiously through the gates of ostentatious mansions as they quickly open and close, swallowing up their chauffeur-driven owners returning from work.

My daughter loves to play hide-and-seek with the sun, which slips behind the houses and becomes visible again at the end of every block, each time a little redder and a little lower in the sky. We have no fixed route—she gets to choose left or right, and we simply meander through the neighborhood following the sun. When we want to head home, we trail after the white moon on the other side.

If we are feeling brave, we cross Norodom Boulevard, but this is not for the fainthearted. Tiny and vulnerable, we sit in the middle of six interweaving lanes of motorbikes. At least they drive slowly and wind around us. Much worse are the oversized SUVs, whose iron-barred bumpers are level with our heads, so that our eyes meet with the conspicuous empty space where the registration plates should be. In these moments I can't help but wonder if the drivers really can see out of those black, bulletproof windows.

But it is worth it, just to get to the east side and creep down one of the tiny alleys where the streets are unpaved and Khmer families sit outside to cook and wash clothes.

Their children follow us, waving and laughing. These alleyways nearly all lead to Street 21, a sleepy dirt lane full of whitewashed bungalows and a handful of colonial villas, beautiful and rundown with that shabby elegance that only the French can achieve. Colorful bursts of bougainvillea spill over their walls. Recent accumulation of wealth among a small elite has led to demolition of many of the traditional houses, replaced by imposing, rarely beautiful mansions, but here I can imagine a Phnom Penh before three decades of war devastated many of the its buildings and pagodas.

We often end this trip with a walk around the pretty green gardens of Wat Svay Popei, the Buddhist temple and monastery between Street 21 and Sothearos Boulevard. The monks welcome us and enjoy talking to visitors. It is a perfect setting in which to seek the inner peace all mothers need to help prepare them for the dinner, bath, and bedtime that await.

Day tours in a cyclo

Georgiana adds: It is also fun to pretend to be a tourist in the middle of the day, when the cyclo canopy protects us from the unrelenting sun. We take a trip along Sothearos down to the riverside, past the fun fair on Sisowath Quay, across the park to the Royal Palace and National Museum, and on to Wat Phnom, where children can meet Sambo, the city's ancient and much loved elephant.

Compassionate riding

Cyclo drivers normally charge a few thousand riel for a half-hour ride. When you think how hard they work, in the heat and the traffic, or if you go out late at night and see hundreds of them fast asleep in their cyclos, their feet up against a tree or lamppost (most drivers virtually live in their vehicles), it is hard not to offer them more money. Especially if you are six months pregnant with a toddler on your lap, and they look so old and thin you wonder how on earth they are going to get you moving. Thank goodness Phnom Penh is flat. Georgiana has been known to get out and help push the bike over the speed bumps.

Giving directions

The one drawback for tourists is that most cyclo drivers do not speak English. This shouldn't matter if you are happy to meander and explore with a map. You just direct them with your hand or learn the words for please turn right/left/go straight on (*bat sdam/bat chweing/trong*).

The Cyclo Centre

The Cyclo Centre is dedicated to supporting cyclo drivers in Phnom Penh. For individuals and groups, they can arrange cyclo tours of the city.

(023) 991-178

www.cyclo.org.uk

Loung Ung dreams with a cyclo driver in Phnom Penh

A long time ago, I read a newspaper story about a poor cyclo peddler in Phnom Penh who spoke of the joys of having two birthdays in one year—the day of his birth, and the day someone paid him $5 for a short sightseeing trip around town. Since reading that article, every time I visit Cambodia, I go for a cyclo ride on my last day in the country.

As I exit Psar Tuol Tom Pong market, my arms heavy with bags of crispy fried fish, green mangos, and pink dragon fruit, I glance at a group of cyclo drivers on the other side of the street. Immediately, they all look up and wave, calling me with the downward curve of their fingers. I slowly make my way to them, but am suddenly stopped by a swarm of motodops that circle me like hungry crocodiles.

No, thank you. I shake my head and continue to make my way to the cyclos. The motorcycle drivers stare at me with disbelief, their faces hardening like stone. On the other side of the street, the cyclo drivers hop on their bicycle pedicabs, waiting eagerly for me to arrive. Finally we meet. I smile and speak to them in Khmer. They all laugh in surprise. They think I am a foreigner. No, I am Khmer, I tell them. They laugh again. I tell them I wish to go on a sightseeing ride in a cyclo. Instantly, each one implores me to climb into his cab.

I search the group to find the oldest and poorest looking driver and walk over to him. Our eyes connect and we exchange smiles. His face is a beautiful, sun-worn structure shrunken by years of hard work and poverty. As he helps me into his bicycle-powered cab, a twang of guilt vibrates in my heart. Even though I am only 105 pounds, I feel big and fat next the man's wiry and lean body. I glance down. His calf muscles ripple. Hardened veins travel across them like the map of his life.

Where to? he asks.

The riverfront.

The short ride is slow and smooth. I sit back and watch people speed by us in their cars, tuk-tuks, motodops, and even bicycles.

Where is your family? I ask him.

He tells me they live in his village.

Like many other cyclo peddlers, he is a poor farmer who comes to the city during the dry season when the earth cracks and his small plot of land refuses to grow the food needed to feed his family. Every year, for a few months, he makes his way to Phnom Penh, bringing with him no more than the clothes on his body. By day he joins the ever-vanishing community of drivers circling markets, restaurants, and hotels looking for riders or vendors who will pay him to transport their produce and products. When the last ray of sun flickers off in the sky and he lays his tired body to sleep in the passenger seat of his cyclo, he might have up to a dollar in his pocket for his hard day of work. Sometimes less.

His voice catches a little as he tells me his story.

I ask what he dreams about.

He dreams of reuniting with his family and working his land.

When the ride ends, I thank him for his story and hand him a $5 note. The disbelieving look, surprised eyes, and happiness start out on his face as a Cheshire cat grin, and then bubble into a throaty laugh. I thank him for the ride and walk away.

Riding in a cyclo

Most of the time, Loung travels by motorcycle taxi in Cambodia. However, for short trips to noodle shops or markets, she often takes cyclos, which can be an enjoyable way to see the city. The cyclo is a human-powered vehicle for hire, usually with one or two seats for carrying passengers in addition to the bicycle seat on which the driver sits. In many Asian cities where they are widely used, this type of rickshaw driving, or a variation on it, provides essential employment for recent immigrants from rural areas, generally impoverished men. In Cambodia, cyclo drivers have lost much of their business to the explosion of cars, motos, and tuk-tuks, which, for a comparable price, can take customers faster to their destinations.

Denise Heywood observes dance traditions in Phnom Penh

Clouds of dust enveloped the taxi as we drove over bumpy, potholed dirt roads to an area of landfill where once there were lakes. This was Russei Keo, a bleak neighborhood northwest of Phnom Penh, where the Royal University of Fine Arts dance school has been forced to move amid the controversial selling of their former premises in the city.

Dance classes start here at seven, before the heat of day, in the new, open-sided halls. I stood outside one watching the students, all girls, aged from six to seventeen, dressed in pink satin bodices and red *sampots*— part sarong, part trousers—that enhanced their long, slender limbs and supple bodies. With bare feet, they moved gracefully through their exercises, backs arched and knees flexed, while their hands, with fingers bent back, unfolded like flowers.

Their pace was slow and hypnotic, with carefully synchronized steps, while their faces remained dreamlike and impassive. All of the expression was instead in their hands. The young dancers were a vision of heavenly beauty, and indeed, many of them would learn the dance of the *apsaras*, imitating the twelfth-century celestial dancers carved on the walls of Angkor Wat.

In Cambodia, dance is the essence of the country's artistic identity. Religious in origin, its traditions hark back more than a thousand years to the great Khmer empire, where dancers performed in temples. The performers lived within the royal palace, and many were princesses, a practice that continued through the twentieth century, until the Pol Pot regime, when 90 percent of them were killed.

The revival of dance has been made possible by performers who escaped the carnage. Two of great significance, Soth Somaly, in her fifties, and Em Theay, in her seventies, have dedicated their lives to passing on their skills. Em Theay, who was a performer at the Royal Palace before 1975, survived the killing fields, but her husband and five of her children died. Still, she has the strength of conviction to help piece together from memory the ancient court dances of the *Ramayana*, the Hindu epic that was reinterpreted in Cambodia as the *Reamker*.

Soth Somaly teaches 130 girls each day, coaxing their agile bodies into seemingly impossible poses, stretching the joints, bending the fingers back, and training them to lie flat while their legs are crossed in a lotus position. By the age of ten, these girls have learned an intricate vocabulary of gestures and start on the repertory of dances, all of which are sacred. With luck, they might enter the National Dance Company. Otherwise, they can perform for tourists.

It was not even noon when the class was over. The girls thanked Soth Somaly with a *sompeah*, bowing and bringing joined hands to the lips, a sign of deep respect. Then they scampered away, laughing, transformed from elegant *apsaras* back to jubilant children, while I negotiated the dust and rutted roads back to Phnom Penh.

Royal University of Fine Arts dance school

Now located at 598, Street 211 in the Russei Keo district, the Fine Arts dance school is about nine kilometers outside of Phnom Penh. The drive out is bumpy, and the school is often flooded during the rainy season. As well as classical dance, the university teaches folk dance, masked dance, theater, and circus arts.

Dance performances in Phnom Penh

There are no regular Royal Ballet performances in Phnom Penh. Occasional performances can be seen at Chaktomuk Theatre on Sisowath Quay. Just outside the capital at Takhmau, the excellent Khmer Arts ensemble dance company has its headquarters, but they too do not schedule regular performances. Two locations that offer alternate shows of classical and folk dances are the Apsara Arts Association, a training school for students, and the Sovanna Phum Art Association. Check the local press for their weekend performances.

www.apsara-art.org
http://shadow-puppets.org
www.khmerarts.org

Dance performances in Siem Reap

In Siem Reap several hotels and restaurants offer evening shows combined with a buffet meal. These are performed for tourists, and whilst the standard is not as high as that of the Royal Ballet, they are enjoyable nonetheless. These include regular shows at the Temple Club on Pub Street, the Apsara Theatre at the Angkor Village Hotel & Resort, and at La Résidence d'Angkor Hotel.

www.angkorvillage.com
www.residencedangkor.com

PHNOM PENH
TO BATTAMBANG

Elizabeth Briel braves the train from Phnom Penh to Battambang

Determined to ride the famously decrepit train from Phnom Penh to Battambang, I arrived at Phnom Penh's Art Deco-style station just after sunrise. Lines snaked around counters. Hawkers howled. Strangers smiled. Cambodia's Pchum Ben Festival was in full swing, so the station was filled with holidaymakers going back to their hometowns.

Every carriage was stuffed with people. They spilled into aisles and down steps, between cars and onto rooftops. I saw several passenger cars, then two "cattle cars" for cargo *and* passengers. These had the most room, so I climbed up and in, losing sight of the two other foreigners I'd noticed in the station. After a two-hour wait, finally we were off, at the lazy speed of around twenty-five kilometers per hour. My car was directly behind the engine, and its frequent horn blasts rattled my eardrums. Now I understood why everyone was concentrated at the *other* end of the carriage. I stuffed small wads of wet tissue in my ears.

The Cambodian train brakes were spectacular—the train slowed, stopped, then lurched violently at unpredictable intervals. Passengers crashed into one another, fell over benches, slipped and tripped in the muddy aisles. Packages tumbled from shelves overhead. Each time, everyone shrieked, then laughed as they got to their feet again.

A uniformed guard strolled by occasionally with an automatic rifle slung over his back. At twilight, I wandered through passenger cars, looking for one with electricity, but none of the lights worked anywhere on the train.

"I've worked these railways since Pol Pot fell," said the conductor, who happily recited the train's timetable: "The Battambang line runs once a week in each direction. From Phnom Penh on Saturdays, then back to Phnom Penh every Sunday. The Sihanoukville line almost never takes passengers anymore. Too dangerous."

"When will we arrive?" I asked.

"Maybe ten, eleven, twelve," the conductor grinned. "Depends on the train, track, how many stops for how long, how many passengers." He waved his hands in an arc that encompassed all these variables and more. "You tired?" he asked me.

I nodded.

"I don't know what you call this in English," he said, and unrolled a piece of fabric.

"A hammock!" I cried.

"Really?"

"Sure."

He patted it free of diesel dust. The train rocked, ready to fall off the seventy-year-old tracks. I quickly learned to keep a tight grip on the window ledge when my hammock swayed too far.

An ancient man played his tabla in the aisle, and candlelight flickered, making the space seem cavernous. Fresh air rushed through the window as we sped past fireflies and rice fields. This, I thought, was *it*. times like these make the sweat, the greasy cans of warm beer, and the slippery toilets of train travel all worthwhile.

Train travel in Cambodia

Passenger trains in Cambodia have been discontinued, though if you turn up on a Saturday morning you will be able to get a ride to Battambang. The train leaves Phnom Penh at 6:20 a.m., or thereabouts, and arrives somewhere between 8:00 and 10:00 p.m., depending on the condition of train and tracks. Those to Phnom Penh leave Battambang on Sundays at 6:40 a.m. and arrive in Phnom Penh somewhere between 7:00 and 10:00 p.m. One major stop takes place midway through the route in the large town of Pursat.

The Cambodia railway is slated for a complete overhaul to open up a trans-Asian railroad from China to Singapore. In Cambodia that means laying new track and extending the line from Sisophon to the Thai border and from Phnom Penh to the Vietnam border. There is a timetable for this work to be completed, but like everything in Cambodia, that schedule is fluid.

SIEM REAP

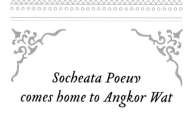

Socheata Poeuv
comes home to Angkor Wat

The first time I visited Angkor, I came with my family, all of whom are expatriate Cambodians. We moved to Texas after my parents' survival of the Khmer Rouge and their escape from Cambodia, and this was my first trip home.

My father had been to Angkor Wat as a young man. He was a traveling salesman and had the opportunity to see every corner of the country. My mother, though she grew up in an affluent Chinese-Cambodian family, had never visited the temple. I found this unbelievable, but she told me that most Cambodians haven't seen their most cherished heritage site. They simply don't have the luxury.

My parents, being the frugal immigrants they are, insisted that our family take advantage of the "Cambodian discount." For Cambodians, a day pass to the temples is free. For everyone else, it's $20.

To prove our Cambodian-ness, my father told us that there were certain rules we had to abide by or we would be found out. First and foremost, we could not dress like Americans. This meant no ball caps, shorts, or tank tops. Although it was at least 30 degrees Celsius and steam-room humid, we had to wear long pants and long sleeves just like proper Cambodians.

I asked my father where this tradition of dress slacks in a tropical climate came from. He didn't seem to know, but there wasn't even a question about it—Cambodian gentlemen always wear slacks. I suspect it has something to do with the French colonial influence, because as soon as Cambodian men are safe in their homes away from prying eyes, they strip off their trousers and slip into sarongs.

The second rule was that we could only speak Khmer when we were at the temples. Easy for my parents, but for my brother and me, who had grown up in America since ages five and two, respectively, it was difficult. Embarrassingly, our vocabularies had been reduced to the most essential communications like "I am hungry," "My hand hurts," or "You're crazy in the head." Although in our twenties, we were only able to sound like bratty three-year-olds.

During our visit to Angkor, we strolled among endless monuments, some half-consumed by the jungle. I was impressed by both the scale and the detail. An entire ancient city, and on each square inch is carved a different character, a different story. I had never seen anything like it in my life.

Although my brother and I did not have the words—in Khmer or English—to express how we felt about what we were seeing, one thing was clear to us. It wasn't the clothing or the language that made us Cambodian. It was our heritage.

I feel that we Cambodians have an inferiority complex. We don't think we're as sophisticated as our neighbors to the west—the Thais. We feel less enterprising than our neighbors to the east—the Vietnamese. And we have that deeply tanned skin that's undesirable among Asians in general. But we do have Angkor, proof that we come from a powerful and beautiful legacy.

Entering Angkor

For admission to Angkor, foreigners have a choice of a one-day pass ($20), a three-day pass ($40), or a one-week pass ($60). Passes can be purchased to run consecutively, or for the three-day and one-week passes, they can be used over the period of a week or a month, respectively. Make sure you confirm details at the official entrance booth. Visitors entering after 5:00 p.m. can enjoy the sunset for free if their ticket starts the following day. The fee includes access to all the monuments in the Angkor temple complex, but does not include the remote temples of Beng Mealea and Koh Ker or the sacred mountain of Phnom Kulen.

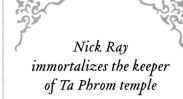

Nick Ray
immortalizes the keeper
of Ta Phrom temple

He was as much an icon of Angkor as the tangled roots that slowly choke the ancient stones of the Ta Prohm temples. Here in Cambodia, man first conquered nature to create, then nature slowly conquered man to destroy. But Nhiem Chun dedicated his life to stemming the tide of nature, bent double, stooping low over the stones to sweep away the falling leaves each day.

I first met Nhiem back in 1995 when exploring Ta Prohm. He was sprightly then, nimbly gliding over fallen pillars, tumbled stones, and moss-clad lintels in search of his quarry, those ever-falling leaves. His face was every bit as chiseled and full of character as the beautiful carvings of the *devatas* that lined the temple's galleries.

Years later he was immortalized by Lonely Planet when his iconic image was selected as the cover shot for the fourth edition of the Cambodia guidebook. It was a definitive photograph, Nhiem standing in front of the "*Tomb Raider* tree," the place where Angelina Jolie had plucked a jasmine bud and fallen through the earth into ... Pinewood Studios. Nhiem soon became an A-list Angkor celebrity himself, and crowds thronged around him, wanting a picture.

Nhiem Chun was about the same age as King Sihanouk, although their lives could have hardly been more different. Nhiem grew up tending buffalo and helping with the harvest, but he had a chance meeting with Angkor curator Henri Marchal in 1941 and began work as a laborer, helping with temple restoration at Angkor. It was the start of a lifelong love affair with the temples, and Nhiem was destined to spend the next sixty-five years of his life working amid the sacred stones.

Nhiem's labor was interrupted and his world crumbled around him when the Khmer Rouge came to power. "In the 1970s, our lives were turned upside down. I could not do my job; I had to work the land," said Nhiem. "You had no choice. You would be killed." More precious than his beloved temples, his sons disappeared during the Khmer Rouge regime. "When the fighting was over, my two sons were still missing," he recalled. "I was told they had been killed by the Khmer Rouge, their throats slit with sharpened sugar palm fronds."

In 2006, the BBC came to Cambodia to film *Who Cares About Art?* and Nhiem Chun was our subject, the loyal guardian of Ta Prohm. We spent several days with him, learning about his life, his loves, and his loss. "The older I get the more I love this place. These temples are the spirit of the Cambodian nation," he mused, wandering about Ta Prohm. "I could have built this temple in a past life. If I did

not have any connection, I would not be here to take care of it today."

Nhiem was not getting any younger and fretted about the future: "I am old now. I can't take care of these temples anymore," he opined wistfully. "But when I am gone, these stones will still be here. These temples are the symbols of our soul. We will not survive if we do not look after our temples."

Like the ancient stones of Ta Prohm, Nhiem Chun experienced light and dark. Living among beauty and brilliance, he also experienced the ugly side of man. But life goes on, and the leaves continued to fall. "If I don't sweep, the leaves will cover the temple. I must sweep," he muttered. Nhiem Chun was a man for all seasons.

Ta Prohm

Ta Prohm is one of the "Big Five" at Angkor, the iconic temple twined with all the incredible tree roots. It is about twelve kilometers from Siem Reap near the royal bathing pond of Sra Srang. It is easily accessible by bicycle, moto taxi, tuk-tuk, or car/bus. Undoubtedly one of the most romantic of the incredible structures of Angkor, this was originally constructed as a Mahayana Buddhist temple during the late twelfth century by Jayavarman VII. Apparently it took eighty thousand people to look after it: no wonder it is such a ruin today. Ta Prohm has been abandoned to the elements, a reminder that while empires rise and fall, the riotous power of nature marches on, oblivious to the dramas of human history. Left as it was "discovered" by French explorer Henri Mouhot in the nineteenth century, its tentaclelike tree roots are slowly strangling the surviving stones. It may be crowded, but Ta Prohm can still make the first-time visitor feel like an explorer of old.

Beating the crowds

This is the challenge for travelers to Angkor these days. The most atmospheric time to visit is at the crack of dawn. Most visitors make for Angkor Wat to see the sunrise, so ignore the crowds and head to Ta Prohm instead. Lunchtime is a fallback option, as most of the tourist buses head back to town.

Movie sets

Despite what some imaginative local guides will tell you, Ta Prohm was not used for the filming of Indiana Jones. However, the romance of the place has not been lost on filmmakers, and it has been used as a backdrop in two Hollywood productions. *Tomb Raider* shot some scenes here in November 2001, as this was the "back entrance" used by Angelina Jolie (aka Lara Croft) to break into the underground crypt. As well, in this same movie, the bad guys pulled down a giant

polystyrene *apsara* blocking the East Gate of Angkor Thom. The following year, Jean-Jacques Annaud brought a truckload of tigers into town and filmed several sequences in Ta Prohm. Look out for the early scenes of *Two Brothers* with the family of tigers gallivanting around the temple, as much of this is Ta Prohm.

Nhiem Chun

I report with sadness that Nhiem Chun passed away in March 2009 at the age of eighty-seven at his home near Ta Prohm. He will always be remembered as The Sweeper of Ta Prohm, and his story is one well worth contemplating as you explore this incredible temple.

Steve McClure sings the "loud song" in Siem Reap

We had just wrapped up two fantastic weeks of shooting interviews and cross-country traveling for a documentary I was working on and had good reason to celebrate. It was our last night in Cambodia. We decided to see what Siem Reap had to offer as a parting gift.

Our crew of four, along with our Cambodian guide, arrived at the Martini Pub & Beer Garden, just across the river from the city's main nightlife area. We were immediately greeted by the sweet sounds of karaoke, which blared from the outside patio—music to my ears. Instantly, I requested a song list and an Angkor beer, not necessarily in that order. After a momentary internal debate, I decided on Stevie Wonder's "I Just Called to Say I Love You" from the list of about ten songs on the "English" list.

I'm no stranger to karaoke, so singing in front of the mix of locals and tourists seemed like a fun challenge. But the Khmers singing onstage before me were actually pretty good. Heck, almost professional. I figured if the locals (talented or not) were brave enough to do it, then so was I.

As I walked onstage, I was greeted only by a lone music stand, a piece of sheet music, and a guy with a keyboard. What? No TV monitors displaying the lyrics? No prerecorded music? No problem.

To my surprise, the music quickly started. Without a visual cue, I missed the beginning of the song. My keyboard-playing cohort decided to take that opportunity to begin singing the song himself. I guess he was trying to help the wounded duck onstage. I gave him a friendly "what the heck are you doing" stare, and soon after, I was off and running. Okay, so I didn't know the song as well as I thought and stumbled a few times, but it was certainly better than trying to fake it through "Hotel California," one of the nine other choices on the list.

I'm not sure if any of my audience had ever seen a poorly performed moon walk, mixed with a bit of "the ro-

bot," combined with a heavy metal version of a Stevie Wonder song before, but after that night, they could definitely say they had. I received a rousing applause—sympathy, maybe?—and returned to our table, congratulated by our Cambodian guide for singing, as she called it, the "loud song."

The Martini Pub & Beer Garden

Reopened in 2009 after a long spell with the doors firmly locked, The Martini Pub & Beer Garden is located just across the Old Market Bridge, near the Siem Reap River. There is no cover charge, and the drinks are competitively priced. Indoors boasts a large nightclub, playing both Western and modern Khmer music. This is a great place for dancing. It is no relation to its namesake in Phnom Penh.

CHAM YEAM TO SIHANOUKVILLE

Jan Polatschek crosses the border to Sihanoukville

The entry from Thailand and the onward trip to Sihanoukville should've been straightforward. However, my first visit to Cambodia began with a sneer. The officious Cambodian border guard at Cham Yeam was not happy, despite pocketing a couple of extra bucks because I had misplaced my passport photos. I spent the night in Koh Kong—a dusty and unappetizing place, even though the hotel was comfortable and had a lovely garden.

I booked myself a seat on a minibus to Sihanoukville. It was scheduled to pick me up at 8:30 a.m. It arrived at 9:15. After just fifteen minutes on a rutted, sloppy dirt road, the driver was stopped by the police. We were abruptly sent back to the police station at Koh Kong.

We waited at the station for no apparent reason. On the porch, we watched the pouring rain and eyed a variety of uniformed guys who carried a variety of menacing weapons.

Finally at 11:30 the driver announced, "300 Thai baht each."

I was happy to pay up and leave. Others travelers were angry. Regardless of their disposition, we collected the money, paid off the police, and got the hell out of there.

Four of the young passengers decided that Cambodia was not for them and returned to the more genteel Thailand. Always tempting for me is the excitement of the unknown, so I decided to continue with the remaining backpackers. We took off through the rain and over the mountain roads. At any moment I expected to be ambushed by bandits or remnants of the Khmer Rouge.

The ride from Koh Kong to Sihanoukville was a scenic and serious six-hour adventure. We crossed narrow, rain-swollen rivers on local ferries that were nothing more than planks of wood lashed together and propelled by outboard motors. Wearing our rain ponchos, we had lunch in an open-sided hut.

On the jungle mountain road again, we approached a steep hill. Another minivan was stuck in the mud about twenty meters from the top. Our driver backed up and floored the gas pedal to gain momentum to get us up and over the hill. No way. Now we were all stuck. What to do? First, everyone pushed our van over the hill. We cheered as we repeated our labors on the second van. Covered with mud from the spinning tires, we washed off in a nearby stream. We felt very proud of ourselves.

We cheered again when we finally arrived in Sihanoukville. Then, unexpectedly, the representative of the tour company refunded the "toll money" exacted by the police. "Welcome to Cambodia."

Thai border to Sihanoukville

There is now a road, National Highway 48, that will take travelers from Koh Kong to Sihanoukville, 220 kilometers away, in less than four hours by bus or taxi. There is also a ferry, but it only runs in the high season, and the bus is much cheaper and more comfortable, anyway.

BATTAMBANG

Anne Best honors the past at a festival in Battambang

Today is the main day of the weeklong Pchum Ben festival, which focuses on the honoring of ancestors. It is a time when families meet up to remember their loved ones. All over Battambang, people are walking or riding motos, armed with rice steamers, flowers, fruit, and other foodstuffs. Dressed in their best clothes, they are headed for their local pagoda or *wat*.

We must get our own offerings for the monks at the *wat* in Ksach Poy. First, we head to Sunrise Café to collect fifty chocolate donuts, which we know will be a hit. Next, we go down to the riverside market for two of the beautifully presented gift hampers that are available at festival times. Wrapped in clear cellophane paper, which is rather surprisingly printed with yellow tulips and daffodils, these include sugar, tinned milk, tinned fish, tea, and in the center, joss sticks, candles, and matches.

The wrapping and presentation of gifts is important in Cambodia, and most shops will have a selection of papers and ribbons to choose from. The gift is then very carefully, economically, and tidily wrapped and tied. Traditionally, Cambodians will not open a gift in the presence of the giver, which can be a bit disconcerting to a Westerner, but here it's considered the polite way to do things.

Eventually, we arrive at the *wat*. It is full of people, music, and activity. At one corner of the temple complex are the stupas, which house the ashes of the deceased. Here, a monk is performing a solemn ceremony in memory of a dead relative as the family stands by with their offerings of food. Small children let off firecrackers, and no one turns a hair. Tolerance reigns.

We move toward the meeting hall, which is the hub of the *wat*. Part temple, part place of assembly, where lay people and monks meet. We put our gifts of food on the tiled floor and wait until the head monk comes over. Prayers are said, blessings are made, and we hand over the donuts and food.

The hall fills up. Soon it will be time for the monks to eat. I sit down on the floor among a group of Khmer women who smile and greet me with clasped palms and bowed heads. They arrange my skirt and generally fuss over me. One has a small baby. She pulls down his pants to show me proudly that he is a boy, and the baby promptly pees all over me. Much laughter follows.

Now the monks file in and take their places along the wall of the hall, seated in order of seniority. Each monk is presented with new robes, mats, and gifts, and each is given a tray piled with dishes. After prayers and chanting, the monks eat sparingly, and in the spirit of the festival, all uneaten food is then shared around with the congregation.

Cambodian festivals

It is worth planning your trip to Cambodia to coincide with some of the colorful annual ceremonies and celebrations. But remember, the festivals are national holidays and can affect the general running of things such as transport, shop hours, etc. Although festivals attract large local crowds and traffic can come to a standstill, the virtual absence of alcohol means that things remain generally good humored and safe.

A couple of the main festivals take place in autumn. Pchum Ben is in late September or early October and centers on the *wats* as described above. The Water Festival begins in late October or early November; essentially it focuses on highly competitive rowing races in which colorfully painted and carved "dragon boats" compete. Provincial heats take place in various towns, and the finals are held in Phnom Penh at the time of the November full moon.

GENERAL CAMBODIA

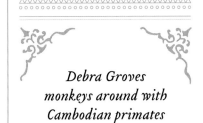

Debra Groves monkeys around with Cambodian primates

When one is traveling in a foreign country, it always pays to be a little cautious and to stay aware of personal safety. I've learnt this from experience, as I've been mugged in Cambodia a couple of times—by monkeys!

The first ambush took place at Wat Phnom in Phnom Penh. I was touring the *wat* with my friend Angela and had a plastic bag with food in it. As I was sitting, just watching the world go by, a huge monkey snuck up behind me and grabbed the bag, scaring the life out of me. I ducked behind Angela, screaming like a stuck pig. The monkey then proceeded to eat the entire bag of food. This obviously wasn't a one-off occurrence for this monkey, as he was extremely obese.

The second incident happened at Siem Reap along a road not far from Angkor Wat. My driver wanted to stop, since he had some bread left over from his lunch, and he wanted to feed it to the monkeys. As a photographer I thought this would make a good photo opportunity, so I laid my camera backpack on the ground and opened it up to get my gear out. I left the bag and walked a couple of meters away to take a picture.

When I turned around, I found a gang of monkeys descending on my backpack with evil intent in their eyes. They were out to grab anything they could get their simian hands on! I shouted at them, and—waving my arms like a lunatic—ran for the bag, scaring them off. But one of them had grabbed my sunglasses. He promptly ran up into a tree and cheekily waved the glasses at me with what I am certain was a mocking look on his face. My driver tossed sticks at the tree to try to get the monkey to drop the glasses. Eventually, the creature broke them in two and hurled them at us. I consider myself lucky. Better a pair of cheap sunglasses than my photography equipment. And now I know: In Cambodia, "better safe than sorry" takes on an entirely new meaning.

Monkey see, monkey do

The Khmer word for monkey is *sva*. They can be found all over Cambodia. You can see them on the side of the roads amongst the Angkor temple complex outside Siem Reap and around Wat Phnom and the post office area of Phnom Penh. They are also often tethered at pagodas and markets around the countryside. While they are cute, they can become aggressive quickly, and a bite from a monkey may mean a round of painful rabies injections.

Denise Heywood weaves a tale of Cambodian silk

Sumptuous silk in dazzling colors is one of the glories of Southeast Asia. The shimmering fabric is irresistible, whether rolled on bolts, folded on shelves, or simply draped in a shop window on display. When people ask me what to buy as a souvenir from Cambodia, I always say silk.

The best pieces include sarongs, called *sampots*, the Cambodian national dress, worn by women and men—a long piece of material that is wrapped around the hips, drawn up between the legs, and tucked in at the waist. The other quintessential Cambodian accessory is the *krama*, a scarf in cotton or silk. Each province has its own *krama* designs. Some produce patterns that resemble Scottish tartans, others regency stripes, and Kompong Cham's, for example, come in shades of burgundy, purple, crimson, indigo, and emerald. All around Cambodia you will see the myriad uses for *kramas*, as turbans, scarves, stoles, sarongs, shorts, swimsuits, towels, hammocks, and most picturesque in my opinion, infant carriers. I once saw a baby in a *krama* swinging from the handlebars of a bicycle. For Khmers, the *krama* is an affirmation of their identity. For travelers, the silk ones are perfect as presents.

At the National Silk Centre at Puok, sixteen kilometers from Siem Reap, I enjoy watching the techniques of silk weaving. The tradition is handed down from generation to generation, and used to be practiced in every village throughout the country, usually by women, who weave at home while looking after their children. Cambodian silk-weaving is intricate and decorative, incorporating patterns of birds such as peacocks, crowns, jewels, flowers, images from Khmer tales, and scenes from Angkor Wat.

This intricately patterned and dyed style is called *Kha Bang Neang Sok Kra Ob*, which uses the complex *ikat* technique, practiced throughout Southeast Asia. I saw one example of this as a weaver wrapped strands of raw silk onto a frame, and then tied the strands with banana leaf threads to create patterns. She then removed the silk to be dyed. She would later remount it on the frame to be retied for the other colors in the pattern. For a weaver using this method, it takes two weeks to weave silk for just one *sampot*. Bags, diaries, wallets, hats, slippers, tablecloths, and napkins are among other accessories made here.

Along with the rural women who have long woven silk as part of their daily lives, the Royal Court of Cambodia maintained a large retinue of silk weavers, who created luxurious, richly patterned textiles in vibrant colors. In Phnom Penh I visited a silk weaving school that opened in 1994 in the home of the last great master weaver, the late Leav Sa Em, who wove silk for King Sihanouk's wife, Queen Monique. Thanks to UNESCO and nongovernment organizations, these valuable skills have been revived and are now part of Cambodia's modern heritage as well as its rich ancient traditions.

Angkor Silk Farm

The Angkor Silk Farm is home to workshops for both the National Silk Centre and Artisans d'Angkor, which produces some of the best work in the country. A guided tour takes you through the whole process and is available free of charge, between 7:00 a.m. and 5:00 p.m. daily. The farm is sixteen kilometers west of Siem Reap, along National Highway 6, on the right-hand side just before the village of Puok. As well, you can visit Artisans d'Angkor's Chantiers-Ecoles workshop right in Siem Reap.

www.artisansdangkor.com

Buying silk around Cambodia

Along with Artisans d'Angkor, mentioned above, in Siem Reap you can find good shops selling quality silk in the market. In Phnom Penh, Wat Than, a Buddhist temple on Norodom Boulevard, teaches land mine victims to weave. The Russian Market (Psar Toul Tom Pong) also has a wealth of silk stalls where you can bargain for various silk items.

Lundi Seng denounces the ancient tradition of coining

When you are in Cambodia and you see people on the street with horrific red or purple welts all over their body, don't be alarmed. They have just undergone a medical treatment. More specifically, the ancient Cambodian practice of "coining."

Personally, I have experienced this firsthand, and I never want to be coined again. While some people report variable degrees of comfort—"It's like a massage"—I can tell you that it is the most painful thing ever. And for me as a child, it was a traumatic experience. However, surprisingly, many Cambodians both inside and outside the country still practice it on a regular basis when they're unwell or experiencing *kchyal chab* (wind illness).

My first coining happened when I was seven or eight years old. I must have come down with a fever. All I remember was lying facedown on the bamboo bed and two adults holding me down by my leg and left arm while my mom held my right arm and tried to coin me at the same time. I cried and screamed, and then screamed some more. Although coining was common practice, it is no wonder that in the late 1970s and early 1980s, with the influx of refugees from Southeast Asia to the West, physicians often misdiagnosed the marks produced by it as child abuse.

Cambodians use coining to try to relieve conditions associated with febrile illnesses, low energy, muscle aches, and stress-related ailments such as headaches, as well as "wind illness." Central to a Cambodian's interpretation of anxiety is the concept of wind, or inner air (*kchyal*). In a healthy person, this wind flows throughout the body unimpeded, much as blood circulates. A Cambodian believes that anxiety-related symptoms are generated when there is a disruption of the proper flow of this wind. For instance, when suffering a panic attack, a Cambodian construes it to be a wind attack. Subsequently, he engages in self-treatment by *koh kchyal* (literally, "scratching the wind") with coining or another practice known as cupping (*cup kchyal*).

To perform coining, a warm oil or Tiger Balm is applied on the skin, which is then firmly abraded with a brass coin or copper disc. The most common target areas of coining are the arms, chest, and back. Afterward, patients carefully observe their skin. If the marks are reddish in color, they will interpret this as minimal wind accumulation in that area. A darker blue or purple is a worrying sign and suggests excessive wind accumulation.

Upon seeing this darker color, the person may initiate further coining or cupping. With cupping, the blocked air is removed with a set of round glass cups. The cups are held to a flame and pressed to the skin in various patterns on the body, where they create vacuums to draw out the wind. Approximately fifty cups are placed on the patient's body in less than five minutes, and then left on for up to fifteen, leaving circular purple marks on the body. Cupping is believed to have a similar effect to coining, and like coining it continues to be a part of modern Cambodian life.

Heal thyself

Coining and cupping practitioners can be found pretty much everywhere in Cambodia, and most older family members are usually well practiced in the art. If you're feeling anxious or under the weather—and if Lundi has not scared you off—ask your Khmer friends to suggest their favorite practitioner.

Mariam Arthur is humbled at a countryside wedding

While in the countryside in Takeo Province, I was invited to attend a wedding. I was with a Khmer friend—the only person there besides me who could speak English—and was grateful that he would be able to explain the various customs I witnessed that day.

The wedding was held at the bride's house, and although the groom paid a dowry, all expenses were covered by her father. In order to help compensate for the cost, everyone attending paid some money to join the celebrations. A table was set up at the entrance to the yard, and respected men of the village counted and double-checked the cash. They entered the amounts in a ledger, to be kept by the bride's father. This book would be referred to when there was another wedding to attend, and a similar gift of money would be made to the next newlyweds, depending on their contribution to the bride's wedding.

Although most city weddings now last just one or two days, rural weddings are still major events, and traditionally last three. Their venues are entered through an arch made of bananas and coconuts still on their stalks, painted silver on one side and gold on the other. Traditional musicians and singers are hired to play during different phases of the ceremony, and a local wise man is chosen to lead the ceremonies. This person is not a religious or government official, but usually a community leader.

Weddings are exceptionally colorful, as they are a time for women to dress up in bright outfits bought just for the occasion and spend a few hours in the beauty shop. The bride alone puts on beautiful silk dresses of different colors—up to twelve over the course of just the wedding day. These are rented and fitted during the wedding, often held together with pins. The groom usually wears traditional Khmer outfits, although some will wear a suit. Suits are also normal attire for male guests, although I noticed that smart casual wear also seems to be appropriate.

At one point during the ceremony, I enjoyed the privilege of participating. *Ma-loo* leaves were wrapped around *sslaw* seeds and dipped in a pink powder known as *kom-bao*, made of ground snail shells. Along with fellow guests, I chewed on some for a bit before spitting it out. This meant I agreed that the couple loved each other and I gave my approval. Guests also took turns tying a red string to the wrists of the bride and groom. It is custom to leave the strings on until they naturally fall apart, signifying that the couple will live a long life together.

Throughout the day, the same as at a wedding back home, a photographer took pictures, including the typical shots of the bride and groom with their bridesmaids and groomsmen. I was next to the photographer snapping a picture when my Khmer friend took my camera and told me to stand in line with the bride. I was horrified, thinking of how upset a Western bride would be if a random guest leaped into her wedding photos. But my friend insisted, so I did as told and hoped for the best.

A few days later, the parents of the bride came to visit me, bringing the wedding photo album. Even though they spoke no English, their message was clear. They turned to every page with a picture of me in it, indicating that they were extremely proud that the *barang* (foreigner) had been an active part of the wedding. I already felt humbled to be able to attend the wedding. I was now even more so, learning that my presence was considered such a blessing to the new bride and groom.

Wedding season

There is an official wedding season in Cambodia, immediately following the end of the rainy season and leading up to the end of May. Wherever you wander—whether in a city or the countryside—you will be hard-pressed not to find a wedding taking place, most often spilling out into the middle of the street. There are also large wedding reception centers such as the Mondial in Phnom Penh, which act as a sort of conveyor-belt for wedding celebrations. During this time of year, it is not uncommon for foreigners to be invited to attend a ceremony—either asked by a new friend or even their moto driver, or drawn in right off the street. Just follow the instructions of your Khmer host—no matter how strange they may seem when viewed by Western standards—and you're sure to make a good impression and have a great time.

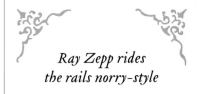

Ray Zepp rides
the rails norry-style

Norries, as they are called in the Battambang region, are small contraptions for riding on the railroad tracks. Used extensively by locals all along the Cambodian railway line, especially in areas far from main highways, to transport local goods and passengers, they are marketed to tourists as "bamboo trains."

Norries are ingeniously simple: a set of wheels, a flat bed of bamboo, and a small generator attached to the wheels. They are becoming increasingly popular among tourists as a fun and adventurous new mode of transportation. If you are riding a motorcycle, you can just load it onto a passing *norry*, travel as far as you want, and then get off and continue your moto journey.

Just before I left Cambodia, I decided to throw a *norry* party. Twenty friends of mine rented a van, bought some food and drink, and even gathered together our musical instruments. We headed north of Phnom Penh about ten kilometers past Udong and turned left toward the railroad tracks. There we found a couple of *norries* ready for departure. We rented two entire *norries*, and off we went across the countryside.

There can be many *norries* traveling along the same railroad track, loaded with sacks of rice, vegetables for market, and even children going to school. We met several along the way. When two *norries* meet on the track, the less heavily loaded one must be completely disassembled and taken off the tracks for the other to pass. Everyone gets off while the driver takes off the generator, the flatbed, and finally the wheels from the tracks. When the other *norry* has passed, he puts the whole thing back together. This is all very amusing the first couple of times, but on a hot day, when you have to stand out in the sun while all this is going on, it can get a little irritating. Be sure to bring *kramas*, sunscreen, and hats or umbrellas to protect you from the sun.

The *norries* let you see a real slice of Cambodian life. They also take you to parts of the countryside where roads do not go. Along our way we passed several old railway stations thoroughly destroyed by the Khmer Rouge in days past. We were taken away from the dust of the main roads, and the ride along the rails was much smoother than any motorcycle trip could ever be.

Down the tracks we stopped for a "country music" session near a small village where the folks supplied some freshly tapped palm wine for our refreshment. My friend Dan is a talented banjo player, and I brought along my recorder to play a tune Dan had taught me called "Long Journey Home." Sitting there playing, we enjoyed the peace of the rural setting without the disturbance of cars and motorcycles.

We had planned to end our journey where the main east-west road to Udong crosses the tracks. This was and still is a major station, with piles of interesting old railway equipment lying around. After we had inspected railway bogies and such, we decided everyone was having such a good time that we should carry on with the *norries* south to a crossing near the temples at Phnom Baset. We telephoned the van to pick us up there.

There are some impressive modern-day temples at Phnom Baset, including a replica of Angkor Wat, built, it is said, by a rich Khmer man who had a dream telling him to build the temple. But it was getting late, so rather than explore, we had a quick snack and headed back to Phnom Penh.

Riding a norry in Battambang

The easiest place in Cambodia to ride a *norry* is Battambang. Any motodop will know where to take you. The *norries* are not allowed to leave from Battambang station, so the motodop will deliver you to O Dambong station, where you will almost certainly see one or two preparing to head off for Phnom Teppedey, about two hours' journey southeast toward Moung Russey. Ray says "almost certainly" because at times when the real train is scheduled to come along, the *norries* vanish. But right after the train passes

is the moment when, at least in the direction of the train, you can travel without meeting any traffic. You can travel by *norry* to Phnom Teppedey and return by moto along National Highway 5.

Riding a norry in Phnom Penh

From Phnom Penh, the easiest way is to ride a *norry* is to go to Udong. You can either take the road that branches left just past the Udong market and go out to a major railway station or go through Udong on National Highway 5 and turn left at one of the towns five to ten kilometers north of Udong.

Riding a norry in southern Cambodia

In the south of Cambodia, the *norries*, which are called *lorries* in this area, are a bit different. There, a hole is cut out of the flat-bed and a motorcycle is inserted. Instead of a generator, the motorcycle engine itself provides the power. The rear wheel is slotted onto the track so that you actually ride the motorcycle on the railroad tracks. There are many *lorries* of this type available in the area around Kampot, where the rail line leaves the main road. Ray once rode one of these *lorries* from the Kampong Trach area all the way to Takeo.

Monk at a monastery near Bakong temple

Paying It Forward

Suggestions for giving back while you're on the road

For me, this chapter is a vehicle to give you the heads-up about things you can do to make a difference when you're visiting Cambodia. That might be just having lunch at a socially responsible restaurant, or it could be contributing to an orphanage that puts a roof over the heads of at-risk children. The need is great, and the number of projects in Cambodia is huge, so those listed here are just a small drop in the ocean of good deeds that you as a traveler can commit to.

Whether providing financial help or sharing your time and skills by volunteering, giving is a personal act. In no place is that more true than Cambodia, where it is all too easy to let your heart rule your head, especially on the streets. Begging is a way of life for many children and adults, and it is something you cannot avoid seeing. To give or not give money directly to those holding out their hands in your direction? This question is examined by two different writers here. Robert Tompkins says *yes*—give just a little, and discreetly. Debbie Watkins says *no*—it can only perpetuate the cycle of begging. If, after reading their opinions, you still don't know where you stand, I suggest you investigate the organizations that other contributors to this chapter have chosen to champion.

To get started, you can help supply rural classrooms, support a music school for the disabled, contribute toward the production of artificial limbs for land mine victims, and give hope to AIDS patients. And remember, giving doesn't have to be formal. It can be nothing more than a choice of how you spend your money while you're traveling. Elizabeth Briel buys her books from a needy young vendor in Siem Reap, Ray Waddington gives street kids a future by dining at Friends restaurant in Phnom Penh, and David Shamash shops responsibly from the silk weavers of Stung Treng. If you're up for a grand gesture, I have examples of that too. Just follow Christina Heyniger, who cycles for education across the country, or Doug Mendel, who donates an American fire truck—yes, a fire truck—to a station in need in Sihanoukville.

Children playing at Angkor Thom temple

Having lived in Cambodia for almost three years now, I naturally have my charities of choice. Among them is Cambodia Living Arts, which is also advocated here by Dickon Verey. This organization does fantastic work with older artists like Em Theay (classical dance) and Kong Nay (music), encouraging them to pass on their talents to the younger generation as well as recording their knowledge and sound for posterity. I have also always been impressed by the sheer bloody-mindedness and determination of Geraldine Cox to get the best for the orphans at the Sunrise Children's Villages (www.scv.org.au). I've visited the old and new centers in Phnom Penh, and the children were, hand on heart, among the happiest I've ever met. I can think of no better reason to give than that.

PHNOM PENH

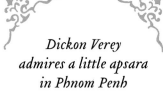

Dickon Verey admires a little apsara in Phnom Penh

She is a perfect little form, poised in concentration. Her back is arched slightly, her chin is raised. Her eyes twinkle. Her hands are tiny, and her palms are bent back. She raises her right leg and balances. Then she starts to sing, and her voice is clear and determined.

I have seen many startling things in Cambodia, but watching this singing *apsara* who lives in the squatter community of Tonle Bassac is one of the most moving. *Apsara* is a form of cultural expression that can stand proudly alongside any other style of dance the world has to offer. It has miraculously survived for centuries and will hopefully continue to do so. As for the girl's own future, it is precarious.

Built by the celebrated Cambodian architect Vann Molyvann, the apartment buildings at Tonle Bassac used to be some of Phnom Penh's most impressive edifices. What remains is now an eyesore on the capital. Some of the buildings have fallen down, and others were destroyed by fire, leaving a broken-down, moldy mass of concrete, stuffed with humanity. If you walk the corridors, you can almost smell the difficulty of the life within.

There are plans afoot to renovate the whole area. New buildings surround old ones, and some villagers have already given up their homes.

The slum is a confusing juxtaposition. Some of it serves as a brothel. Whilst this goes on, children take lessons. Ninety students (boys and girls) study traditional music and dance within the building and its surrounding shantytown. Kong Nay, possibly the most gifted *chapei* player in Cambodia, taught and lived there until recently. Despite the conditions, there is considerable pride and sense of community.

Just nine years old, the little *apsara* is incredibly dedicated. She goes to school from Monday to Saturday, and each day she takes four hours of dancing and singing as well. On Sunday all of the classes get together for a group lesson. Days off are rare. Her classmates are similarly determined. There are few ways out of the slum, and dancing and singing could offer a different future for a lucky few.

The little *apsara* and her classmates are sponsored by Cambodian Living Arts (CLA), an organization focused on keeping Cambodia's very unique and precious culture of dance and music alive. While visiting a slum might not be everyone's idea of a holiday outing, I urge you to get in touch with CLA if you are in Phnom Penh. Visit the little *apsara*'s class. It is an experience you will not soon forget, and a way that you can contribute not only to Cambodia's heritage but also to its future.

Cambodian Living Arts

The Tonle Bassac community is located in central Phnom Penh near the Bassac River in Chamkamon district. For information about visiting, go to the CLA website.

www.cambodianlivingarts.org

Molly Jester finds boundless love in Phnom Penh

On one of my frequent trips to the capital, I was fortunate to visit the burn ward at the Children's Surgical Centre (CSC). The center performs surgeries for burns, eye problems, cleft palates, and orthopedic issues, all free of charge, and although it primarily provides care to children, its mission is to serve "children of all ages."

Many of the patients I saw had been horribly disfigured in vicious acid attacks. The majority were young women of childbearing age, but there were some men there too. Even sadder, though, were the children. Acid is an imprecise weapon. It splatters and can hurt more people than the intended victim, making it even more damaging than the attacker may have planned.

While the hospital offers free surgical care, like most hospitals in developing countries, it does not have enough nurses. So the patients are taken care of after their surgeries by relatives. It is heart-wrenching but touching to see

PHNOM PENH PROVINCE

family members caring so warmly for their loved ones who often no longer resemble the person they remember. Love knows no bounds.

While at the hospital I was struck by one caregiver in particular, a little girl of nine who was taking care of her mother. I do not speak Khmer, and yet I had never felt I understood someone more. Her eyes spoke volumes, and I could feel her love for her mother and her pain at witnessing all her mother had suffered.

I talked with a hospital staffer, and she explained that the girl's mother, Yem, had been burned by her father's girlfriend. The girlfriend hoped if she disfigured his "first wife" then the man would leave the woman and marry her. That did not happen. The attacker ended up in prison, and Yem ended up horribly burned, as did another one of her children, who just happened to be in the line of fire.

The staffer also told me that the hospital had a hard time releasing patients like Yem because many of them had no homes to go to. The patients also needed jobs to survive, but because of their disfigurement they would have a hard time getting them. With the need to empower victims to rejoin society, Kanya Massage was started by caring staff at the CSC who realized they needed to create jobs for the patients they treated who were still physically able to work.

Several women who are truly survivors now had employment giving absolutely fabulous massages. I had the opportunity to visit Kanya Massage with some friends, and I must admit, I was going out of pity, thinking I would give these women some work. I assumed the massages would be mediocre at best, but that I should do something to help. I was wrong. The women were well trained, and my friends and I agreed that far from being charity cases, they gave some of the best massages we ever had.

Children's Surgical Centre

Run by victims of acid attacks, and including a support network for survivors, Kanya Massage closed down in 2008. A new massage business with the same principles is slated to open soon after the publication of this book. Please contact the surgical center for more information.

www.csc.org

Ray Waddington makes new friends in Phnom Penh

One evening I decided to eat dinner at Friends in Phnom Penh. Since it's primarily a place for the vocational training of street kids pursuing their careers in culinary arts and restaurant management, as well as a nonprofit fundraising outlet, my expectations of both ambience and cuisine were quite low. Still, from the description in my guidebook, it seemed like a cause worthy of my support.

How wrong I was in my low expectations. The restaurant was plush and spotlessly clean, and I felt out of place partaking of this almost formal dining experience wearing sandals, shorts, and a T-shirt. The food was excellent, too, as was the service. I decided to find out a bit more about the organization that had started the Friends restaurant.

Roughly translated from Khmer as "good friends," Mith Samlanh is a Cambodian nongovernmental organization set up in the mid-1990s by a Frenchman, Sébastien Marot. At that time Sébastien was just passing through Phnom Penh on his way to Japan. But like many who see firsthand what life is like for the city's street kids, he became involved unintentionally and decided to do something to help.

Sébastien told me about some of those early experiences: seeing kids living on the streets, sometimes alone and sometimes with their family, begging for money, clothes, or food. I was sure I hadn't seen it to the same extent he had, but his recounting reminded me of scenes I had witnessed in the last few days, and I could at least understand what he was describing. He also explained how Mith Samlanh grew out of these experiences and how it now functions.

My guidebook hadn't pointed out that the café is just one small part of what this NGO does. In fact it has many programs that are carefully designed to meet the different needs of kids who are on the streets of Phnom Penh for various reasons. In the end, though, all the programs are aimed at reintegrating these children into society.

Since my visit Mith Samlanh has grown tremendously to become a successful, international organization, now also working in other Asian countries like Thailand, Laos, and Pakistan. Sébastien has been awarded the Order of Australia for his work, and he is still a key part of Mith Samlanh. As for me, I learned a valuable lesson—a simple guidebook recommendation combined with a little curiosity can lead a person to a rich understanding of people and place.

Friends

Friends is located near the National Museum in Phnom Penh. Its sister venue, Romdeng—at 74, Street 174—serves up delicious meals based on recipes from the provinces of Cambodia.

215, Street 13
(023) 426-748, (012) 802-072

www.friends-international.org

Hing Channarith admires the return of dignity in Phnom Penh

Early in the morning at the entrance of the Kien Khleang National Rehabilitation Centre, I walked toward the reception desk among many disabled people, including amputees and children with polio. There I was welcomed by the center's manager, who was going to be my escort on my visit that day.

First on the tour, a description of the devices that the center produces: wheelchairs, artificial limbs, and braces. The manager then talked me through the center's activities: physiotherapy, prosthetics, orthotics, and wheelchair use.

In the physiotherapy room, where adult and child patients receive treatments prior to fitting a prosthetic device or receiving a wheelchair, I watched a small group of children afflicted with polio, who were practicing with their braces and wheelchairs in the playground area. Next door is a room where technicians produce artificial legs and braces. One of the technicians showed me the process of casting the stump of an amputee to ensure a comfortable fit.

At the gait-training area, where amputees are fitted and practice with their prostheses, patients learn how to walk with artificial limbs on obstacle courses that include climbing up stairs, walking along a small bridge, kicking a ball, and riding a bicycle. I was so pleased to witness these activities and the dignity that is restored to these individuals when they can walk once again. During my visit, I spoke with an amputee who lost his leg to a land mine accident, and he told me how happy he was with his artificial leg, which enabled him to live an almost normal life at home.

At the wheelchair workshop, where many technicians are physically disabled themselves, workers produce and repair wheelchairs and walking frames. They can usually produce nearly fifty per month. One of the technicians was blind, another victim of a land mine explosion, but he could assemble the wheels on a wheelchair as well as any seeing person could. The center had restored his pride not only by helping him heal but also by giving him a job that he could be good at and therefore giving him a place of respectability back in society.

Kien Khleang National Rehabilitation Centre

The center is situated along National Highway 6A, across the Tonle Sap River, about fifteen hundred meters from the Japanese Friendship Bridge in Phnom Penh. Its goal is to restore the lives of thousands of Cambodian land mine survivors and other disabled people. Donations contribute to the production of prosthetics and rehabilitation, as well as meals and dormitory housing for patients staying at the center.

www.csc.org

SIEM REAP

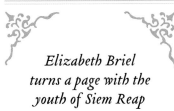

Elizabeth Briel turns a page with the youth of Siem Reap

After a glass of wine with a friend one evening, I crossed Sivatha Street toward home. We'd just been discussing my new photo students—a group of precocious teenagers from the community of booksellers in the high-density tourist areas of Siem Reap: Pub Street and the Old Market (Psar Chas).

As I passed a dark alleyway, someone called out, "Hi, teacher, how're you?"

"Who's that?" I asked, keeping my distance from the darkness.

"It's me, Rom," said an adolescent voice from somewhere on my right. A light flickered on between slats of wood. He'd been arranging the books in his cart. "You want to buy any books?" he said with a smile, that particularly Khmer expression visitors rave about. It illuminated everything around him. Even a large-lettered sign on his cart said, "My name is Rom. I used to beg but now I sell books. How can you resist this smile?"

"Hmm ..." I looked at his selection, a typical assortment of French- and English-language books, most of them sensationalist and related to Pol Pot-era atrocities and associated political turmoil. Comparing these books with those of neighboring Thailand, its syrupy tourist lit bordering on braggadocio, I often wonder how it would feel lugging around books whose titles and cover photos scream of abandonment and despair. How would I feel about tourists with high-denomination bills who eagerly snapped up stories about the destruction of my country? The bookselling kids seem to get on with things and don't dwell too much, as perhaps their parents have tried to do.

"Tonight I can't choose, so I will have to get one tomorrow."

"Oh, but teacher, just one book, that's enough. Look at this one—*Brother Number One*! Very good, original, not a copy..."

Even I knew better than to believe that one. "I'll see you in the morning at Psar Chas for breakfast, okay?"

The next morning he didn't show up. My assistant, Ret, said she knew where he was. "He's still sleeping."

"How do you know? Did you see him?"

"Yes," she said. "He's inside his cart. Not far from here."

We shuffled through dust and motorbikes to Pub Street and spotted his cart. Rom had folded the top down so it provided some shelter—but no security—for himself and his ten-year-old brother, who was curled up next to him. They blinked as Ret woke them up.

"Hey, Rom, what time did you get to bed?" I whispered.

"Maybe four thirty," he croaked.
"Why so late?"
"The last tourists went home at that time."
"Okay, but if you want to talk on the radio today and take some pictures, come to breakfast in ten minutes," I said.

He arrived shortly afterward. Whether for the food or the cameras, I didn't know. But it didn't really matter. He showed up, and that's what counted.

Helping young street vendors

When buying a book from a book cart, be sure to have a chat with the vendor, too. This turns the interaction into something that's more than a mere exchange of dollars. The few weeks Elizabeth spent with the child booksellers of Siem Reap weren't nearly enough, but you can learn a lot from someone in just an afternoon. While their version of the truth can be ... ahem ... flexible, especially when it comes to money, it can be a mutually rewarding experience to share some time with them.

Let's make a deal

Naturally, book prices are negotiable, but bargain with a smile and don't push the vendor far. Elizabeth has heard Westerners verbally abusing kids because they wouldn't come down in price by 50 cents. Buy in volume if you want to get a discount that's fair to you both.

After all, these kids did beg once, and selling these books to you is what will keep them from doing it again. And don't give them, or any kids on the street, extra cash. Give it to NGOs who can distribute it to the kids who need it most, like the Green Gecko Project in Siem Reap.

www.greengeckoproject.org

Joanna Owen learns through teaching in Siem Reap

We arrived tired and exhausted off the bus from Phnom Penh, welcomed by the beautiful setting sun over Siem Reap. Coconut trees were silhouetted against the pink sky, and water buffalo wallowed in the cooling water of the rice fields. It wasn't long until we were relaxing with a cold Angkor beer in hand.

We were staying at Earthwalkers', a friendly guesthouse set up by some Norwegian backpackers who wanted to give something back to a country they fell in love with. The place encompasses a warm sense of homeliness, combined with the fact that it makes you, the guest, feel like you are contributing in some small way to the local community. Through a commitment to responsible tourism, guests are encouraged to stay longer and experience more than just Angkor Wat.

Amazing as they are, the wonders of Angkor push the wealth of tourism right up against the stark poverty of Cambodia. Self-preservation and a hunger for life are everywhere as kids and adults struggle to come to terms with their past, present, and future. Through Earthwalkers', we met some of the children from Sangkheum, a center that provides school support, general education, and selected vocational training to orphans and disadvantaged children.

Watching the kids' enthusiasm as they performed traditional *apsara* dances made me feel that even the smallest contribution could make a big difference. As a result, my love for Cambodia and hope for its future generations began to grow. I asked the question aloud, "What can I do?"

"You can speak English, can't you?" the Earthwalkers' fund volunteer coordinator responded. "Come back and teach."

So I did!

I returned during the wet season and spent three months volunteering with Schools for Children of Cambodia, an English charity providing free education. The children were always enthused and motivated, despite having nothing. Their resourcefulness when it comes to enjoying life makes me smile, even now, especially the vision of them using water lily stems fresh from the ponds for jump ropes. Every day was an adventure as I cycled past the lush green rice fields, through the flooded roads from the swollen Tonle Sap River, where excited kids making the most of the rainy season dove and swam.

For the first time in my life I truly understood the meaning of the word *humble*. Teaching the kids English every day was the easy part. My hardest day was saying goodbye. I had grown used to working with no electricity in the middle of nowhere with kids with no shoes, filthy clothes, and a distinct smell. Turned out I couldn't stay away long, and I have already returned once again ...

Earthwalkers' guesthouse

Now under Thai management, Earthwalkers' offers special rates for long-term volunteers. Here you will find great Khmer food, hot showers, and the opportunity to join in many community enrichment activities, including building water filters and teaching English.

Sala Kanseng Village
Sangkat 2
Siem Reap
(012) 967-901

www.earthwalkers.no

Sangkheum Center for Children

Since 2001 Sangkheum Center has provided support to more than two hundred disadvantaged children and a home for forty-eight orphans or neglected and abused children between ages four and seventeen. In earnest it lives up to the meaning of its name: hope.

SIEM REAP PROVINCE

171

Chey Village
Teukvil Commune
Siem Reap

www.sangkheum.org

Schools for Children of Cambodia

Providing free education, SCC also trains Khmer teachers and pays a better than average wage to eradicate the necessity of children paying additional classroom fees to learn. It also offers volunteers the chance to work with the children on various projects, such as English, arts, or sports.

Svay Dangkum
Siem Reap

www.schools4cambodia.org

Anna Hassett lends a helping hand outside Siem Reap

After a chance meeting with Debra Groves in Phnom Penh, I took up her offer to call in on "her village" when I was in Siem Reap. Debra, who left a wedding photography business in Australia to volunteer in Cambodia, was introduced to life in Prasat Char when asked to aid a needy family, whose father was dying of tuberculosis. Encouraged by the villagers' eagerness to help themselves, she went on to adopt the village and formed an organization called Helping Hands.

The forty-five-minute moto ride to Prasat Char from Siem Reap provided a real slice of rural life. Traveling through the scenic countryside, we passed rice fields, locals in ox carts, bicycles stacked high with produce, and small settlements of traditional wooden dwellings. The trip out to the village and the whole experience of meeting and seeing how the villagers live provided a fresh perspective on the region, beyond the Siem Reap tourist strip and well-trodden Angkor temple sites.

Prasat Char has not been inundated by visitors, and the villagers enjoy welcoming those who do come. They were keen, when I was there, to show off various Helping Hands projects. These varied from a new bridge that enables access in and out of the village during the wet season to new bicycles to vegetable gardens developed from a seed bank to small businesses.

A female village leader invited us into her home to discuss an English program community members had slated as the next priority. After my visit, just three weeks' worth of solid work on the part of the villagers—with donations from Helping Hands supporters worldwide—saw completion of the planned school building for just over $3,500.

Sopeap, a charming young Khmer man, is the sole teacher for the 270 children from the village's 280 families. He is keen on involving visitors, whether in formal teaching situations or just informal chats with small groups of students. There are opportunities for volunteers to help improve English and other skills and contribute to the fun through organizing activities around particular interests. The children have, for example, completed a garden around the school, and another visitor organized craft activities. Adult literacy is also an emerging area of village interest, and classes have recently begun.

Debra and her Cambodian assistant Chanti, who helps run Helping Hands, both have a good deal of infectious enthusiasm, but they are not the least bit pushy about bringing people on board. Most importantly, they are just happy to link up—and share their inspiring experiences—with like-minded people.

Helping Hands

While running Helping Hands, Debra supports herself financially in Cambodia as a photographer. She can be reached through the Helping Hands website.

www.helpinghandscambodia.com

KOMPONG CHHNANG

Aaron Horwitz asks "who will?" for the orphans of Cambodia

In the summer of 2007, a good friend and I embarked on a no-frills, whirlwind backpacking tour around Southeast Asia. I knew it'd be the trip of a lifetime, and sure enough, when I returned to the States two months and five countries later, I was a changed man. The experiences I'd had and the sights I'd seen had an indelible impact, but nothing hit me harder than the poverty-ravaged children on the streets of Cambodia.

"Meester, you buy postcard, one dolla!" they would cry as they walked alongside me and tugged at my shirt (and my heartstrings), trying to sell the same tired souvenirs that all the other children sold, while their parents reaped the monetary benefits. Most of these kids would never have a chance to go to school or ride a bicycle, simple things we take for granted. In fact, many would end up abandoned altogether, left alone on the streets to fend for themselves before they even finished losing their baby teeth.

KOMPONG CHHNANG PROVINCE

While sitting on my dad's plush couch in the living room of his mansion high in the Hollywood Hills, I couldn't shake these images. But what could I do? I was just one man, and an unemployed one at that. So when a friend I met along the way, a lovely young Australian woman named Georgie Walsh, informed me of a new project she was embarking on, I nearly jumped out of my seat.

Before and after my time in Southeast Asia, Georgie was volunteering as a fundraising coordinator at a rather large orphanage just outside Phnom Penh. The orphanage, which at the time housed seventy-two children, seemed like a shining beacon of hope in an otherwise dark territory. But as Georgie spent more time there, she learned that all was not well.

The orphanage, as she would uncover, was run by several Cambodians who were secretly siphoning donors' money for their own personal use. The men were having generous contributors transfer money into their personal accounts rather than the official ones Georgie had set up, and spending it on whiskey and cigarettes instead of children's necessities like toiletries and schooling. As an example, there was only one toothbrush for all the boys to share and one for all the girls.

Unable to tolerate it, Georgie left the orphanage, but her attachment to the children of Cambodia was not broken. She had made alliances with several influential Westerners while in Phnom Penh, including Gerald

Trevor and Jane Oliver. These two, like Georgie, were strong in both influence and spirit, and together their mutual love for the children drove them to create a wonderful new orphanage all of their own, free of corruption and government influence.

It started small, with a simple soup kitchen in an apartment, but a short time later, the Who Will orphanage was founded. After being informed by Georgie of the plans to start the orphanage—which would include housing units and a school and library—I organized a fundraiser with some friends in Los Angeles to see if I could help. Jane and Georgie sent me a blueprint for the new orphanage, along with detailed biographies and countless photos of each of their children, so I could provide all attendees with more than enough information on where their donations were going.

I was also given staggering financial figures. For a mere $70, we could feed the entire orphanage for a week. It only cost an additional $2 per child per day to send each to school and buy them clothing. Apparently, I wasn't the only one blown away, as our modest fundraiser managed to raise over $6,000.

Since we donated, the feedback from Who Will has been outstanding. They keep us updated with detailed letters and stories from the children and photos of their escapades. Our money is spent exactly how we ask it to be, and we always feel secure when we make donations, seeing in the smiling faces of each of the children their modest hopes and dreams slowly becoming realized due to the care and love they receive.

I constantly hope and dream of the day I can go visit them at their new stomping grounds, so I can give them all massive hugs—Georgie, Jane, and Gerald included. If you ever happen to be in the Kompong Chhang area, please do them, yourself, and me a favor and drop by to say hello. You never know; it could change your life.

Who Will

Since this essay was written, Who Will moved the children from their Phnom Penh home to their brand-new children's village near Kompong Chhang in central Cambodia. The number of children being looked after and schooled has now reached forty-five. Telephone and email contact information can be found on the orphanage website.

www.who-will.org

KAMPOT

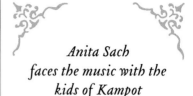

Anita Sach faces the music with the kids of Kampot

A spur of the moment decision in 1988 was to change the direction of my life. I was traveling around Vietnam, developing programs for a specialist tour operator in the UK, when I was invited to tag along with a dozen Americans visiting Cambodia. Tourist numbers were a mere trickle at the time, and Phnom Penh airport was a shell of a building with cows and dogs wandering through as we cleared immigration. The hotels were basic and the infrastructure poor. Many of the residents of the city were still squatting in wrecked apartment blocks, with no running water and noxious open sewers.

My strongest memory from that first visit was the friendliness and generosity of the people. Our arrival caused great excitement as it meant that Cambodia was back on the tourist map, if only in a very small way. We each adopted a cyclo driver who took delight in showing us around. Using a combination of Pidgin English and French, we learned of their personal experiences during the Khmer

Rouge years. Nobody had gotten away unscathed, and many were the only survivors from their family. But they were unfailingly cheerful and very reliable. From that time on I was hooked, and on subsequent visits I always returned home having been humbled by the people I met, their optimism, and their warmth.

This was to happen again in 1999, when I was researching the Bradt guide to Cambodia, although this time it wasn't a Cambodian who inspired me, but a young British woman. In a *Daily Telegraph* article, I had read about Catherine Geach and how she had set up the Kampot Traditional Music School for handicapped and orphaned children. I spent an hour in her company, touring the school and meeting the children and staff. An accomplished musician, Catherine had worked at the Royal University of Fine Arts in Phnom Penh, where she realized that there was a role for her in reviving Cambodian traditional Pin-Peat and Mahouri music. In 1994 she set up a school in Kampot, where orphaned, abandoned, or disabled children are taken care of, educated, and taught about the rich culture of Khmer music and dance.

Catherine herself had lived in Cambodia since 1991 and spoke the language fluently. Her whole demeanor had become distinctly Cambodian, and she moved with extraordinary grace. At the time she lived onsite, in one small, plain room, so that she could guide the staff and be on hand for the children. The sense of fun and love was palpable, and the children were excited by and curious about our visit. There were simple but neat dormitories, classrooms, a dining room, and bathroom, and most importantly, a future for these disadvantaged kids. Educated to the age of sixteen—something we take for granted in the UK—learning to be proficient musicians, and reviving tradition in a country whose culture had been devastated, all thanks to Catherine and her extraordinary team.

Kampot Traditional Music School

Although Catherine is no longer based in Cambodia full-time, her legacy continues. The staff ensures that the children are educated and cared for and learn about Cambodia's traditional music, so that they in turn can hand down this skill to future generations. The school is located two blocks off the riverfront in Kampot, behind the Old Market. It is open from 8:00 to 11:00 a.m. and 6:30 to 9:00 p.m. Monday through Friday. There is no charge to visit, but donations are welcome.

www.kampot-music-school.com

Dickon Verey gives as he takes tea and cake in Kampot

If you are looking for something a little different, Kampot is definitely worth a visit. The town features classic old colonial architecture, as well as being the natural jumping-off point if you want to seek out the abandoned hill station at Bokor or relax at the quiet beach at Kep. Until the late 1990s, Kampot was rarely visited because Khmer Rouge lived in the surrounding countryside. Nowadays that has changed, and new restaurants and guesthouses have sprung up to handle the increase in tourist numbers.

My favorite place to spend a few hours when I'm in Kampot is the Epic Arts Café. The café was the idea of Hal and Katie, expatriates who have spent the last five years in Cambodia. A husband-and-wife combo, they arrived in Kampot and discovered that there were no cafés to suit their penchant for four o'clock tea. As both of them take being English very seriously, this was clearly a situation that needed to be remedied. Along with lack of a proper venue for afternoon tea, they also realized that Kampot lacked training and job opportunities for locals with disabilities. As a result the café was founded, supported by Epic Arts, an NGO run by Katie, dedicated to helping Cambodians with disabilities through the arts.

Vee (known for her high-pitched giggle) and Chuon run the kitchen, churning out all manner of delicious cakes and tasty snacks—the carrot cake and jam sponge being particular favorites of mine. They also produce a selection of thirst-quenching beverages. Their "lemon juice" (*krouch-ma*) is amongst the best I have had in Cambodia. Recently they started mak-ing various savory items, the highlight of which is an excellent quiche.

Menus provide detailed explanations on how to make your requests using Khmer sign language. I must admit that ordering from the deaf waiters and waitresses is something of an experience, but at the same time this very much incorporates the unique Epic spirit.

While at the café, take the time to chat with Katie or Leakhana, who can be found in the office behind the kitchen. Check out a workshop going on upstairs; Katie is well-known for her energetic dance routines. Or slip next door to Hal's office, where you can learn about his work for a local NGO, Sahmakum Teang Tnaut, which focuses on housing and community infrastructure. In every way, Katie and Hal are working to better the lives of Cambodians, and you can begin to help, too, simply by ordering tea and cake the next time you're in Kampot.

Epic Arts Café

The café is located in the center of Kampot, three blocks from the river and on the same street as the old (and unused) market. It is open from 7:00 a.m. to 6:00 p.m. Profits fund dance, music, and arts workshops for deaf and disabled Cambodians.

www.epicarts.org.uk
www.teangtnaut.org

SIHANOUKVILLE

Doug Mendel gets fired up about helping out in Sihanoukville

I could not have imagined—at the tail end of a six-week trip through Asia in 1997—that three days in Phnom Penh and Siem Reap would so captivate my heart and lead me on an adventure unlike any other. The strikingly beautiful, caring, and giving people; the heat and humidity that permeated every inch of my body; the culture's simplistic, Buddhist, and bonding nature have lured me back many times to soak up everything that is Cambodia.

On my third trip in 2001, I was in Sihanoukville, a busy beach town on the southwest coastline. Walking back to my guesthouse, I saw a fire station, which caught my attention since I am a volunteer fire fighter in the United States. Returning home I had an idea that maybe I could help that one station in Sihanoukville. I talked to my fire chief to see if the department had anything that could be donated to a needy station, eight thousand miles away from the Colorado Rockies.

Two years later I visited Sihanoukville armed with three boxes of station wear shirts, pants, and boots. It was the start of a great friendship with that Cambodian fire station. During the past years, the station has received much-needed bunker gear (coats, pants, helmets, boots, Nomex hoods, gloves) so that the men are better protected when fighting fires. When the fire captain asked me for a fire truck in 2004, I told him, "Give me two years, and I'll have one for you." Although it may have seemed like an impossible request, with lots of patience and media exposure, I was able to stay true to my word. In 2006 I delivered a donated fire truck from Breckenridge, Colorado, to the fire station in Sihanoukville.

Because Cambodia was under civil war for a couple of decades, various levels of the infrastructure are in great need of assistance. Since I was a volunteer fire fighter, it was the fire stations in Cambodia that caught my attention. I started small with a few boxes of donated gear, and now I'm helping eight stations across the country. I bring up to eight hundred pounds of supplies to help the various stations on each of my regular visits. If you are as fortunate as I am to discover a cause that speaks to you—and there are many in Cambodia to choose from—you can soon find yourself making a valuable contribution that will help the country just as much as it enriches your own life.

Finding your cause

Along with supporting Cambodia's fire fighters, Doug also helps organizations in Sihanoukville that assist disadvantaged street children (M'Lop Tapang) and disabled children (The Starfish Project), by providing clothing, stuffed animals, games, school supplies, toothbrushes, and toothpaste.

www.mloptapang.org
www.starfishcambodia.org

STUNG TRENG

David Shamash supports the silk weavers of Stung Treng

Stung Treng is a rather nice little town—a bit scruffy, but possessing a certain charm. A big market with the best coffee ever and a hotel with lovely views over the Sekong, a river that flows into the Mekong a mile or so away. However, Stung Treng's problem is that just about everyone regards it as a stepping-stone on the way to or from the nearby border with Laos. A new road and bridge have made an overnight stop here almost unnecessary.

But back in 2003, my wife Diana and I decided to visit. We were sitting on the terrace outside our hotel room when someone came up and handed us a leaflet about a new project aimed at educating women in basic literacy, hygiene, and child care, and then training them as spinners and weavers of silk. As we, unlike most other Westerners, were spending a few days exploring the region, we took off on our rented bicycles to visit the project, a few kilometers out of town.

When we got there we were welcomed by Chan, the general manager, and given a tour to show us the spinning, dyeing, and weaving processes, as well as the kindergarten where there was a full-time teacher to look after the workers' children. What was really noticeable was the smile on every face. We had never seen so many people happy to be working, earning a good living producing beautiful things. The products were stunning: beautifully soft silk scarves, bags, and throws in subtle colors, all set out for sale in the showroom, and at irresistibly low prices too.

When we got back to England, we wanted to help the project, so my company sent enough money to cover the year's deficit. In that way they could go forward into the next year free of financial worries. Since then further funding from us and others has enabled the project to grow from employing less than thirty to nearly one hundred, thus supporting several hundred people who were previously living in poverty in the surrounding villages.

That chance encounter on the hotel terrace not only changed the lives of so many Cambodians but also has drawn us back to Stung Treng time after time, to visit a project that is now an essential part of our life too.

Stung Treng Women's Development Centre

The center is located about four kilometers from town. Go along the river, past the new bridge across the Sekong, and you will find it on your left. As well as touring the workshops, take time to visit the showroom and have a drink or snack in the café. You can also visit a Mekong Blue showroom on Street 130 in Phnom Penh, which opened with funding from the Lonely Planet Foundation.

www.mekongblue.com

GENERAL CAMBODIA

Dougald O'Reilly gets friendly with Cambodia's at-risk heritage

Cambodia is famed for its jungle-clad temples peering through the foliage, mysterious smiles on huge stone faces. This heritage is one of its most important resources, yet it is alarmingly under threat. As interest in the ancient Khmer empire grows, so has the demand for artifacts from Cambodia's past. This has led to the most heartrending and wanton destruction of some of humankind's greatest creations.

Beautifully sculpted temples lost in the forest, untouched for centuries, are being hacked away and dismantled. Archaeological sites containing the remains of pre-Angkorian peoples are being churned up in search of booty, human remains scattered across empty fields. Valuable sites have been destroyed, and with them any chance of understanding the rise of this ancient civilization.

It is illegal to purchase antiques in Cambodia, and doing so can lead to arrest and punishment, as some unfortunate individuals have already discovered. Still, many people—including travelers—continue to do so without giving it a second thought. It is possible to help preserve Cambodia's heritage simply by not participating in this trade. If tourists cease buying relics such as stone and glass beads, pottery, and stone tools, the market will shrink.

Beginning in 2003, travelers can help promote heritage, arts, culture, and social development in Cambodia by patronizing shops and businesses that display the Heritage Friendly logo. This logo means the business has been certified by an independent organization and seeks to reward those who care about Cambodia and give back to the local community. If the current rate of destruction continues unabated, there will be little left of Cambodia's ancient past, and what does remain will be irreparably damaged. So during your visit, help those who help Cambodia by shopping in Heritage Friendly establishments.

Heritage Watch

Heritage Watch is a nonprofit organization dedicated to the preservation of Southeast Asia's cultural heritage. It was founded in 2003 as a result of a sharp increase in the destruction of Cambodia's precious treasures, especially the looting of ancient temples and cemetery sites nationwide.

www.heritagewatchinternational.org

Don Gilliland finds sustenance for AIDS patients in Cambodia

It was December of 2000, just two days before the end of the year, and I was stranded in Cambodia. A short Angkor trip had turned into a multiweek ordeal after I lost my passport. Getting a replacement from the embassy was a relatively simple matter, but because I now lacked an exit visa, I was forced to play the waiting game. With government ministries closed for the long holiday period, processing my application might take up to three weeks. I barely had enough money to last me three more days, so what could I do?

I did have one friend who lived in Phnom Penh, but she was visiting her family in the United States at the time of my crisis. I sent her an email, and I received a prompt reply, inviting me to stay at her apartment. She told me her friend Beth would give me a key. I phoned Beth and arranged to meet her at a bakery on Sihanoukville Boulevard. When she walked through the door, I did a double take: the woman before me was a short, almost pixie-like figure, wearing a loose white shirt and black trousers—and sporting a shaved head. With a big grin she stuck out a hand and introduced herself: Beth Goldring, Zen Buddhist nun.

During our conversation I found out that Beth was originally a university humanities teacher in Chicago and a veteran human rights worker in the Middle East. We discovered that we both liked to travel and shared a passion for the music of Richard Thompson. Ordained as a Zen nun in 1995, Beth made her first visit to Cambodia in May 1996 with the Dhammayietra (annual peace walk) and relocated to Phnom Penh that October. Four years later she formed Brahmavihara/Cambodia AIDS Project, a Buddhist organization that provides chaplaincy and social work services to destitute AIDS patients.

Many AIDS patients are ostracized by Cambodian society and even abandoned by their own families. Brahmavihara helps provide them with a voice and to make peace with their suffering. From its inception Brahmavihara has worked closely with organizations that provide food, money, and medicine, helping people to access available resources. Since the introduction and availability of free antiretroviral medicines, the social work side of Brahmavihara's mission has expanded even further. But its primary focus remains being a resource for those dying without access to Buddhist spiritual support. With her extremely capable Khmer staff, Beth offers chanting, meditation, healing touch Reiki, and a range of other emotional and spiritual resources.

"The most gratifying thing for me about what we do," says Beth, "is seeing the beauty that arises, even under terrible conditions, as people make peace with their lives and deaths.

I think the hardest thing is adjusting to major new issues. Right now we are dealing with patients developing cancer on top of their AIDS, and with new forms of tuberculosis for which medicines aren't available. Thankfully, the Buddha's teachings are really useful precisely when we reach our limits and need to develop deeper compassion."

The work that Beth and her staff do takes an incredible amount of courage, compassion, and dedication. Unfortunately, it also requires money. In late 2006 Brahmavihara launched a website that explains their mission, shares the personal histories of some of their patients, and outlines their expenses and estimated budget. Take a look and learn more about how you can help this life-affirming cause.

Brahmavihara

Brahmavihara/Cambodia AIDS Project is overseen by the Empty Hand Zen Center in the United States. Even though Brahmavihara is located in Cambodia, donations made to it through the center are tax-exempt under U.S. laws. Checks should be made out to Empty Hand Zen Center and must include a notation that they are for the "Cambodian AIDS Project," otherwise the donation will not reach Brahmavihara.

45 Lawton Street
New Rochelle, NY 10801

www.brahmavihara.cambodia
aidsproject.org

goldring@forum.org.kh

Christina Heyniger cycles for education across Cambodia

I have been cranking the pedals on my mountain bike since dawn, over bumpy dirt roads through a cool mist into midmorning heat. As I marvel at the panorama unfolding before me—the green of rice paddies and fields of dry crops, village houses on stilts adorned with bright pink curtains fluttering over doorways and windows—I repeatedly wonder whether I really have it in me to cycle like this for fourteen days.

I am riding my bike across Cambodia.

I have never been on a multiday bicycle trip in my life, and yet here I am, panniers loaded, tires pumped, helmet buckle neatly snapped in place—on my first day of a two-week journey through the rugged beauty of rural Cambodia. I've joined a PEPY trip (Protect the Earth, Protect Yourself), during which I'll discover not only that I can cycle for days through the countryside but also that as a participant in a program to support Cambodian school kids, I can also make a small contribution to meaningful improvements in the lives of deserving children.

PEPY's Cambodia cycle ride takes us from Siem Reap, through Phnom Penh, and down into Sihanoukville, stopping along the way to deliver school supplies and teach classes about environmental awareness to Cambodian kids. A centerpiece of the program is the Bike-to-School Program, in which bicycles are awarded to primary school kids with excellent academic performance and attendance, to help them continue their education through secondary school—schools that are not within walking distance of their villages. Since its first ride in December 2005, PEPY has raised over $100,000 to support American Assistance for Cambodia, Japan Relief for Cambodia, and the PEPY Ride School.

My PEPY trip turns out to be an adventure in every sense. Our travel route is varied and rough. We all have to carry our own gear, and we stay in villages and small towns, experiencing the "real" Cambodia as we go. I learn that traveling from the seat of a bike, propelling myself through a country rather than sitting sheltered on a bus, allows for a communication with the environment and its people that is unmatched.

Frequently kids wave at me from their work in the fields, energetically yelling "hello!" as I ride along. Motos and carts pulled by water buffalo slow as they grind past me, drivers and passengers craning their necks to get a look at this cycling oddity in the funny shorts and big helmet. Everyone smiles.

On the few days we ride the main roads, flatbed trucks overflowing with workers honk politely to let me know they're coming up behind—the people on board all waving and smiling, point-

183

ing at me as they fly by. One woman, her head wrapped in a red-checked *krama*, drives by on a moto, a wicker basket filled with greens strapped on the seat just behind her. She stops to talk to someone, and I pedal past her, waving. Later, she overtakes me again, slowing and beeping, and this time we wave at each other like old friends as she chugs past.

As the days pass, I come to understand this type of easy acceptance and familiarity as the common currency in Cambodia. It becomes so in our group, as well, as our team of foreign cyclists quickly develops a strong camaraderie. I notice also the ease with which we adapt our pace to natural rhythms—rising early, resting in noonday heat, relaxing and laughing over group dinners before falling into bed each night.

In the end I feel the trip expands my mind and heart. The physical effort of biking tires me. The constant presence of welcoming Cambodian people and the vast countryside comforts me. The school visits educate me in the challenges of developing-world education. And in interacting with kids I would never otherwise have met, I reunite with that oft-neglected sense of playfulness and joy of which we busy Westerners seem to so frequently lose sight.

PEPY cycle tours

If you would like to participate in a PEPY ride across Cambodia, more information can be found on the organization's website.

www.pepyride.org

Robert Tompkins ponders giving great and small

As soon as my wife and I entered Phnom Penh's bustling Russian Market, we were approached by a girl no older than fourteen, who carried a baby wrapped in a dirty blanket. "Baby sick," she said with outstretched hand. Strolling vendors, most of them disabled or very young, wended their way through the welter of constricted passageways. A woman whose face was badly disfigured by burns struggled to smile as she displayed her assortment of postcards. With a touch like a feather, a ragged child put her hand on my arm and then gestured to her mouth.

Anticipating the heat, we had brought half a liter of water each, and soon we were taking the last sips of the now warm and bitter liquid. After we purchased more, a young girl dressed in a filthy white dress approached and pointed at the bottle. When we gave her one, she drank greedily, finishing it in three long gulps. We gave her the second bottle, and she quickly vanished down a crowded lane.

Displaying a T-shirt with a skull and crossbones and the words "Danger Beware of Landmines," a vendor smiled and suggested, "Cheap souvenir from Cambodia." Farther down the aisle a man on crutches dragged himself in front of us, pointed to his missing leg, and then gave the poignant utterance, "Boom. Give me money."

Like water around a rock, the throngs flowed past a mother who had parked herself and her baby in the middle of an aisle, her hand outstretched for alms. Alongside were stalls of grains in swollen bags and fruit sellers with heaps of rose apples, bananas, mangos, and rambutan. A vendor of books and postcards pointed at his prosthetic leg and then to his mouth. With a barely audible whisper, a mother carrying a baby extended a battered metal bowl and stared with imploring eyes. Proffering a garland of jasmine flowers, a girl of about six stood expectantly, her face unsmiling and cheerless.

A cynic might dismiss the expressions on the beggars' faces, the sadness in their eyes, as a well-honed skill calculated to rip at the heart and thereby induce giving. We are not cynics. The looks in their eyes still haunt.

Three hours later, we left the immense souk, having seen about half of what the market had to offer, but more than enough wretchedness. As we entered the Foreign Correspondents' Club, a teenager wearing a Nike baseball hat pushed a wheelchair containing an armless and legless man who growled, "Give me money. Give me money."

We chatted for a while with two NGO workers who had been in Phnom Penh for just over a year. They told depressing stories: parents making their children beg instead of sending them to school, organized gangs forcing children to beg and then stealing whatever money they made, the sex junkets from Japan and Korea that exploited the desperation of young girls.

"When I first arrived in Cambodia," one said, "I bought new clothes for two street kids wearing filthy rags. Two days later, I saw them huddled in a storefront, dressed in dirty tatters again."

"You get used to it after a while," the other observed, taking a sip of his Angkor beer. "Frequency brings a degree of emotional immunity. You can't let the despair gnaw at you. You become acclimatized, almost impervious."

"Then the helping can start."

Their stories continued with their witnessed incidents of human suffering, of lives without hopes and dreams. We left the FCC drained and returned to our hotel, where we attempted to purge the imagery of limbless land mine victims, expressionless children gesturing to their mouths, and pleading mothers carrying infants. It was impossible. We were left with the question: What can we do?

Both of the NGO workers had agreed that money should be given to beggars, even though many charity workers were opposed to this on the grounds that it only encourages more begging. "Give a little," we were told, instead, "perhaps 500 riel, maybe 1,000, and make larger donations to the local charity organizations."

While this would not help us forget what we had seen, it was a reminder that contributing in both large and small ways is essential to help alleviate the pain that is so much a part of Cambodia's daily life.

How to give

You have to follow your heart regarding the city's many beggars. If you do give, try to do so discreetly, or you will be swarmed by very insistent others. Along with money, bottled water is always welcome.

Debbie Watkins defines the meaning of responsible tourism

Let's get a few things clear about what responsible tourism is not.

It is *not* descending on a small village in the middle of nowhere armed with a huge supply of beer (or something stronger) and getting trashed. It is *not* buying ancient tribal artifacts because they'll look good on your sideboard at home. It is *not* giving to beggars.

Not giving to beggars, you may ask?

Surely that's helping the poorest people, and a very responsible and worthy act? For you, the tourist visiting from a country that provides for its needy, to see people who obviously have nothing asking you for only a small sum of money is a heartrending experience. "Maybe," you think, "by giving them just a dollar they will be able to feed themselves today." "Maybe," you think, "I can help them get back on their feet and find some work."

This is unfortunately rarely the case, and all too often you are in fact encouraging someone to remain a

beggar. Whatever their circumstances, beggars have no incentive to try to better themselves if they get enough money by begging. One of the negative impacts of giving in a developing country is the cycle of a "dependency society"—one that has become so conditioned to receiving something for nothing that it grows to expect it.

So what can you do to break this cycle? Give something back in a way that you know will be put to good use.

In Cambodia, there are many not-for-profit organizations that are working directly with "street people." Rather than just blindly giving, they are working together with those who want to help themselves, with those who need rehabilitation and want to make something of their lives.

Some projects have outreach workers, who go onto the streets to provide education and medical care, or social workers, who listen to young people's stories and try to help them reconcile with their families. Drug rehabilitation, safe houses to sleep in, and vocational training are all provided to those who want to make a fresh start. Centers provide care for rape victims and victims of human trafficking, often barely in their teens. Other groups offer homes and land for whole families, education for children, livelihood training for parents. The entry requirements for these are often tough—no alcoholics, gamblers, or those who are not prepared to work.

Projects like this are happy for you to visit, to see the work that they are doing. Talk to the people they are helping—see how they feel about the opportunities they've been given, about the hope they now feel for their future. When thinking about how you can pay it forward, remember the saying: "Give a man a fish, and he has food for a day. Teach a man to fish, and he has food for the rest of his life."

Opt for the rest of his life.

Giving in Cambodia

A number of NGOs are happy to show you around their projects if you request an appointment. As well, socially responsible tour operators such as Carpe Diem Travel include visits to such organizations as part of their itineraries and also cover bank charges and manage how donations are spent for travelers who wish to help.

www.carpe-diem-travel.com

Recommended charities

The Cambodia Trust

Set up to help Cambodia's disabled population, the trust's programs range from rehabilitation and job training to human rights advocacy.

www.cambodiatrust.com

Friends

Based in Phnom Penh, this organization works with street kids. Goals include rescuing children from human trafficking, providing basic education, and offering job skills training through programs such as running a restaurant for travelers.

www.friends-international.org

Kantha Bopha Foundation

Started by Dr. Beat Richner, this foundation has built five hospitals providing free health care for children and a maternity ward serving mothers with HIV.

www.beatocello.com

Sunrise Children's Villages

This group is involved in helping orphans in Phnom Penh and Siem Reap with education and health care. Through various programs, you can sponsor an individual child, provide items from the organization's "wish list," and even visit and spend time with the children.

www.sunrisechildrensvillage.org

RESOURCES FOR THE ROAD

Practical advice to help you prepare for your travels

When visiting many countries, knowledge of history is not essential to a satisfying travel experience. This is not true for Cambodia. You *must* find time to do some research before you leave home. Studying the timeline of Angkor, especially, will help you appreciate the temples: their development, building styles, and the great god-kings who built them. It will also explain why France had such a strong interest in and influence over Cambodia, and that in turn will lead you on to the terrible excesses of the Khmer Rouge and how that has affected everything and everyone in modern-day Cambodia. The scars of the Pol Pot time still run deep, even though over half the population was born after the regime ended.

For grasping Cambodian history and culture, books are the natural place to start. In the 1990s it was almost impossible to find books about Cambodia, but that has changed dramatically. This chapter reflects that growing library with a well-rounded sampler, as writers weigh in on contemporary classics such as *Cambodia Now* and *Sideshow*, as well as lesser-read volumes like *The Mekong Exploration Commission Report (1866-1868)—Volume 1*. While their lists are selective, the subject matter is comprehensive, taking Cambodia from prehistoric times to the present. As well, they fan out to include Khmer comics and cookbooks.

Sadly, Internet resources about Cambodia are lacking. It remains one of the least exposed Southeast Asian countries on the web. That said, there are some useful, well-established online resources, and I have done my best to gather them here. In that same vein, I have chosen a small but what I feel is important collection of films, from the well-known *The Killing Fields* to the more obscure but essential *The Tenth Dancer*. Whilst its neighbor Vietnam has had its fair share of movies made about it, Cambodia is still behind on that front, although documentary filmmakers have begun to cast their net over the country, and the situation improves year after year.

Buddhist novice smiling at Angkor Wat

As the writers here prove, there are many ways to "research" Cambodia, from discovering its unique brand of rock 'n' roll music from the 1960s to studying the Khmer language. And if I haven't convinced you that a little background homework will make your trip all the better, I'm sure you'll realize it for yourself once you arrive. If that's the case, this chapter can still be of help by directing you to a local bookstore or sending you to two phenomenal resources. Once you've spent time at the Documentation Center of Cambodia or Bophana Audiovisual Resource Center, you'll be addicted to the story that makes up Cambodia's rich history.

Book Recommendations

Editor's Choice: Books

A Cambodian Odyssey
by Haing Ngor, with Roger Warner

If you thought Haing Ngor's acting performance in *The Killing Fields* was spellbinding, then I urge you to read his miraculous memoir and realize that his own personal story was even more harrowing and heartwrenching than any Hollywood movie could portray. Haing Ngor, who won an Academy Award for his performance as Dith Pran in the film, sadly was murdered by a street gang in Los Angeles in February 1996.

Images of the Gods: Khmer Mythology in Cambodia, Laos & Thailand
by Vittorio Roveda

The temples of Angkor are a magical draw for visitors to Cambodia. The structures themselves are incredible, but it's the intricate carvings that adorn their walls and doorways—telling the lives and legends of Hindu gods and heroes—that few understand better than Vittorio Roveda. His definitive 544-page tome is the culmination of meticulous research into these sculptures that many marvel at but few fully understand.

River of Time
by Jon Swain

A nostalgic, passionate, and personal love story from a journalist who lived through the Vietnam and Cambodia wars and survived, when many of his fellow journalists didn't. He includes a firsthand account of life in the French Embassy in the first days of the Khmer Rouge takeover in Phnom Penh, a scene perfectly encapsulated in the movie *The Killing Fields*. Swain was *The Sunday Times*'s correspondent in Paris for many years.

When Broken Glass Floats:
Growing Up under the Khmer Rouge
by Chanrithy Him

Khmer Rouge survivor stories have become fairly commonplace in the last decade, but Chanrithy Him's story is so well written, so expressive, and so painful that it's a must for anyone interested in this period of Cambodia's turbulent history. It's a truly inspiring story of survival and courage in the face of adversity. Today, Chanrithy Him is a public speaker, classical dancer, writer, and aspiring screenwriter. Her sequel, *Unbroken Spirit*, has yet to be published.

Runners-up
Along with these top choices, I must give honorable mention to a handful of books that are definitely worth checking out—some of which are noted by *To Cambodia With Love* writers in the following sections. They include my recommended temple guide, *Ancient Angkor* by Claude Jacques and Michael Freeman; memoirs from Somaly Mam (*The Road of Lost Innocence*), Geraldine Cox (*Home Is Where the Heart Is*), and Kari Grady Grossman (*Bones That Float: A Story of Adopting Cam-*

bodia); novels by Geoff Ryman (*The King's Last Song*) and Christopher J. Koch (*Highways to a War*); and David Chandler's chilling exposé of the Khmer Rouge's detention center Tuol Sleng (*Voices from S-21*).

Shopping for books
A wealth of books about Cambodia can be found in shops in Phnom Penh (Monument Books, etc.) and Siem Reap, as well as at the airport. For used copies of books, check out the reliable AbeBooks website.

www.monument-books.com
www.abebooks.com

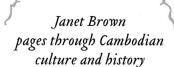

Janet Brown
pages through Cambodian
culture and history

Cambodia Now
by Karen Coates
photographs by Jerry Redfern

Travelers to Cambodia are aware of the country's past—the glorious history of the Angkor Empire and the inglorious era of the Khmer Rouge years. It's a very Western desire to see a happy ending while traveling in that corner of the world—but it isn't there, at least not to the untutored eye. Karen Coates and Jerry Redfern lived in Phnom Penh in 1998, when the city was wracked by turbulence, trauma, and the aftermath of tragedy. Talking to everyone they can, they chronicle in *Cambodia Now* how people in a broken country struggle to stay alive—and how they try to help each other. This book will break your heart while it opens your eyes. It is essential reading for anyone who plans to spend any time in Cambodia. Unfortunately, although this was written in the late '90s, this book still describes Cambodia, now.

Crossing Three Wildernesses
by U Sam Oeur

Cambodia, U Sam Oeur explains, is a land of dreams and spirits, haunted by its history. His autobiography preserves seventy years of his country's turbulent past, from the days of French colonialism through the horror of the Khmer Rouge, and gives a colorful depiction of a culture that was almost destroyed by the regime of Pol Pot. Born a farmer's son in 1936, U Sam Oeur began his education as a naked schoolboy in a country village and finished with a Master of Fine Arts in creative writing from The University of Iowa. After living in the United States for seven years, he returned to Cambodia in 1968, married, and became a United Nations delegate months before the Khmer Rouge entered Phnom Penh and the horror of the Pol Pot years began. This is one of the few accounts written by an adult survivor of that era, describing an amazing and terrible odyssey. U Sam Oeur now lives in Texas, where he writes poetry and translates Walt Whitman into Khmer.

The Gate
by François Bizot

A Khmer-speaking Frenchman, François Bizot hunted for old manuscripts and art that would illuminate the religion and customs of ancient Cambodia. A man whose only gods were Saul Steinberg and Charlie Parker, Bizot inhabited a world that was "enameled with paddy fields, dotted with temples, a country of peace and simplicity." Then the war in Vietnam spilled over the border into Cambodia and, while working thirty miles from Phnom Penh with two of his Cambodian colleagues, Bizot and his companions were captured by a group of Khmer Rouge. He was the only prisoner held by the infamous Duch who was given his freedom—and later one of the only foreigners to witness the haunted emptiness of the evacuated city of Phnom Penh. His story, lived in Khmer, written in French, and translated into English, provides a stunning testimony to the horrors of the Pol Pot time.

Highways to a War
by Christopher J. Koch

Phnom Penh was a city that flourished and floundered and fell between the years of 1965-1975. A city "of charmed peace ... which no longer exists, which will never exist again," Phnom Penh attracted journalists "like a whole mislaid life" that was both exotic and familiar. A war lay beyond the enchantment of the city, down the highways, and journalists traveled to it in taxis. One of them was Mike Langford, a photographer who drew closer to the war as he fell in love first with Phnom Penh, then with its inhabitants, and finally with a Khmer journalist whose fierce love for her country fed Langford's own passion for it. The attachment that Cambodia still inspires in so many foreigners is well described in this novel of a vanished world and some of the people who dissolved with it.

The Road of Lost Innocence
by Somaly Mam
www.somaly.org

When Somaly Mam was told by a European Union representative in Phnom Penh that "there are no prostitutes in Cambodia," her response was blunt and immediate. "Madame," she told the representative, who had lived in Cambodia for "at least a year," "You're living in a world of air-conditioned hotels and offices. This isn't an air-conditioned country. Go outdoors and take a look around." Nobody knew better than Somaly that the representative was misinformed. Not only was she the founder of an organization that helped women who worked in brothels in her own neighborhood, she had also been sold into prostitution herself when she was sixteen. For three years, Somaly was a slave, living in a world of filth, violence, and fear. It is difficult to read about her years as a prostitute; it must have been excruciating to write about them. Her book is a document of courage and persistence—read it, give it to others, and help wherever and however you can.

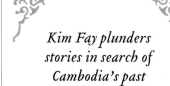

Kim Fay plunders stories in search of Cambodia's past

One of the most interesting parts about writing a historical novel is the background reading. When that novel happens to be about colonial-era Cambodia and the looting of the Angkor temples, it gets even better. Hours that I should have spent writing were instead lost in books ... about thieves, explorers, and the history of the Khmer. While I could easily recommend fifty wonderful volumes, I have pared my list down to a modest five, which I feel give an eclectic, rather than comprehensive, view of Cambodia's cultural heritage and life during French colonial rule.

Angkor and the Khmer Civilization
by Michael D. Coe

To complement Dawn Rooney's essential *Angkor* (see page 48) and get a deeper understanding of Cambodian history, including the ancient civilization that led up to the Angkorean period, this book is your next step on the road of Khmer scholarship. A bit more academic, it is still an enjoyable read, especially when it comes to descriptions of daily life in the Khmer kingdom. It also contains a fascinating chapter on the decline of the classic Khmer period, which sheds light on how the country evolved to the place you see when you visit today.

Silk Roads
by Axel Madsen

While this is not a very well-written book, the story (a true one) carries it. In the early 1920s, a young French couple, Andre and Clara Malraux, decided to rob a Cambodian temple—using the misguided reasoning that the government had no right to claim such treasures for itself. Communism was a passionate hobby for many bored intellectuals at that time, and it brought with it an audacity that can only occur during certain eras. In this case, the wake of dissatisfaction that followed WWI. Armed with this conceit, the Malrauxs stormed into Cambodia and ripped a massive bas-relief from the walls of Banteay Srei. As for how their story ended, you must read the book. If you can, also try to get your hands on Clara's *Memoirs*. Told in her own voice, the story becomes one of gender and social hierarchy as well as adventure.

The Royal Way
by Andre Malraux

Andre's version of looting a Cambodian temple, here in fiction form, is telling in its masculine tone and overt rebuttal to the real life situation he endured. *The Royal Way* serves as an illuminating companion story for those whose interest is piqued by *Silk Roads*.

A Pilgrimage to Angkor
by Pierre Loti

I recommend that you read this short book in one sitting, while perched somewhere quiet in the Angkor Wat complex—perhaps out back by the moat overlooking the temple. Despite the crowds of tourists, it is still possible to drift back to 1901, as Loti describes his brief visit to the temples—in a present tense voice, which gives his story a nice immediacy. Although he can tend toward the cynical, his writing is overly dramatic at times. It must be read in context. In the twenty-first century, Angkor Wat still has the ability to take the breath away. Imagine what it must have been like more than a century ago, to be one of the first Westerners to view this incredible place.

Travels in Cambodia and Part of Laos
by Francis Garnier

Officially *The Mekong Exploration Commission Report (1866-1868)—Volume 1*, this book shows Cambodia before the arrival of Western influence. Cambodia was just a few years into its era as a French protectorate when the commission arrived, and so Garnier's views are of a largely untouched culture. One fun thing about this book, though, is not to read it to see how much Cambodia has changed, but to note the ways in which it hasn't, which is particularly evident in descriptions of the countryside and a journey up the Mekong River.

Dougald O'Reilly
expands his understanding
of Angkor

I first saw the temples of Angkor in the pages of a *National Geographic* magazine in the mid-1970s. Fascinated, I longed to know more about the ancients who built these monuments and to explore this enchanted place. Sadly, Cambodia was far from enchanted for almost thirty years, and the land was inaccessible, isolated. I had to delay my rendezvous with Cambodia's past until 1994, when the chance to visit arose.

I was captivated immediately by the country's unique mix of charm and dark foreboding. At that time, the temples were not overrun with tourists, but the Khmer Rouge periodically made incursions into Siem Reap and purportedly owned the country roads after nightfall. Cambodia, thankfully, has come out of that nightmare, and today every corner of the country is as safe as any other country in the region.

As my academic interest in Cambodia grew, I searched for resources that would help to explain what had motivated the people to build such incredible monuments, to explain the meaning of the exquisite carvings. I discovered many excellent examinations of Khmer history, including Michael D. Coe's book *Angkor and the Khmer Civilization* and Charles Higham's *The Civilization of Angkor*. For those intrigued by the iconography of Cambodia's ancient temples, the works of Vittorio Roveda are not to be missed, beginning with his magnum opus, *Images of the Gods*. And for those who would like to know more about the rise of Southeast Asia, you may find my own *Early Civilizations of Southeast Asia* to be useful, as it explores the original

polities of Burma, Malaysia, Thailand, Cambodia, and Vietnam.

As a unique complement to these titles, I would recommend a charming artifact of colonial Cambodia, *The Monuments of the Angkor Group*, by Maurice Glaize, the conservator of Angkor in the 1930s and '40s. Written in 1944, it is an excellent resource peppered with interesting tidbits, including suggested itineraries and recommendations such as this: "A trip to Beng Mealea ... can be combined with a hunting party, since the region is rich in both small and large game and wild animals; - tigers, panthers and elephants." Clearly, not everything in this time capsule of a guide stands the test of time, but one thing has not changed—the unforgettable beauty and rich history of the Angkor temples.

The Monuments of the Angkor Group

For a free download of *The Monuments of the Angkor Group*, go to The Angkor Guide online.

www.theangkorguide.com

Kent Davis patterns his reading on ancient Angkor design

An ancient geometric pattern, the quincunx is a design in which four points form the corners of a square or rectangle and a fifth point sits at the center. It has been used for centuries throughout the world, from the Yucatan to the Solomon Islands, from Byzantine churches to ancient Indian temples. In Cambodia, the most prominent quincunx is the five towers that form the topmost level of Angkor Wat. Indeed, many Khmer structures prominently feature this quincunx layout. Adding to the mysteries of Cambodia, there is no single accepted modern theory of why the ancient Khmer held the quincunx to be so important, but it was clearly essential to their culture.

In keeping with this legacy, I have decided to use the quincunx to create a small library of recommended reading. My own Cambodian library has grown to more than 160 volumes, and perhaps yours will, too, eventually. But these essential five books will anchor your journey of exploration, and all are sure to enhance your love and understanding of Cambodia before, during, or after your visit.

Art & Architecture of Cambodia
Helen Ibbitson Jessup

This book is compact, lavishly illustrated, and filled with insights into the artistic soul of Cambodia. Jessup co-curated the only two international exhibitions of Khmer art to tour museums in the past forty years. Her wonderful introduction provides essential knowledge for a deeper enjoyment of your Cambodian travels.

Cambodia
by Michael Freeman

Freeman has focused much of his professional work as an author and photog-

rapher on Southeast Asia. His book is a kaleidoscope of personal accounts that weave Cambodia's past, present, and future into a single tapestry. The result is a delicious mélange: thought provoking, practical, humorous, sometimes shocking, but always entirely fascinating.

The Gods Drink Whisky
by Stephen T. Asma

This is one of the most astounding traveler's tales I have ever read. Asma, a professor of Buddhism in an American college, is invited to travel to Cambodia to teach Buddhism. His electrifying journey delivers the dichotomy of Cambodian life with full force: Eastern and Western, ancient and modern, peaceful and violent, rich and poor. With compassion and hope shining through it all.

Of Gods, Kings, and Men
by Jaroslav Poncar and Thomas S. Maxwell

Although this book deals only with Angkor Wat reliefs, I include it for two reasons. First, Maxwell's scholarly analysis offers readers a chance to plumb the depths of Khmer beliefs. Second, to see Poncar's photographic work. Since 1993, Poncar has lived, breathed, loved, and visually captured the heritage of this land. Viewing this world through his eyes reveals perspectives rarely discovered by most visitors.

Sideshow
by William Shawcross

Shawcross centers his political investigation on the 1970s, the decade that changed Cambodia more than any in history. He carefully documents the painful events and consequences that divide Cambodia's glorious past from its promising future. His brilliant account holds humbling lessons on power, statesmanship, and responsibility for every world citizen.

Christine Dimmock is fascinated by Cambodia's recent past

Attracted to its gaudy saffron and red cover, not to mention its catchy title, I bought *Gecko Tails* after my first trip to Cambodia in 1999. I credit this book with my most important words of Khmer, *ot panyahar*—no problem. This phrase in several different languages has served me well during my travels over the years.

I'm unashamed to admit that I am attracted to the Wild West atmosphere that was Cambodia during the United Nations Transitional Authority in Cambodia (UNTAC) era of the early 1990s. It is this time that is the subject of Carol Livingston's funny and tragic book, and my favorite quote from *Gecko Tails* says it all: "Many soldiers, Buddhist verses tattooed in Pali across their chests, necks, or arms to protect them from bullets, carried booty. One wore a tea kettle on his head and held a ceiling fan. Wires trailed in the dust; bunches of plastic flowers sprouted from his uni-

form." Essentially, this was a place where logic did not exist.

Arriving in Cambodia "looking for something to write about," the author joins acclaimed journalist Tim Page, now older, wiser, and still full of shrapnel from his Vietnam War days, for ganja-laced chicken soup and a sorry visit to Phnom Penh's last remaining opium den. With a nonviolent election, she mingles with the expatriate fraternity of news reporters continually looking for ways to amuse itself, usually involving bars, nightclubs, and rumors. The inimitable Foreign Correspondents' Club is born. UN staff eat MREs (meals rejected by Ethiopians), and Livingston and friends travel around the country hitching rides with NGOs and United Nations Military Observers (UNMOs) looking for the latest scoop.

After the elections, "national reconciliation" becomes the buzz, but factional fighting continues to plague the poor Cambodians who are just trying to get on with their lives. Poorly paid civil servants sign attendance books each morning, then leave their offices to work as moto drivers or English teachers. Half the nation's budget comes from foreign aid. The Khmer Rouge make headlines around the world by capturing three foreigners from a train in an attack in a coconut grove near Kep—Englishman Mark Slater, Australian David Wilson, and Frenchman Jean-Michel Braquet. The men's pleas that they are too young to die are seen on worldwide TV, but they are murdered nevertheless. It is an event

I remember well, although it pales in comparison to Livingston's description of the little publicized abduction and murder of three other foreigners she knew—and the implications of being a journalist in such a place at such a time.

Cambodia was once a last frontier. It is different now. A gun is just a kitsch monument on a roundabout near the Japanese Friendship Bridge in Phnom Penh. But the past will never be forgotten thanks to Livingston's account of what was all at once Cambodia's most hopeful, flawed, thrilling, incomparable, and ultimately disappointing time period.

Gecko Tails

Written by Carol Livingston and published by Phoenix, *Gecko Tails* can be ordered online at Amazon. com or purchased in various markets and shops in Siem Reap and Phnom Penh, including Monument Books and the airport.

COMIC BOOK RECOMMENDATIONS

Matt Ames marvels at the lasting legacy of Khmer comics

After marching around the broad streets of Phnom Penh for the better part of a morning, without any real goal in mind, I decided to have a look inside a Western-style store called Pencil. There in the book section I stumbled across a handful of colorful, eye-catching pamphlets, which quickly revealed themselves as the gorgeous works of art that are Khmer comics.

When I first laid eyes on the comic books of Cambodia, I knew I was in love. They revealed primary colors, epic violence, monsters, and a sense of graphic design that was both crude and creative. Most were written in Khmer, but that didn't matter. Their images of love, war, and mythical beasts—with Khmer script typeset in a bold 3-D format—were amazing. One of the comics I found that day, *The Fallen Areca Flower*, was written in English, its stilted, charmingly broken text bubbles telling the story of young lovers kept apart by a meddling relative.

That night back at my guesthouse, I decided upon a mission. To find more Khmer comics. The next morning I took a tuk-tuk to the Russian Market and began my search there. Later on, after much maneuvering among stalls in the day's heat, I uncovered the mother lode at the Psar O Russei market. On the second floor, in the book section against the far wall, a female vendor had a shelf chock-full of comics. She must have had over fifty different titles, including some two-part series.

At first, she and her friends seemed a little surprised by me, possibly because the Psar O Russei is the least touristy of the city's markets and sees relatively few foreigners. Even more perplexing, I was interested in reading material I couldn't read. Recognizing a serious shopper when she saw one, however, she pulled out a plastic stool so I could sit and peruse my newfound obsession.

Her collection yielded many wonderful surprises. I found comics with men riding dragons, naked giants hovering over villages, warriors losing arms in battles, zombie women menacing terrified lovers, *apsaras* floating over ponds, and kings and queens coping with indiscernible yet ominous challenges to their leadership. A few even contained stills from old Cambodian movies, arranged in story format, starring Kong Som Eun, a male heartthrob of the 1960s and '70s.

Throughout the rest of my travels, I occasionally shared my new comic collection with Cambodians as a fun way to break the ice. Outside of Phnom Penh, people were surprised and asked where I'd bought them. A teacher in Sen Monorom even translated *Boxing District* for me, the tale of a champion boxer who gets mixed up with the wrong crowd. In Battambang, the older monks seemed to think they were trashy, while the younger monks gobbled up the colorful soap operas.

Somewhere along the way, I realized how amazing these comics really were, beyond their immediate visual impact. Somehow, the printing plates for many of these books had survived the Khmer Rouge era, escaping cultural destruction to see resurrection as cheap pop entertainment. In a country that lost so much of its heritage, this one legacy at least had survived.

Khmer comic books

You can start your own Khmer comic book collection by visiting Pencil Super Center on Street 214 in Phnom Penh. The Russian Market, known to all motodops and tuk-tuk drivers, may yield a few treasures, as will the equally well-known O Russei Market. Comic books can also be found at some of the stationery bookshops, such as Peace Book Center.

www.pbc.com.kh

COOKBOOK RECOMMENDATIONS

Phil Lees
cooks up a selection of
culinary resources

Written resources about Cambodian food are notable for their almost complete absence. While the de rigueur explanation is that generations of food culture were lost under the Khmer Rouge regime, this is not true. Khmer cuisine traditions are passed down orally rather than in writing, with many recipes often accompanied by an appropriate folktale. Most recipes survived the Khmer Rouge as a testament to the endurance of the Cambodian people and their devotion to their unique culinary heritage.

For those Westerners who want to take a deeper look at Cambodian food, ex-*Bangkok Post* journalist Nusara Thaitawat's *The Cuisine of Cambodia* is the only Khmer recipe book written in English by a Cambodia-based author. Along with recipes for favorites such as fish *amok* or *samla karko*, Thaitawat documents recipes for the Chinese- and French-influenced "royal cuisine" and includes beautiful photography, rural folktales, and an esoteric chapter on deep-fried insects. Other titles worth searching out include *The Elephant Walk Cookbook* (from the restaurant of the same name), by Longteine de Monteiro and Katherine Neustadt, and *The Food & Cooking of Cambodia*, by Ghillie Basan.

With the paucity of physically published material, another place to turn is the Internet. The best online resource is Mylinh Nakry Danh's Khmer Krom Recipes. Mylinh methodically records recipes from her native Kampuchea-Krom, the ethnically Khmer part of Vietnam's Mekong Delta region. She often does not differentiate between thousands-year-old recipes and those added from other cultures' cuisines in modern times, but the website is nonetheless an accurate portrayal of the eating habits of southern Cambodia. For the hardcore foodie and market shopper, the spotter's guide to the Cambodian cornucopia of herbs, fruit, and vegetables is invaluable.

Khmer Krom Recipes
www.khmerkromrecipes.com

Phnomenon
Phil's own blog, Phnomenon, transcribes the current street food and dining scene in Phnom Penh and provinces farther afield, with some degree of both weight and occasional humor. His approach is broad ecumenism, and his goal is to capture food traditions and the collision of modern and ancient Khmer culture.

www.phnomenon.com

BOOKSTORES

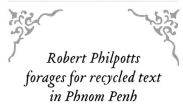

Robert Philpotts
forages for recycled text
in Phnom Penh

Where I come from, urban commuters often find opportunities for reading fiction confined to time on the train, with books being digested in courses lasting as long as a journey. But when the commuter turns into a traveler, then hours in a pleasant café or whole days on a beach may offer the chance to become absorbed in a novel without needing to break the thread as carriage doors open.

In general, on the road throughout Asia, maintaining a supply of inexpensive reading material can be a perennial difficulty, with English-language works often being hard to locate. In Phnom Penh, though, it is fairly easy to find Indian editions of out-of-copyright classics in student-orientated stationery stores, and there are also a handful of good general secondhand bookshops. This is providential since anecdotal evidence seems to show that travelers are more inclined to take reading risks when a long way from home. For example, a fan of Marian Keyes's might forego a copy of *Under the Duvet* on the shelf and whisk away Malcolm Lowry's *Under the Volcano* instead.

The first secondhand English-language bookshop that opened in the postdemocratic Kampuchea period was Bert's Books, which published Ray Zepp's classic *The Cambodia Less Travelled*. The second was the London Book Centre. Although both of these enterprises have closed, the newcomers have done a respectable job of filling the space they left behind. Better still, they are within easy walking distance of the Royal Palace.

D's Books, which advertises itself as "Asia's Number One Choice for Books" and has a presence outside Cambodia, operates two well-stocked shops run by pleasant staff. The smaller of the two venues, close to the Foreign Correspondents' Club, tends to carry general stock, whilst the other, on Street 240, also sells textbooks and a substantial number of children's books—handy for those traveling with kids. Look out for the blackboards in these shops, where special offers are sometimes chalked up, restaurant-style.

While I like D's, my favorite bookshop is Bohr's Books, named after Niels Bohr, the Nobel Prize-winning physicist. The owner, the friendly and approachable Chea Sopheap, has a passion for science, hence the name of his store. But he also has an interest in fiction and maintains as wide a selection as possible within the confines of his ground floor unit.

As a Khmer entrepreneur making headway outside the usual run of guesthouses or bars, Sopheap is unusual. Originally from a rural farming background, as a boy he endured the privations of the Khmer Rouge period. He did not find the path to building his small business easy, but there is something about the shop he has created, with its simple but carefully chosen shelves and welcoming atmosphere, that marks it out as special. It is little wonder it is well patronized by the expatriate community.

A second, family-run bookshop called Kepler's Books (after the astronomer Johannes Kepler) has just opened in Kampot. With the support of expats and travelers, I hope these stores will continue to thrive, and that we might see an Einstein Books in Battambang or a Rutherford Bookshop in Siem Reap sometime soon!

D's Books

Street 178 (close to the riverside)

Street 240 (near the junction of Norodom Boulevard)
Phnom Penh

Bohr's Books

5, Sothearos Boulevard
(near Wat Ounalom, one block from Sisowath Quay)
Phnom Penh

Kepler's Books

25, Ekreach Street
Kampot

www.keplerbook.com

MOVIE RECOMMENDATIONS

*Editor's Choice:
Movies*

The Killing Fields

Hollywood movies about Cambodia can be counted on one hand. The film that resonates in everyone's perception of the country is Roland Joffé's 1984 epic. The incredible performance of Haing Ngor—a doctor by profession—in his first film role won him an Oscar and brought to life the pain and suffering endured by the Cambodian people under the Khmer Rouge. The film won three Academy Awards in total. It should be in everyone's collection.

New Year Baby
www.newyearbaby.net

Socheata Poeuv's soul-bearing documentary examines her parents and their survival through the Pol Pot regime. At the heart of the story are decades-old family secrets—to reveal any of them here would be to spoil the poignancy of how the Khmer Rouge drastically affected family life. This is a moving portrayal that brought a lump to my throat, and I'm sure it will do the same to you.

S21: the Khmer Rouge Killing Machine

Vann Nath, the most famous survivor of S21 (or Tuol Sleng as its better known), confronts his former jailers and torturers in this astonishing award-winning documentary by Rithy Panh. Reenacting the ghastly crimes committed on over fourteen thousand people that were imprisoned, tortured, and murdered by the Khmer Rouge staff of S21, this film is a chilling look at Cambodia's darkest years.

Year Zero: The Silent Death of Cambodia

It was *Daily Mirror* journalist John Pilger's 1979 expose on Cambodia that sparked my interest in this faraway country as I sat in my comfy armchair at home in Cheltenham, England. Pilger's revelations about the brutality of the Khmer Rouge and the injustices inflicted on the Cambodian people made me sit up, take notice, and embark on a love affair that just grew stronger with time. The film is one of the most influential documentaries of its time, and over $45 million was raised as a result of it. Pilger went on to make another four documentaries about Cambodia.

Andy Brouwer meets Cambodia's tenth dancer

Around the same time as I first came to Cambodia in 1994, I watched a memorable documentary that focused on the fledgling revival of Cambodian classical dance. It featured one of the survivors of the Khmer Rouge regime, which killed nine out of every ten of the country's dancers—hence the film's title, *The Tenth Dancer*. The survivor's name was Em Theay, and it was clear that she was a remarkable woman. Little did I know that years later I would meet her and discover that she was an even more exceptional individual than I first thought.

I was acting as the local fixer for a documentary about Cambodia, thirty years after the end of Pol Pot's iron-fisted rule. We'd interviewed Vann Nath, the famous painter of Tuol Sleng prison, and now it was the turn of the living icon of Cambodian royal court dance. Dressed in her finest clothes, her toothless grin spreading from ear to ear, Em Theay arrived with her eldest daughter, also a leading classical dancer. She was seventy-eight years old, and the prospect of talking about dance—her lifeblood for so many decades—was something she was eagerly anticipating.

With the help of a translator, Em Theay launched into the story of her life, a tale of funny moments interspersed with the sadness of the Pol Pot years and the subsequent struggles to resurrect her beloved dance traditions. She was chosen to dance at the age of seven by Queen Kossamak, for whom her parents worked as domestic servants. She grew up in the Royal Palace and was a dancer and singer in the King's Royal Ballet until the Khmer Rouge took over her country. At that time she was forty-three and was sent to live in Battambang, where her talents did not go unnoticed—her captors encouraged her to sing and dance as well as work in the fields.

In 1975, when the Khmer Rouge came to power, twelve of Em Theay's eighteen children were alive. By the end of the Khmer Rouge period in the late '70s, seven more had died and only five were left. Her spirit unbroken, Em Theay returned to Phnom Penh, where her knowledge and skills of the traditional arts were put to use as a teacher at the National Dance Company and the Royal University of Fine Arts until a few years ago.

She told her moving story with such grace and dignity that it was impossible for those present not to feel the emotion of the moment, and as I listened in awe, I quickly wiped away the tears before anyone could see. But laughter is never far from Em Theay's lips. She even surprised the cameraman on a couple of occasions by springing up from her chair to demonstrate the wealth of postures and movements that she knew by heart and had passed on to countless students over the years, including her own children and grandchildren. As she finished her tale with more of her amusing stories about her students, I found myself unsure whether to laugh or cry. She ended the session by sitting on the floor and handing me countless photographs of her family and some of herself, yellowing with age, but obviously precious items and memories. Clearly, her desire to pass on the secrets of the royal court dance has been undiminished by time.

In March 2009 Em Theay and her daughter lost everything in a house fire.

Irreplaceable documents of dance and family history—her treasured notebooks, which contained the record of many important sacred songs and dances, along with those yellowing photographs, which she kept hidden from the Khmer Rouge on pain of death—were gone forever. A benefit concert and a screening of *The Tenth Dancer* have raised much-needed funds to assist her. While such support helps, nothing can be done to retrieve her invaluable possessions. Yet she continues on, undaunted. Her life has been—and still is—an incredible journey. She is not only a true survivor, she is also a vital link to Cambodia's glorious past.

The Tenth Dancer

Sally Ingleton's 1993 documentary is a testament to the resilience of Em Theay and the rest of the Cambodian classical dancers and their dedication to resurrecting this vital link to Cambodia's past.

www.singingnomads.com/tenth
www.360degreefilms.com.au/the-tenth-dancer

Geoff Ryman
raps about contemporary
Cambodian music

Cambodia has some of best popular music in the world, but you'll have to hunt for the good stuff. Most of it aspires to the likes of Bon Jovi, Mariah Carey, or ABBA, and Preap Sovath—

Cambodia's superstar—is so prolific that he has only occasional flashes of brilliance. But at its best, Cambodian music is a mix of devastating verse, serious intent, phenomenal beats, and a mélange of traditional and modern sounds. No other current music has such stories to tell, such a range of sources, such a love for the past, so much hope for the future. Better yet for Westerners, a lot of it is in English.

Tony Re-al and Master Kong Nai

I can't listen to "Brothers and Sisters," by Tony Re-al with his group SEAsia, without getting emotional. Tony left Cambodia as an infant, and the song describes the moment watching a documentary that he realized he was a Cambodian. His music mixes rap beats with traditional instruments played live, a diversity that is evident throughout the album, beginning with its first track, sung by Master Kong Nay, who looks like a genetic duplicate of Ray Charles. Kong Nay plays a traditional string instrument, the *chapei*, to which he improvises with a howling gravelly voice verse that is both classic and modern. If anything, he sounds like a Delta bluesman.

Kong Nay is often heard at the Sovanna Phum Theatre in Phnom Penh at one of the regular Friday or Saturday night shows. I highly recommend that you go to Sovanna Phum, whatever is playing, whether it's the company's own shadow puppet extravaganza or traditional theater. The first time I went, I was battered by a performance by Kong Nay, and then elated by a dance piece that blended traditional Cambo-dian ballet and Indian classical dance with big-band jazz sampled from a French film.

DJ Cream and A Ping

Tony Re-al also works with another key Cambodian music figure, DJ Cream, aka Sok Visal. Visal in turn partners with a stable of Khmer and Khmer-American rappers, including A Ping. A Ping's "Chivit Leu Boeung Kaplhoak" breaks open 1960s Cambodian pop from Sin Sisamuth to create a moving story about a raped karaoke girl, and his "Chivit Setrey" samples "Beauty School Dropout" from the musical *Grease* to tell other stories of Cambodian women.

The Mujestic collective, Prach Ly, and Silong

At the core of the Mujestic collective of Khmer-American rappers, you will find the undisputed king of Cambodian rap, Prach Ly. Prach's music reveals grim stories of survival, warfare, politics, and threatened culture. Meeting him is a bit like meeting the young Nelson Mandela: he has a clear-eyed focus on moral responsibility, a trait not common in most Western rappers. Any of the chapters from his three-part album "Dalama" are worth picking up. Prach also works closely with Silong, a Seattle-based Khmer-American. Silong samples from a huge range of sources, from Angelina Jolie to Mozart, and his superbly crafted work is featured on his album with the group Second Language.

Meeting the musicians

Where Cambodia's local musicians hang out changes continually. Once I met Prach Ly, Silong, and Tony Re-al quite by accident at a noodle shop on Street 178, but the young rappers have such respect for Cambodian tradition that you might also find them helping out at the headquarters of Cambodian Living Arts off Street 105. Founded by flute player Arn Chorn-Pond, this wonderful organization supports performing artists and also runs classes in Cambodian music for young people. Prach Ly has been heavily involved with their work in preserving the community of Bassac, where masters such as Kong Nay taught and lived.

Listening to live music

There is a small live rock scene in Cambodia, and although most of it involves expats from around the world, there are still some local gems. Thom Thom is a totally Khmer outfit and, like many other such bands, plays at the Zeppelin Café. You can also follow DJ Cream's recommendations for good music: "Any disco bar in town—Golden Boss or Golden City or Pacific Kiss. Any beer garden, during weddings ..." Bottom line, wherever you are in Cambodia, keep your ears open and you're sure to find yourself introduced to the country's energetic music scene.

Shopping for music

For good Khmer and Khmer-American rap in Phnom Penh, try the music shops in the square around the Central Market, or even better the music stalls in the fairground across Sihanouk Boulevard from the Buddhist Institute. *Hip-hop* is now a Cambodian term, although it covers many different kinds of music, but rather than requesting the genre, ask for the good artists by name: DJ Khleng, DJ Sdey, DJ Sope, DJ Cream, A Ping, Prach Ly, Phnom Penh Bad Boyz, DJ Boomer, and Lisha. What you get will be grab-bag pirate compilations, but every one of them will have a gem. For more about Cambodian rock from the 1960s and early '70s, continue on to the next essay.

Sovanna Phum Theatre

159B, Street 99
(Corner of Street 484)
Phnom Penh
(023) 987-564

www.shadow-puppets.org

Cambodian Living Arts

37, Street 105
Phnom Penh

www.cambodianlivingarts.org

Zeppelin Café

49, Street 86
Phnom Penh

Mujestic

At the Mujestic music collective website, you can hear downloads of songs by members of the collective and find out when they are performing in Cambodia. The website is temperamental, so if it doesn't come up one day, try back the next.

www.mujestic.com

Current events

If you want to check out some shows in Cambodia, the following blogs offer up-to-date listings as well as reviews of current shows.

http://lengpleng.blogspot.com
http://phnompenhgigs.blogspot.com

Sheila Scoville rocks out in Phnom Penh

Besides learning what diseases to worry about and memorizing cultural dos and don'ts, preparing for a trip to Southeast Asia also meant seeking out some local music. Luckily, much of the legwork had already been done by a few specialized record labels, which collected songs from the countries on my itinerary and released them on CD. All I had to do was place my orders.

Of the popular music of Thailand, I had to admit its instantly gratifying, sugary high was hard to resist. But once its kitschy thrill wore off, Thai pop proved a little thin and wearisome. Rather than inspiring an immediate affinity, Vietnamese street music, atonal and otherworldly, intrigued but definitely promised to be an acquired taste. Then along came a collection of Cambodian pop rock dating from the late 1960s and early '70s.

Much about the Khmer music made it a hit, both instant and enduring, so much so my boyfriend played the album I'd ordered for weeks leading up to and throughout our four-month trip. Heavy reverb guitars, backed by twist 'n' shout beats and bass, recalled early American psychedelic and garage music. But it was the soul-shattering vocals that sparked a new music love affair for us.

A couple of singers in particular, Sin Sisamuth and Ros Serey Sothea, packed a rawness that hurtled across the language divide. Though they belted out in their native Khmer, these Cambodians hadn't lacked any one of Western rock's critical elements—heady, newfound freedom, the celebration of reckless youth, and the rebellious joy of subverting their parents' music. They had totally gotten it! This was the soundtrack of a revolution that demanded you dance, dance, dance till the end of this crazy, old world—prescient given the times to come.

A quest to learn more about Khmer rock became the focus of the week that my boyfriend and I spent in Phnom Penh, where we scoured markets for music stalls and information about the fate of Sin and Ros. Sadly, neither survived the Khmer Rouge regime, although details of their deaths remain unknown. We did, though, find the location of Sin's former home, as well as a store run by Chlangden Production, which still releases their music. Between the two of us, we left the country with over twenty CDs and a newfound appreciation for one of Cambodia's lesser-known cultural legacies.

Purchasing Khmer music

Along with the venues mentioned in the previous essay, the Russian

Market provides a good hunting ground for Khmer music from the 1960s and '70s. The proliferation of music shops in Phnom Penh has also expanded the choices available, and Chlangden Production on Street 107 remains a useful source. To buy CDs or MP3s of the Khmer-Rocks series, go to the website below. You can also hear Sin and Ros on the soundtrack for the movie *City of Ghosts*, along with various other Khmer and French singers.

http://khmerrocks.com

WEBSITE RECOMMENDATIONS

Editor's Choice: Websites

Angkor Wat Apsara & Devata: Khmer Women in Divine Context
www.devata.org

Kent Davis poses this question to one of the world's most fascinating archaeological mysteries: Why do carvings of women dominate Angkor Wat, the largest ancient religious monument on earth? This is an area that has seen little scholarship, and Davis's effort to change that include a massive digital archive, comprehensive listing of (combined with photographs and articles about) temples featuring *apsaras* and *devatas*, and studies of ancient Cambodian dance.

Cambodia: Beauty and Darkness
www.mekong.net/cambodia

This website provides an interesting archive of articles, documents, and photographs about Cambodia, with an emphasis on the country's recent past and most significantly the era of the Khmer Rouge. Of particular interest are the first-person oral histories—individual stories that give voice to the 1.7 million who died during that time. The photography section offers rare glimpses of Cambodia, from a set of 1981 photos of Khmer Rouge soldiers to a collection from 1991 of daily life just before UN peacekeeping forces entered the country.

Cambodia Travel Guides
www.canbypublications.com

This web version of a series of print guides features major locations in Cambodia, including Phnom Penh, Siem Reap/Angkor, Battambang, Kampot, Kep, and Sihanoukville. Along with accommodation and dining information, this is a great resource for travel times and routes. Its maps are excellent, and its updates essential in a country where change is constant.

The Phnom Penh Post
www.phnompenhpost.com

Updated every afternoon with the day's print stories, this website is the best way to keep up with news in Cambodia. In the Lifestyle section you will find articles about current art exhibitions, local events, and culture—the waning tradition of magical tattoos, perhaps, or the craft of mask-making. Check out the Siem Reap Insider section if you plan on spending time in that area.

Tales of Asia
www.talesofasia.com

Considered one of the most important resources on Cambodia, Gordon Sharpless's long-standing website includes a comprehensive guide to Siem Reap and Angkor and a special emphasis on the overland route between Thailand and Cambodia. Additional articles by the website's readers are a nice touch.

Cambodia Tales
www.andybrouwer.co.uk

Kim Fay adds: No listing of Cambodia websites would be complete without including *To Cambodia With Love*'s own Andy Brouwer. Andy's sites— Cambodia Tales and his blog— include extensive travelogues, photographs, book reviews, and bibliography. My personal favorites are his stories of exploring out-of-the-way temples. He does a terrific job of capturing the spirit of the country's forgotten relics, while at the same time always sharing his love of the people he encounters along the way.

LEARNING THE LANGUAGE

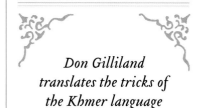

Don Gilliland translates the tricks of the Khmer language

I was having dinner with a Cambodian family at their home in Siem Reap one evening when the subject of farm animals came up. Or so I thought.

"I want to buy a cow," the oldest child, a twelve-year-old boy, told me. "I only have one."

I was puzzled by his statement. Just an hour earlier I had watched him and his sister walk two cows down a dirt road and secure them inside an open-air shed next to their thatched-roof house. I assumed these two cows belonged to the family.

"But you have two cows already," I pointed out. "Why do you want another one?"

"No," the boy whined, "I only have one cow. And it is very old." With that declaration he pulled on the leg of his frayed black pants ... and I finally realized what he'd been trying to say.

It was *kao*, the Khmer word for pants, which sounds the same as *cow* in English. This child was a fairly gifted English speaker as a result of selling postcards to tourists outside the Angkor temples, but he hadn't yet learned how to say *pants* or *trousers* in English. No, he didn't want any more cattle, just a clean pair of britches.

This wasn't the first time I'd encountered language misunderstandings, but it did inspire me to study Khmer more. Unlike Thai or Lao, Khmer is not a tonal language. In other words, you won't have to worry about learning an assortment of high, low, rising, and falling tones. But where Khmer rears up and kicks you in the head is with its vowels. As one course book stated, "Many of these vowel sounds have no comparable sound in English." Hey, no kidding! Another book noted there are twenty-three vowels in Khmer; but taking into account their long and short versions and factoring in diphthongs, you end up with about sixty different sounds. I don't know about you, but my tongue dries up at the very thought of so much work.

My first full-fledged leap into studying Khmer came via ***Colloquial Cambodian*** by David Smyth (published by Routledge). I had also studied Thai using books that Smyth had written, so I was familiar, and comfortable, with his system of transliterating, or "Romanizing," the words into English. I've heard some linguists criticize his system, but for my language learning tastes, Smyth's method is easier to use than the "proper," or more technical, phonetics that linguists prefer. The course comes with a book and a CD (although my original copy in the late 1990s had cassettes). The book

includes lessons, conversations, and a supplemental dictionary. It also has exercises on how to write Khmer script, a daunting challenge that I have yet to tackle.

To supplement that course I bought two pocket-sized dictionaries. One of those was Tuttle Publishing's ***Practical Cambodian Dictionary***. Compiled by Smyth and Tran Kien, it conveniently uses the same Romanization system that Smyth used for *Colloquial Cambodian*. The other one, Seam and Blake's ***Phonetic English-Khmer Dictionary***, wasn't as easy to for me to use because of its different, and more awkward, way of transliterating Khmer words into English. But I found it handy to have for the simple fact that it would sometimes include a word that the other dictionary didn't … and vice versa.

For example, if I wanted to know how to say *boring* in Khmer, I discovered that the Seam and Blake book has no such listing, but the Tuttle book has *bored*. Although not exactly what I wanted, it was close. Okay, how about *borrow*? For this word the Seam and Blake book does have a listing, but Tuttle doesn't. Sticking to the "B" section, the Tuttle book tells you how to say *broken* but Seam and Blake give you no help on that at all. Yep, you need to have both dictionaries, which conveniently include Khmer script next to each entry. Inevitably, after I've botched the pronunciation of a word, I can point to the Khmer script and ask a Cambodian to pronounce it correctly for me. If nothing else, it's always a good icebreaker at parties.

In recent years, yet another small book surfaced—at least from street vendors in Phnom Penh. Simply titled **Khmer Phrase Book**, it includes "everyday phrases" and a minidictionary. In the preface to the book (white cover with a collage of photos on the front) there is a note from "the compiler," but no information as to who actually compiled or published the thing. It uses a system similar to the Seam and Blake volume and also has Khmer script next to each word. Its advantage over the other two minidictionaries is that it includes some phrases you might actually use. Thankfully, whoever put this book together realized that most travelers in the twenty-first century no longer send telegrams or buy film for cameras, so they have wisely ditched such out-of-date terms and included phrases about such activities as email and making photocopies.

Another relatively recent entry into the Cambodian language learning pool is **Cambodian for Beginners**, by Richard K. Gilbert and Sovandy Hang. It's published by Paiboon Publishing, the same company that released *Thai for Beginners* and similar books for learning Burmese and Lao—although in the Cambodian version phonetics are used to Romanize the words. The Cambodian course comes with a book and two CDs. The book follows the lessons on CD and also has additional lessons for learning how to write the language. Overall, it's a good introduc-

tion, but I think *Colloquial Cambodian* has got a bit more substance.

For serious study of the written and spoken language, you can look for books by Franklin Huffman, most written in the 1970s. **Modern Spoken Cambodian** and **Cambodian System of Writing and Beginning Reader**, along with an extensive dictionary, are just some of his output. Another vintage title that you can still find in Phnom Penh bookshops is the lime-green-colored **English-Khmer Phrase Book**. It was produced by the United Nations Field Operations Division in 1991 and prepared by Robert K. Headley (who also compiled a dictionary in the 1970s) and Kassie S. Neou. This "phrase book" is oddly shaped and impossible to fit in your pocket, but it does have a variety of useful phrases.

If you sincerely want to learn the language, the main thing is to keep trying. You'll no doubt make a few mistakes and become frustrated by those slippery vowel sounds, but when you ace a phrase and are rewarded with one of those delightful Cambodian smiles, you'll agree it's worth the effort.

RESEARCHING CAMBODIA

Tiara Delgado remembers the past in Phnom Penh

From 1975 to 1979, Cambodia was ruled by the genocidal Khmer Rouge regime. An estimated 1.7 million Cambodians died from starvation, disease, forced labor, and execution. Despite the passage of three decades, the legacy of genocide still resonates in Khmer society today. Talk to your motodop or cyclo driver and inquire about the "killing fields." Most locals over a certain age will tell you they are survivors and can recount the number of relatives they lost.

I believe a visit to Cambodia will be much more rewarding if tourists understand how much suffering Khmers have endured. Their ability to reconstruct a society and culture that was nearly destroyed will be even more impressive, the accomplishments and progress they have made even more appreciated.

As a documentary filmmaker I found the Documentation Center of Cambodia (DC-Cam) to be an incredible resource. Started in 1995 by Yale University's Cambodian Genocide Project, DC-Cam collects and preserves evidence from the Khmer Rouge regime. Promoting "memory and justice" are the dual ambitions of this nonprofit organization, which serves as a major source of information for academics, lawyers, activists, and the general public. The all-Cambodian staff is helpful and resourceful. A good assortment of books published by DC-Cam is available for sale, as well as video documentaries and issues of "Searching for the Truth," DC-Cam's fascinating quarterly magazine.

DC-Cam is nestled between two restaurants—Shiva Shakti and Java Arts Café—both great places to browse through any materials you might purchase, or to simply reflect on the significance of what you have just experienced. I trust that after learning about Cambodia's tragic history that the resilience and strength of Khmer people will astound you even more.

Documentation Center of Cambodia

In 1997 DC-Cam became an independent research institute and opened a Public Information Room, which offers the opportunity to conduct research using the organization's immense collections. If you would like to access DC-Cam's many valuable resources, you can fill out an online application form at their website.

66, Preah Sihanouk Boulevard
(Near Independence Monument)
Phnom Penh
(023) 211-875

www.dccam.org

Java Arts Café

This café is an ideal place to relax and enjoy homemade food, great coffee, and contemporary art exhibitions all under one roof.

www.javaarts.org

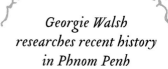

Georgie Walsh
researches recent history in Phnom Penh

When I arrived in Phnom Penh in 2006, I was an "old hand" in Asia, not to mention a longtime visitor to Cambodia, though that was my first time in the capital. A friend suggested that I visit the Bophana Audiovisual Resource Center, telling me it would be well worth my time.

I was already a big fan of Bophana's founder, Rithy Panh. His documentary, *S21: The Khmer Rouge Killing Machine*, captivated me, as did its subjects: former prison guard Him Houy and former Tuol Sleng prisoner Vann Nath, who was at that time exhibiting his latest collection of paintings at Bophana.

The Bophana building, known in Phnom Penh as the "White House," was architecturally beautiful and symbolic to the city in the 1960s. The whole place had a calm and cool atmosphere. There was a small café downstairs that also served as a gallery, and hanging on the walls were the experiences of Tuol Sleng prison

that Vann Nath had painted. I appreciated having the time and space to take in these images without the busloads of tourists and snapping cameras of the Tuol Sleng museum.

I was there to do some research about Phnom Penh in the 1980s, and after explaining this to the front desk assistant, I was introduced to research analyst Sok Koung. He shared that Rithy Panh had been inspired to preserve Cambodia's audiovisual history because, after decades of wars, coups d'état, and genocidal madness, the few archives that had been spared would not survive another decade.

Mr. Koung then handed me over to a bright young French woman, Aurélie Collado, who was able to tell me more about the future and purpose of Bophana. Not only does the center preserve audiovisual history but it also helps to reinforce education by producing and facilitating foreign and local filmmaking. Recently completed projects included shooting traditional Cambodian folktales and distributing them to children in the provinces with on-the-road screenings.

Aurélie sat me down at one of Bophana's many computers, and I was able to search a database collection of about nine hundred documents relating to Cambodia taken from different media: video, audio, photography, and the written word. Unfortunately almost all of it was in French or Khmer, but for me that was okay because I had already read much about Phnom Penh in the 1970s and '80s—to be able to

RESEARCHING CAMBODIA

see what that era looked like was a valuable experience, in and of itself. I spent the afternoon behind a computer screen and would return many times to get lost amidst the audio and visual archives that are not available anywhere else. I would also return to attend events and screenings of new documentaries about everyday life and wonderful people making a difference in Cambodia.

I've kept tabs on Bophana's progress via email updates I receive about the documentaries and events they host, and I was impressed to see that Rithy Panh's latest film, *The Sea Wall*, had been a great success and was featured in the Cannes International Film Festival. I recommend Bophana to anyone wanting to explore the

history of this incredible country, as well as what the next generation of Cambodian filmmakers have to offer.

Bophana Audiovisual Resource Center

Tell your motodop or taxi driver that Bophana is located near the Alliance Française (Le Centre Culturel Français du Cambodge) on Street 184. Hours for exhibitions and archive consultation are listed on the website.

64, Street 200
Phnom Penh
(023) 992-174

www.bophana.org

Elderly man in Kompong Khleang village

Statue on monastery roof near Bakong temple

Epilogue

Peter Walter takes his sons
on a local detour in Siem Reap

The dilapidated taxi sped along a lonely stretch of freshly paved road between Sisophon and Kralanh. It was ferrying me and my two oldest sons, Nathan and Alec, hastily toward Siem Reap, home of the millennium-old temples of Angkor. The road had improved dramatically since our first trip together the previous year, and was now completely surfaced—offering yet more evidence of the rapid development shaping modern Cambodia.

Siem Reap, or more specifically the Angkor complex, is one of my favorite places on earth. Ancient temples, bridges, archways, and other structures stretch across hundreds of square kilometers, offering a vast and breathtaking display of human design and engineering rarely found elsewhere in the world. The detailed illustrations carved into massive sandstone blocks are exquisite and reasonably well preserved, and the scale of even single temple complexes is truly impressive. The little boy in me still relishes the thrill of exploring these ancient temples. With my boys in tow, there would be nothing stopping us from climbing up and down the steep temple faces and scurrying through every last passageway we could find.

Over the last decade, I have watched Siem Reap town and the infrastructure that supports Angkor grow tremendously with the increasing numbers of tourists. While this has clearly benefited the country and many local residents of Siem Reap, it has also created other problems, including temple deterioration, traffic jams, and pollution. The growing crowds are, at times, a distraction from the full enjoyment of Angkor's serenity and mystical aura. Indeed, it can be difficult these days to find quiet spots in some temple areas, while in others, snapping a photo without tourists in the background is a real challenge.

Man sweeping Angkor Wat temple

Despite my mixed feelings about the changing face of Siem Reap, there are many reasons I enjoy returning. Temples aside, the town itself has a certain charm and has managed to remain pleasant overall despite the onslaught of recent development. Both in town and around the Angkor temple area, there is a relaxed atmosphere that's easy to settle into. And once I am out amongst the forests and temples, it's wonderful to drink in the fresh air and watch the passing jungle from an open-air tuk-tuk. The enormous trees towering above often block the direct sun, creating an ethereal, leaf-filtered glow that lingers over the clearings. While usually quiet, the forests occasionally come to life with shrill cries of cicadas that pierce the air, contributing to that slight sense of wild that still lingers at Angkor.

There is also another treasure there that continues to draw me back—the people of Angkor, whose ancestors built everything here. From Bong, the hotel clerk at my favorite Siem Reap hotel, to Yon, Yet, and other vendors who make a living selling their goods to visitors, I've gradually developed friendships with various residents throughout my many visits. By my getting to know them, the experience of visiting Siem Reap has transcended temples and jungles and helped me to more fully appreciate Cambodia, its people, and its culture.

These personal experiences have also provided me an invaluable opportunity to teach my children about the reality of life for those in circumstances different from our own. Instead of being just another holiday, our family visits to Angkor now include regular stops to see the people we know who greatly appreciate our friendship and encouragement as they struggle through the challenges of daily life with remarkably positive resolve.

Bong was one of the first Cambodian people I met on my initial visit to Siem Reap. At the time, he was single and worked around the clock at a traditional guesthouse in order to save money for his future wife and family. While a hotel employee by night, he doubled as a motorbike taxi driver by day—impressing me greatly with his work ethic. I also liked his relaxed style, and I hired him to show me around the temples of Angkor. He took me to the usual sites but also led me to places off the tourist trail that I could appreciate at my own pace. He was the first to open my eyes to the wonders of Angkor.

My brother, Tim, and I met Yon and her sisters, Yet and Triap, in 2002 after a midafternoon exploration of the famous Bayon temple. In our exploratory zeal, we had worked up quite a sweat and were looking forward to cooling off with a few cold beers. Yon was the first of the vendors to rush out to greet us, and we followed her to a few seats under the shadow of the Bayon. While Tim and I sated our thirst, the three sisters chatted with each other and friends and chased other customers. Their shop offered a great spot to relax, its warmth complementing the amazing view of the pyramid-shaped temple with its large, mysterious faces carved in stone.

The talented cook my sons have dubbed the Angkor Wat Breakfast Lady is another friend who operates a little "café" consisting of a few tables and chairs under the shade of a large old tree overlooking Angkor Wat. From her chairs, the view is picturesque, the front face of the temple flanked by two large square ponds teeming with flowering purple lilies. The Breakfast Lady was one of the early pioneers to set up shop there, and after my initial visit, I've never been able to pass up her dangerously delicious scrambled egg, cheese, and baguette sandwiches, laced with onions and chili sauce. She offers pancakes as well, but I'm sold on the house specialty, along with a good, hot cup of tea.

In the eight years since I first met the Breakfast Lady, there are many people we've gotten to know, kept in touch with, and lost track of. Whenever I come to Cambodia, I always call on these friends to see how they're doing. Sometimes we try to help in small ways, donating school supplies, books, outgrown toys,

and clothes to local children. Other times, we stop by merely to say hello and to remind our friends that we continue to think about them even while we're away.

These days, the Breakfast Lady is doing well, with her business benefiting from the growing numbers of tourists. Her menu seems to have expanded as well, and fortunately, she's managed to hold on to her choice spot near Angkor Wat. Eight years on, Bong is now married and has a three-year-old son, with hopes for more children. He's been promoted to assistant hotel manager and can no longer afford the time to take me around on his motorbike, but he always makes sure I have a good guide.

Yon and her sisters now run two different shops located near the Bayon and Ta Keo temples. Yon is married and has a baby boy, and Yet sounds like she's well on her way to marriage soon. Their father, with whom I can converse in Thai, has kindly invited us to their home on a few occasions, cooking a real Cambodian village meal for us and showing the boys around their rice farm. Their mother usually smiles bemusedly and says very little due to the language barrier. She busily keeps the house running, but clearly enjoys the diversion from her daily routine.

On the last day of our most recent visit, Nathan and Alec learned how to steer the cows using the yoke under the supervision of Yon's father, who took them for a few laps around the field. Later, as they played games with the village kids who had trailed us, I reflected on how fortunate I was to be able to show my boys the many facets of Angkor. Indeed, there is so much there to appreciate in both the ancient and the modern, in the temples and the people descended from those responsible for their creation. But as amazing and impressive as the temples are, they are only part of the grander treasure that Angkor, and indeed Cambodia, have to offer when one takes time for the occasional "local" detour.

Women sifting grain on the way to Koh Ker

Apsaras on a wall at Banteay Kdei temple

Juanita Accardo
(Pg. 125, 129)

Juanita is a regular visitor to Cambodia. She adores Ratanakiri and treats it like her second home. When she's not traveling, she's back in the United States working at St. Mary Medical Center in Long Beach, California.

Matt Ames
(Pg. 198)
www.philosophyinc.com

If Matt is not in Cambodia, he is probably in Roanoke, Virginia, studying data visualization, working on art projects, making music, or writing and directing short films. Matt would like to especially thank the monks of Wat Tahm-rai-saw in Battambang for their friendliness and willingness to answer a bunch of stupid questions.

Mariam Arthur
(Pg. 37, 157)

Mariam has traveled the United States extensively and went global in 2006. Her writing career started in California for regional newspapers. She transferred her skills to Hollywood in 2000. She has resided in Cambodia since 2007, where she lives within view of the Royal Palace with her cat, Tigger.

Anne Best
(Pg. 28, 66, 152)

A London-based anthropologist, Anne Best is the author of *The Monk, the Farmer, the Merchant, the Mother: Survival Stories of Rural Cambodia*. This book tells the true stories of the lives of four simple country people. Now elderly, they reflect on the events of their lives and talk about the traditions of Khmer village life.

Andrew Booth
(Pg. 46, 51)
www.asiatravel-cambodia.com
www.iamcambodia.org

British-born Andrew has such eclectic talents and absurd determination, most would agree he is the man to have with them on a desert island. When not obsessing over the logistics of bespoke itineraries for his travel company ABOUTAsia, Andrew can be found spending its profits for the education of Cambodian rural poor through the IAMCAMBODIA Foundation, where he is cofounder and director.

Adam Bray
(Pg. 111)
www.fisheggtree.com

Adam Bray is a writer and photographer based in Mui Ne, Vietnam. He has contributed to more than a dozen guidebooks for countries in Southeast Asia, including Insight Guides' *Laos & Cambodia*, DK's Eyewitness travel guide to Cambodia and Laos, and Thomas Cook's *Travellers Cambodia*—as well as numerous books in the To Asia With Love guidebook series. He is also regularly featured on CNNGO.com and CNN.com.

CONTRIBUTOR BIOGRAPHIES

Classical dancers at Preah Khan temple

Elizabeth Briel
(Pg. 92, 144, 169)

http://elizabethbriel.com

Elizabeth Briel is an artist and travel-writer with an Asian focus. She has recently illustrated her first book, *H is for Hong Kong*, photographed her second, *Lost & Found: Hong Kong*, and is writing another about her quest through Thailand, Laos, and Vietnam in search of the perfect paper. Currently she is based in Australia and Asia. In Cambodia, she ran a solo charity project teaching photography to kids while working as a radio DJ.

Janet Brown
(Pg. 191)

The author of *Tone Deaf in Bangkok*, Janet loves Cambodia from the perspective of a Bangkok resident but harbors dreams of someday being very, very old in Kratie. Look for her forthcoming *Clueless in Cambodia* sometime in 2030!

Cristiano Calcagno
(Pg. 16, 61, 90)

Italian-born Cristiano Calcagno lives with his wife in Kompong Thom, where he has worked for many years. In his spare time he conducts field research into the ancient sites around his home province ... and rides his bike.

Hing Channarith
(Pg. 167)

www.ccaf-cam.org

Hing Channarith is the CEO and founder of the grassroots NGO the Cambodian Children's Advocacy Foundation (CCAF). He formerly managed the Kien Khleang National Rehabilitation Centre's Veterans International Cambodia just outside Phnom Penh for a decade.

Karen Coates
(Pg. 27, 30, 56, 100, 121)

www.karencoates.com

http://ramblingspoon.com/blog

Author of *Cambodia Now: Life in the Wake of War*, Karen Coates splits her time between the American Southwest and Southeast Asia. She's covered Cambodia for publications around the world since 1998, when she worked at *The Cambodia Daily*.

Kent Davis
(Pg. 49, 195)

www.devata.org

www.datasia.us

Kent Davis is a publisher, author, translator, and educator with twenty years of Southeast Asian work and travel experience. In 2005, he founded DatASIA Publishing and initiated an independent research project documenting, cataloguing, and analyzing the sacred women whose portraits fill the walls of Angkor Wat and other Khmer temples.

Tiara Delgado
(Pg. 212)

www.globalvisionvideo.com

From Los Angeles, California, Tiara Delgado is the founder of Global Vision Video production company. In addition to working on documentaries, she has been a news correspondent for CAM-TV in Long Beach, California, and is currently a contributing journalist for *The Khmer Post* newspaper, also in Long Beach. She has been traveling to Cambodia since 1999 and has resided for the past two years in Phnom Penh, where she works as an English teacher.

Christine Dimmock
(Pg. 24, 75, 197)

Christine Dimmock is a volunteer tutor for migrants and refugees in Australia, who first traveled to Southeast Asia and Cambodia in the 1990s. Her travel adventures also took her to Afghanistan in the early part of the last decade.

Kim Fay
(Pg. 44, 73, 86, 193)
www.kimfay.net

Raised in the Pacific Northwest, Kim Fay first traveled to Southeast Asia in 1991. Since that time, she spent four years living in Vietnam and has traveled back frequently, writing about the region. As an expert on travel literature and Vietnam, she has been a guest speaker on NPR and has written for numerous publications, including *Travel + Leisure*. She is the author of *Communion: A Culinary Journey Through Vietnam* and creator and series editor of the To Asia With Love guidebooks. She lives in Los Angeles.

Don Gilliland
(Pg. 18, 181, 209)
www.bangkokdazed.com
www.dasabookcafe.com

Don Gilliland is originally from Orlando, Florida, where he worked as a dishwasher, cook, and record

store manager. He moved to Thailand in 1996 to work for Tower Records. He taught English for a few years before getting the retail itch again, opening the Lazy Mango Bookshop in Siem Reap in 2002 and Dasa Books in Bangkok in 2004.

Steve Goodman
(Pg. 59)
www.stevegoodman.com

Steve Goodman is an American who has lived in Phnom Penh since 2005 working as a professional photographer and part-time guitar player. In 2002, after a twenty-two-year career as a software company executive in San Francisco, he began an exciting adventure traveling extensively and shooting photos throughout Southeast Asia.

Antonio Graceffo
(Pg. 89)
http://speakingadventure.com

Antonio Graceffo is a martial arts and adventure author living in Asia. He is the author of the book *The Monk from Brooklyn* and the host of the web TV show *Martial Arts Odyssey*, which traces his ongoing journey through Asia, learning martial arts in various countries.

Debra Groves
(Pg. 137, 153)
www.helpinghandscambodia.com

Debra Groves is an Australian photographer working in Cambodia. She left her own wedding photography business on Australia's Sunshine Coast to

CONTRIBUTOR BIOGRAPHIES

move to Cambodia in April 2005, a year after her first visit. She is the founder of the charity Helping Hands.

Anna Hassett
(Pg. 172)

Anna Hassett's travels to Cambodia have included spending time at the Helping Hands charity outside Siem Reap.

Christina Heyniger
(Pg. 183)

Christina Heyniger is a consultant, writer, and lecturer working with governments, entrepreneurs, and community tourism interests to develop and market eco/nature/adventure tourism products and services. Her company, Xola Consulting, has supported clients in countries around the world, including Argentina, Brazil, Bhutan, Cambodia, China, Ecuador, Peru, India, Mexico, Montenegro, Morocco, Nepal, and the United States.

Denise Heywood
(Pg. 84, 142, 154)
www.deniseheywood.co.uk

Denise Heywood is a lecturer, journalist, author, and photographer. She has lived in Paris, New York, and Cambodia, where she worked as a journalist for three years. Now based in London, she has written books on Luang Prabang and Cambodian dance, including *Cambodian Dance: Celebration of the Gods.*

Aaron Horwitz
(Pg. 173)
www.causecast.org

Aaron Horwitz is a Los Angeles-based filmmaker and writer who has a passion for Asia and spent a good part of 2008 shooting in Thailand. He is also a cofounder of the charity Who Will? We Will! which organizes annual fundraisers for several small, independent NGOs. He is currently working for Causecast and aiming on a return to work in Southeast Asia again soon.

Mark Hotham
(Pg. 19, 101, 136)

In 2001 Mark set off to spend eighteen months traveling India, Sri Lanka, Thailand, Malaysia, China, Laos, and Vietnam before arriving in Cambodia in 2003. Unable to tear himself away, he found work in the Australian Embassy in Phnom Penh and settled down for two and a half years. He now lives and works in the travel industry in the UK.

Soumya James
(Pg. 23, 46, 54)

Soumya is writing her doctoral dissertation in the Department of History of Art and Visual Studies at Cornell University in the United States. She is studying the cultural role of the divine feminine during the Angkor period. Her experiences during fieldwork led to a greater appreciation for the people and places in Cambodia.

Helen Ibbitson Jessup
(Pg. 87)

Helen is an art historian specializing in the architecture and sculpture of Cambodia and Indonesia. She has curated exhibitions that have traveled in the USA, France, Japan, Germany, Switzerland, and The Netherlands. She is the founding president of Friends of Khmer Culture and a trustee of the The United States-Indonesia Society.

Molly Jester
(Pg. 165)
www.stopexploitationnow.org

Molly spent many years working on issues related to homelessness and street-living youth in the United States. She first traveled to Southeast Asia in 2001 and fell in love with the region. She's the president and founder of Stop Exploitation Now! established in 2005 to fight exploitation and abuse in Southeast Asia.

Phil Lees
(Pg. 32, 200)
www.phnomenon.com

Phil is an Australian living in Phnom Penh and an avid foodie. He pens Phnomenon, Cambodia's first food blog. Lonely Planet's guide to the greater Mekong called him "the unofficial pimp of Cambodian cuisine."

Peter Leth
(Pg. 123)

Peter is an American who has explored all corners of Cambodia for both work and play. He currently lives in Phnom Penh with his wife and daughter.

Martin Lum
(Pg. 62)
http://web.mac.com/morpheuslibrum

Martin advises the Victoria government in Australia on health. He loves traveling.

Roy McClean
(Pg. 104)

rmcclean.com

Roy is currently based in Australia and Asia. He spends his time breathing and making shapes with his body (also known as Chi Gung, Wing Chun, yoga, and meditation). He enjoys riding old bicycles through the back streets of low-rise cities.

Steve McClure
(Pg. 70, 149)
www.rainfallsfromearth.com

Steve is an award-winning writer/ director and cofounder of Ghost-2-Eleven Entertainment. His first feature documentary, *Rain Falls from Earth: Surviving Cambodia's Darkest Hour*, is narrated by Oscar-nominated actor Sam Waterston and features personal stories from victims of the Khmer Rouge regime in 1970s Cambodia.

CONTRIBUTOR BIOGRAPHIES

227

CONTRIBUTOR BIOGRAPHIES

Doug Mendel
(Pg. 37, 178)
www.dougmendel.com

A former volunteer firefighter in Colorado, Doug first came to Cambodia in 1997 and has since donated equipment to six of Cambodia's fire stations, including two fire trucks. He also set up the Douglas Mendel Cambodian Relief Fund.

Howie Nielsen
(Pg. 119)

A former dentist in the United States by profession, Howie is a passionate bird-watcher and now trains local guides for the Sam Veasna Center for Wildlife Conservation in Cambodia.

Caroline Nixon
(Pg. 26, 36, 97)

Serving as a medical student elective in Chiang Mai, Thailand, in 1980 started Caroline's passion for traveling throughout Southeast Asia. Her favorite destinations are Myanmar and Cambodia. Her favorite pastimes include floating on rivers, cooking, and eating with friends.

Dougald O'Reilly
(Pg. 71, 180, 194)
www.heritagewatchinternational.org

Dougald received his PhD in archaeology in 1999 and was hired the same year by UNESCO to teach at the Royal University of Fine Arts and pursue his research interests in Iron Age settlements in Cambodia. He founded Heritage Watch, an NGO that promotes the preservation of heritage assets in Cambodia, in 2003. The author of *Early Civilizations of Southeast Asia*, he is currently a lecturer at The University of Sydney in Australia.

Joanna Owen
(Pg. 170)
www.hopeforcambodia.org.uk
www.angkorhotels.org

Following Joanna's first experience with Siem Reap, she made it her home and runs a successful responsible-tourism business with her partner, Thomas. She has just completed an MA in Responsible Tourism Management and set up HOPE, a UK-based charity supporting young adults in Cambodia.

Daniela Papi
(Pg. 115)
www.pepytours.com

Daniela is the founder of PEPY, a hybrid organization encompassing an education development organization and an edu-venture tour company based in Siem Reap. She has been living in Cambodia since 2005 and is always looking for ways to escape the cities—often by bicycle on one of PEPY's bicycle adventures.

Robert Philpotts
(Pg. 98, 201)

Robert has been writing about Cambodia since UNAMIC times, "but I consider, as far as my books are concerned, what I produce is a bit like white rice without *prahok*. This is why I spice the texts with pen and ink drawings." His books include *A Guide to Phnom Penh, The Coast of Cambodia, A Post of Independence*, and his latest, *South of the Heart.*

Socheata Poeuv
(Pg. 31, 93, 146)

Socheata made her filmmaking debut with the award-winning film *New Year Baby*, which was broadcast nationally in 2008. She was formerly on the staff at NBC's Dateline and TODAY shows and ABC's World News Tonight. She's also the CEO of Khmer Legacies, an organization whose mission is to document the Cambodian genocide through videotaped testimonies by having the younger generation interview the older generation.

Jan Polatschek
(Pg. 150)
http://travelwithjan.com

Jan is a native New Yorker and now lives in Thailand. Using Bangkok as his hub, he travels in Asia, the Middle East, and beyond. He writes about his travel adventures and posts photos on his website, and several of his essays appear in To Asia With Love guidebooks from ThingsAsian Press.

Geoff Pyle
(Pg. 71)

After living in Cambodia for a while, Geoff finds it hard to keep away from the place—the people, the history, the landscape, the food ... though it is the architecture, the old stuff and the 1960s stuff, that really gets him going.

Nick Ray
(Pg. 116, 147)

Nick hails from Watford, UK, and after trying his hand at tour leading he hooked up with Lonely Planet in 1998 and has worked on more than twenty titles since. He lives in Phnom Penh and leads and lectures on tours for top travel companies and international organizations. He also works as a location scout and manager for television and film. Projects have included *Tomb Raider, Two Brothers*, and countless documentaries for the BBC, Discovery Channel, and National Geographic.

Dawn Rooney
(Pg. 47)

Dawn is an independent scholar and an art historian specializing in Southeast Asia. She has authored nine books on the art and culture of the region. An American now residing in Bangkok, her *Angkor: An Introduction to the Temples* was first published in 1994.

Geoff Ryman
(Pg. 204)

Geoff is a Canadian living in London. He has published eight novels and a volume of short fiction and has coedited a collection of Canadian fiction and a volume of stories that are collaborations between writers and scientists. His novels and short stories have won fourteen awards. His book on Cambodia, *The King's Last Song*, was inspired by a visit in 2001 to an archaeological dig at Angkor Wat. He has twice run workshops in Cambodia in creative writing.

Anita Sach
(Pg. 175)
www.travelprojects.co.uk

Anita works as a freelance travel writer and editor, develops tour programs to Asia for tour operators, and leads group tours to the region. She is the author of guidebooks on Cambodia, Vietnam, and Bangkok and regularly writes online guides to Phnom Penh, Saigon, Hanoi, and Bangkok.

Sheila Scoville
(Pg. 41, 207)

Sheila lives in Austin, Texas, playing in her band No Mas Bodas, selling music at Waterloo Records, and thinking about her trip to Asia at least five times a day. She misses the scenery, cheap massages, kindness of complete strangers, and street food (especially sticky rice desserts) the most.

Lundi Seng
(Pg. 156)

Lundi is a doctor practicing rehabilitation, occupational, and physical therapy in Long Beach, California. In January 1979 he fled with his family to Thailand and resettled in Michigan in December 1980.

David Shamash
(Pg. 35, 179)

For the last fifteen years property company director David has been donning his backpack and traveling to the farthest reaches of Cambodia by boat, pickup, or motodop. As a board member of Mekong Blue in Stung Treng, he helped develop the project so that it now supports a large segment of the local community.

Gordon Sharpless
(Pg. 57, 113)
www.talesofasia.com

Based in Siem Reap, Gordon has lived and worked in Cambodia for nearly a decade. He is the writer and publisher of the Tales of Asia website and since 2004 has owned and operated Two Dragons Guesthouse in Siem Reap. He is married with two children.

Robert Tompkins
(Pg. 20, 184)

Robert is a Canadian writer, editor, and e-educator. A regular contributor to ThingsAsian.com, he and his wife, Doris, live in Cedar Valley, Ontario, a rural community thirty-five miles north of Toronto. Bob publishes articles internationally through his freelance agency, Travel, Ink. He is also the editor of *Futurescapes*. Currently, he is involved in an online editing and tutorial service called The Wordsdoctor.

Georgiana Treasure-Evans
(Pg. 83, 102, 139)
www.motherland1.blogspot.com
www.healingspirits.co.uk

Georgiana is a mother, writer, yoga teacher, and healing arts practitioner. During her four years in Cambodia she traveled widely in Southeast Asia with her husband and two small children. She now lives in Herefordshire, UK.

Loung Ung
(Pg. 15, 141)
www.loungung.com

Loung is the author of two memoirs: *First They Killed My Father: A Daughter of Cambodia Remembers* and *Lucky Child: A Daughter of Cambodia Reunites with the Sister She Left Behind.*

Glyn Vaughan
(Pg. 33, 35)
www.allearscambodia.org

Glyn is director of All Ears Cambodia, a local NGO fighting against ear disease and deafness. It focuses on the weakest and hardest hit, providing free medical treatment for some of the most vulnerable groups in Cambodia.

Dickon Verey
(Pg. 64, 164, 176)
www.fedacambodia.org

Dickon lived in Cambodia from 2003 until the beginning of 2006. During that time he volunteered for a number of NGOs. His main work was building a youth and community center in the village of Ksach Poy near Battambang for FEDA. He now lives in Vietnam.

Christine Thuy-Anh Vu
(Pg. 42)

Christine writes and edits work about the arts, culture, and science. Serving as art adviser to several international collections, she has also been an executive director to a Vietnam-based international arts organization.

A Fulbright Fellow in Contemporary Vietnamese Art, she has received other honors and fellowships for her research in Europe and the USA in psychology, gastronomy, and contemporary art.

Ray Waddington
(Pg. 131, 166)
www.peoplesoftheworld.org

Ray is the president of The Peoples of the World Foundation, a secular, apolitical, nonprofit organization based in the USA. He established the foundation to fund educational scholarships for indigenous people after witnessing their lack of educational opportunities and the negative impact this has on political representation. He recently celebrated his one-millionth kilometer of international travel and is preparing a travel/humor book based on his experiences.

Georgie Walsh
(Pg. 213)

Georgie first went to Phnom Penh to work on a memoir set there in the 1980s. This fell through, but she kept herself busy by editing, teaching, exporting textiles, starting a soup kitchen, cofounding an NGO, and selling some paintings, just to name a few activities. More recently she's been based in Bangkok and Luang Prabang, where she is working as a freelance journalist.

CONTRIBUTOR BIOGRAPHIES

CONTRIBUTOR BIOGRAPHIES

Peter Walter
(Pg. 75, 77, 126, 217)

Peter Walter is the Southeast Asia managing director for L.E.K. Consulting. A native of Lakewood, Ohio, he has lived with his family in Bangkok for nearly ten years. Whenever he gets the chance, he enjoys spending time exploring the region with his wife, Lyle, and their three boys.

Debbie Watkins
(Pg. 88, 110, 186)
www.carpe-diem-travel.com

With husband Marc, Debbie created Carpe Diem Travel in 2001 after a career in banking in the UK. Carpe Diem is a social enterprise travel business, reinvesting profits in the communities its customers visit.

Rachel Wildblood
(Pg. 21, 95, 108)
http://rachelwildblood.com

UK-born, Rachel is a freelance consultant specializing in waste and environmental management. She worked for various NGOs in Cambodia over a four-year period from 2005 after arriving as a volunteer.

Mick Yates
(Pg. 25, 52)
www.yatesweb.com/Cambodia/Cambodia.htm

Mick is an innovative leadership researcher, teacher, and author. In 2001, Mick was elected to Save the Children's U.S. board of trustees. Reflecting a long-term interest in children's issues, the Yates family supports a Cambodian school development program in a remote area of the country.

Ronnie Yimsut
(Pg. 36, 94)

Born and raised in Siem Reap, Ronnie fled Cambodia after witnessing the massacre of nearly his entire family under the Khmer Rouge regime. Ronnie is currently a senior landscape architect for the U.S. Forest Service, a published author, and a social and environmental justice issues activist.

Ray Zepp
(Pg. 159)
www.diucambodia.org

Ray came to Cambodia in 1995 as part of the Georgetown University project to rebuild the National University of Management. His travels in the hinterland prompted him to author his *Cambodia Less Travelled*. He now resides in Battambang and has written the tourist guide *Around Battambang*. He has also started the new Dewey International University in Battambang.

CREDITS

CREDITS

INDEX

INDEX

EDITOR & PHOTOGRAPHER BIOGRAPHIES

Andy Brouwer

British-born Andy Brouwer made his first trip to Cambodia in 1994. That white-knuckle ride hooked him for life. His annual visits didn't satisfy his craving, so he upped sticks to Phnom Penh in 2007. As well as having a serious interest in temples, books, and pretty much all things Khmer, he is a lifetime supporter of Leeds United and has an insatiable passion for the music of Steel Pulse and Ennio Morricone.

www.andybrouwer.co.uk

Tewfic El-Sawy

Tewfic El-Sawy is a New York City-based freelance photographer who specializes in documenting endangered cultures and traditional life in Asia, Latin America, and Africa. He is particularly interested in photographing cultural ceremonies and religious and tribal rituals. He leads photography tours to India, Sikkim, Indochina, Indonesia, and the Himalayan Kingdoms of Nepal and Bhutan. His images, articles, and photo features have been published in various magazines and other publications.

www.telsawy.com

To Vietnam With Love
A Travel Guide for the Connoisseur
Edited & with contributions by Kim Fay
Photographs by Julie Fay Ashborn

To Thailand With Love
A Travel Guide for the Connoisseur
Edited & with contributions by Nabanita Dutt
Photographs by Marc Schultz

To Cambodia With Love
A Travel Guide for the Connoisseur
Edited & with contributions by Andy Brouwer
Photographs by Tewfic El-Sawy

To Myanmar With Love
A Travel Guide for the Connoisseur
Edited & with contributions by Morgan Edwardson
Photographs by Steve Goodman

To Shanghai With Love
A Travel Guide for the Connoisseur
Edited & with contributions by Crystyl Mo
Photographs by Coca Dai

To North India With Love
A Travel Guide for the Connoisseur
Edited & with contributions by Nabanita Dutt
Photographs by Nana Chen

To Japan With Love
A Travel Guide for the Connoisseur
Edited & with contributions by Celeste Heiter
Photographs by Robert George

To Nepal With Love
A Travel Guide for the Connoisseur
Edited & with contributions by Cristi Hegranes
Photographs by Kraig Lieb

THINGSASIAN PRESS *Experience Asia Through the Eyes of Travelers*

"To know the road ahead, ask those coming back."
CHINESE PROVERB

Whether you're a frequent flyer or an armchair traveler, whether you are 5 or 105, whether you want fact, fiction, or photography, ThingsAsian Press has a book for you.

To Asia With Love is a series that has provided a new benchmark for travel guidebooks; for children, Asia comes alive with the vivid illustrations and bilingual text of the *Alphabetical World* picture books; cookbooks provide adventurous gourmets with food for thought. Asia's great cities are revealed through the unique viewpoints of their residents in the photographic series, *Lost and Found*. And for readers who just want a good story, ThingsAsian Press offers page-turners—both novels and travel narratives—from China, Vietnam, Thailand, India, and beyond.

With books written by people who know about Asia for people who want to know about Asia, ThingsAsian Press brings the world closer together, one book at a time.

www.thingsasianpress.com